COGNITION IN A DIGITAL WORLD

Edited by

Herre van Oostendorp

LEA LAWRENCE ERLBAUM ASSOCIATES, PUBLISHERS
2003 Mahwah, New Jersey   London

Lawrence Erlbaum Associates, Inc., Publishers
10 Industrial Avenue
Mahwah, New Jersey 07430

Cover design by Kathryn Houghtaling Lacey

Library of Congress Cataloging-in-Publication Data

Cognition in a digital world / edited by Herre van Oostendorp.
   p. cm.
   Includes bibliographical references and indexes.
   ISBN 0-8058-3506-7 (cloth : alk. paper) — ISBN 0-8058-3507-5 (pbk. : alk. paper)
    1. Human information processing. 2. Cognition. 3. Human-computer interaction.
  4. Web sites—Psychological aspects. 5. World Wide Web—Psychological aspects.
  6. Internet—Psychological aspects. 7. Multimedia systems—Psychological aspects.
  I. Oostendorp, Herre van.

BF444 .C63 2003
153—dc21
                                           2002024438
                                                   CIP

Books published by Lawrence Erlbaum Associates are printed on acid-free paper,
and their bindings are chosen for strength and durability.

Printed in the United States of America
10 9 8 7 6 5 4 3 2 1

Contents

Contributors

Jerry Andriessen
Department of Educational Studies, Utrecht University, The Netherlands
J.Andriessen@fss.uu.nl

Richard Duschl
Department of Educational and Professional Studies, King's College London,
   UK
Richard.duschl@kcl.ac.uk

Kirsten Ellenbogen
Department of Educational and Professional Studies, King's College London,
   UK
Kirsten.ellebogen@kcl.ac.uk

Gysbert Erkens
Department of Educational Studies, Utrecht University, The Netherlands
G.Erkens@fss.uu.nl

Frank Fischer
Department of Applied Cognitive Psychology and Media Psychology, University
   of Tuebingen, Germany
Fischer@uni-tuebingen.de

Susan Goldman
Department of Psychology, University of Illinois, Chicago, USA
SGoldman@UIC.edu

Jeffrey Goldstein
Department of Social and Organizational Psychology, Utrecht University, The Netherlands
J.Goldstein@fss.uu.nl

Kristina Groth
Department of Numerical Analysis and Computer Science, Royal Institute of Technology, Stockholm, Sweden
Kicki@nada.kth.se

Valerie Gyselinck
Department of Psychology, University René Descartes, Paris, France
Gyselinck@psycho.univ-paris5.fr

Päivi Häkkinen
Institute for Educational Research, University of Jyväslylä, Finland
phakkine@ktl.jyu.fi

Anders Hedman
Department of Numerical Analysis and Computer Science, Royal Institute of Technology, Stockholm, Sweden
Ahedman@nada.kth.se

Sanna Järvelä
Department of Educational Sciences and Teacher Education, University of Oulu, Finland
sjarvela@ktk.oulu.fi

Ann Lantz
Department of Numerical Analysis and Computer Science, Royal Institute of Technology, Stockholm, Sweden
Alz@nada.kth.se

Jonathan Lazar
Department of Computer and Information Sciences, Towson University, USA
Jlazar@towson.edu

Heinz Mandl
Institute of Educational Psychology, University of München, Germany
mandl@edupsy.uni-muenchen.de

Heimo Müller
Fachhochschule Technikum Johanneum, Graz, Austria
heimo.mueller@fh-joanneum.at

Nanno Peters
Department of Educational Studies, Utrecht University, The Netherlands
N.Peters@fss.uu.nl

Jenny Preece
Department of Information Systems, University of Maryland Baltimore County,
  USA
Preece@umbc.edu

Henry Rodriguez
Department of Numerical Analysis and Computer Science, Royal Institute of
  Technology, Stockholm, Sweden
Henrry@nada.kth.se

Eva-Lotta Sallnäs
Department of Numerical Analysis and Computer Science, Royal Institute of
  Technology, Stockholm, Sweden
Evalotta@nada.kth.se

Kirstin Severinson Eklundh
Department of Numerical Analysis and Computer Science, Royal Institute of
  Technology, Stockholm, Sweden
Kse@nada.kth.se

Simone Stroomer
TNO Human Factors Research Institute, Soesterberg, The Netherlands
Stroomer@tm.tno.nl

Ed Tan
Department of Literary Studies, Vrije Universiteit Amsterdam, The Netherlands
Esh.tan@let.vu.nl

Hubert Tardieu
Department of Psychology, University René Descartes, Paris, France
Tardieu@psycho.univ-paris5.fr

Carrie Tzou
Doctoral student Northwestern University, Evanston, USA
Tzouct@northwestern.edu

Herre van Oostendorp
Institute of Information and Computing Sciences, Utrecht University, The Neth-
  erlands
Herre@cs.uu.nl

Erica de Vries
Laboratoire des Sciences de l'Education, University of Grenoble II, France
Erica.deVries@upmf-grenoble.fr

Susan Williams
Curriculum & Instruction Department, University of Texas, Austin, USA
Susan.williams@mail.utexas.edu

Preface

Herre van Oostendorp
Utrecht University

Massive changes are occurring in society regarding the delivery of information to individuals and the way individuals process this information. These changes happen at work, at home, and in schools; the Internet and the World Wide Web (WWW) are changing people's working lives, leisure time, work settings, and educational environments. Multimedia on the Internet, but also as stand-alone applications, such as games on CD-ROM, are everywhere. It is important for the functioning of individuals and groups to have insight into these developments and consequences. For instance, the integration of many functions into one computer system can be very confusing. This applies on an individual level but also on an organizational level. It is now possible to work, follow the news, read serious information, relax, be amused, diverted, and so on using a PC, almost at the same time. What do all these changes imply?

All these changes and their consequences have traditionally been investigated largely within the domain of sociology, semiotics, mass communication, and so on. Detailed discussions from within cognitive psychology have been lacking. The purpose of this volume is to remedy this lack. In other words, the focus of this book is on the cognitive effects of the modern, digital environment on individuals. But besides that, even more important is the question of what conditions we can stipulate for adequately processing information in multimedia environments. For instance: What are the cognitive conditions of human beings in view of the integration of text, images, sound (speech), and data as frequently is the case within multimedia? It is also instructive to think about the consequences for human cognition of the large databases that are now available in principle. How can we handle so much information? The problem for human beings becomes more of a metacognitive nature than a classical cognitive one (Goldman, 1996). That is, knowledge management and strategies that people have to employ are getting more important than being able to store large amounts of data into one's memory. Consequently, tasks and their related work flow can drastically change our normal way of working because of increased digitization. Another issue concerns the question of whether hypermedia, with the ability to crosslink text documents do effectively assist in the construction and updating of mental models. Further issues are the role of working memory with multimedia information processing (Mayer & Moreno, 1998); or what we can say about the role of computer games (on CD-ROM or Internet) on the cognition and emotion of individuals, and so on.

The amazing growth of the WWW enables people to extract information and communicate despite difficulties of distance or differences in time. Consequently, it is worthwhile to know more about the characteristics of information usage on the WWW. Much of the communication of Internet users, for instance, the communication between members of an interest group or a community, involves exchange of factual information. However, a large amount of the communication is strongly empathic. Better support for the factual information exchange has to be designed, while at the same time supporting empathic communication (Preece, 1999). This suggestion indicates that more knowledge from a sociopsychological perspective is needed to be able to design appropriate tools.

During recent years, a whole new and attractive application area has been developed, that of Computer-Mediated (Collaborative) Communication (Goldman, 1996; Scardamelia, Bereiter, and Lamon, 1994; Suthers, 1999). Increasingly, communication between individuals occurs with the aid of computers (or the Internet). This may concern communication as a goal in itself, but it also may concern communication needed to solve certain tasks (e.g., collaboratively designing a building or making decisons in a control room of a complex factory). The tools used here can be characterized by their highly interactive nature. However, despite a large number of studies on computer-mediated (collaborative) communication, not much is known about the specific mutual relationships between the nature of interaction and communication on one hand and performance (learning, problem solving, and decision making) on the other. In particular, more insight is needed in the crucial characteristics of the interaction and produced discourse, and the relationships with quality of task performance. In this volume, the emphasis is on the cognition part, particularly on the psychological analysis of the ongoing communication and discourse, and not on the interface or technological part.

To summarize, the three main topics of this volume are: *Conditions and Consequences of Multimedia Information Processing.* Massive changes in society concern the delivery of information to individuals and the way they (have to) process this information. What cognitive (and emotional) conditions can we stipulate for adequately processing information in a multimedia environment and what are the effects?

In chapter 1, *Tardieu and Gyselinck* discuss studies that emphasize the need to consider the limitations of cognitive resources available to a user of a multimedia sytem. Those systems must be adapted to the cognitive limitations of the user, especially those of working memory. Chapter 2 by *Goldstein* reviews research on the effects of electronic games. It particularly examines the effects and appeal of violent games, and considers the uses of computer games in educational and therapeutic settings. *Tan and Müller* argue in chapter 3 how developments within television archives will bring about a reshuffling of tasks such as production, storage, distribution, and production of video materials. On the basis of a developed digital video archive system (VINE), they show how these tasks will become integrated into being done by one person.

Sociopsychological characteristics of information usage on the World Wide Web. On the basis of insights of reciprocal understanding and social perspective taking theory, *Järvelä and Häkkinen* (chap. 4) develop a sociocognitive model for analysing Web-based interaction. They show that, with this framework, a useful tool is available for analyzing the quality of asynchronous discussion going on during Web-based learning in teacher education. The chapter by *Severinson Eklundh, Groth, Hedman, Lantz, Rodriguez and Sallnäs* (chap. 5) investigates implications of Web-based information exchange for people in knowledge-oriented professions. In particular, their focus is on how the Web's potential for communication and its accessible information infrastructure affect the strategies of "knowledge workers" for acquiring and spreading professional information. The Web can support multiple forms of communication, each with its own criteria, each with its own form of "community." *Lazar and Preece* (chap. 6) introduce the concepts of *usability* and *sociability* as important determinants of online communities. They present a discussion of success factors for online communities.

Analysis of computer mediated (collaborative) communication. It is important to examine the interactive and discourse aspects characterizing communication that is computer mediated. Multimedia research in educational settings traditionally focused on reading and studying as main learner activities and on memory and comprehension as main performance variables. *De Vries* argues in chapter 7 that the cognitive skills necessary for functioning in a digital world range far beyond basic skills like reading and writing. Students need to become proficient in skills such as defining problems, finding information, and collaborating, which brings about a need for new process and performance measures. *Stroomer and van Oostendorp* (chap. 8) discuss how communication in group or team tasks is analyzed, based on a review of a number of studies. In this review, the focus is on the *sensitivity, reliability,* and *validity* of the categorization schemes for analyzing the communication used in the studies reviewed. During the last few years, many studies have been conducted on the technological feasability and aspects of the delivery of courses as well as on the implementation of video conferening technology in organizations. These studies mostly indicate encouraging subjective experiences of learners. However, little is known on how learners really collaboratively learn in video conferences and how the conditions of interaction in video conferencing influence the processes of collaborative knowledge construction. *Fischer and Mandl* (chap. 9) discuss theoretical aspects as well as results of empirical studies into video conferencing, focusing on the aspects of interaction and collaborative knowledge construction. Also, *Erkens, Andriessen, and Peters* (chap. 10) focus on the interactional processes in computer-supported collaborative learning. Their main question concerns the relation between the nature of interaction and communication on one hand and performance (learning and problem solving) on the other. *Goldman, Duschl, Ellenbogen, Williams, and Tzou* (chap. 11) finally discuss how an electronic conversation environment (Knowledge Forum) can support collaborative knowledge building of students. They show how this environment can be used to scaffold students' argumentation in science.

These topics represent issues that have received little attention in published articles, at least yet, as far as they concern the cognitive and sociopsychological aspects of human functioning in a digital world. Nevertheless, they are important issues for cognitive psychology and also from a practical perspective, such as instructional matters, design of digital information itself, and interface design.

The focus of this book is not on education nor on intentional learning processes in formal school settings, although this aspect and or setting is mentioned in some chapters. However, the focus is rather on how people solve intellectual tasks in general (some of them can be typical, school learning tasks).

Intended Audience

This book has been written and edited with doctoral students and researchers interested in cognition in a modern, digital, multimedia environment in mind. The volume is relevant to the disciplines of social sciences (particularly psychology, mass communication, and educational sciences), computer science (information systems and human computer interaction) and

arts (psycholinguistics and discourse analysis). I hope this volume can help
to bridge the gap(s) between these three worlds.

REFERENCES

Goldman, S. R. (1996). Reading, writing, and learning in hypermedia environments. In H. van
    Oostendorp & S. de Mul (Eds.), *Cognitive aspects of electronic text processing* (pp. 7–42).
    Norwood, NJ: Ablex.
Mayer, R., & Moreno, R. (1998). A split-attention effect in multimedia learning: Evidence for
    dual processing systems in working memory. *Journal of Educational Psychology, 90,* 312–320.
Preece, J. (1999). Empathic communities: Balancing emotional and factual communication.
    Designing multimedia for human needs and capabilities [Special Issue]. *Interacting with
    Computers, 12*(1), 63–78.
Scardamalia, M., Bereiter, C., & Lamon, M. (1994). The CSILE–project: Trying to bring the
    classroom into world 3. In K. McGilly (Ed.), *Classroom lessons: Integrating cognitive theory and
    classroom practice* (pp. 202–229). Cambridge, MA: MIT Press.
Suthers, D. (1999, January). Representational support for collaborative inquiry. Proceedings
    of the *32nd Hawai'i International Conference on the System Sciences (HICSS-32),* Maui, Institute
    of Electrical and Electronics Engineers, Inc. (IEEE).

Part I

CONDITIONS AND CONSEQUENCES OF MULTIMEDIA INFORMATION PROCESSING

Working Memory Constraints in the Integration and Comprehension of Information in a Multimedia Context

Hubert Tardieu
Valérie Gyselinck
Laboratory for Experimental Psychology, Université René Descartes, France

Multimedia systems are developing quickly and will continue to do so in the near future, especially in instructional fields. A multimedia system typically requires the integration of different types of information: verbal information presented visually or auditorily (e.g. words, sentences, or short texts), pictorial information presented visually in a static or dynamic way (illustrations, photographs, schemas), and sound information. Systems that allow users to navigate between different sources of information with the use of hypertext structures are often considered to be multimedia systems, even if only one type of information is provided (for example, verbal information presented visually). The development of technologies is intended to provide the users with quick and easy access to a large amount of information and a choice between different forms of presentations. Thanks to multimedia systems, the instructional process can be made more flexible, rich, and individualized. From a psychological point of view, however, the question arises as to what extent the use of all these overelaborate systems are beneficial to the learning process. The temptation is strong to simply assume that using multiple forms of displaying information, using realistic and vivid presentations, and providing multiple possibilities to interact with a learning system results generally in better learning (Schnotz, 1999a). Despite all technical innovations, however, the acquisition of information through any technical system is subject to the constraints of human information processing. Thus, people involved in the creation and use of this kind of material must then consider a series of relevant questions. In particular, thought must be given to how various sources of information have to be integrated by the user, either simultaneously or successively. This holds true across whatever goal the user has: either instructional, professional, amusement, or other. Further, one has to consider to what extent the user is able to integrate different types of information. For instance, which rules guide selecting the number and nature of simultaneously presented information? What are the sources of individual differences in processing ability from multimedia systems?

Research is currently being conducted that investigates the efficacy of using multiple forms of displaying information such as seen in multimedia systems (see, e.g., Dobson, 1999; Schnotz, 1999b). One of the first and most common integration the user has to achieve when manipulating a multimedia system is the integration of verbal information and pictorial information (e.g., a picture or movie). In this chapter, we propose to focus on the constraints imposed on the user faced with multiple forms of information. The majority of empirical studies are conducted mostly in instructional fields. We present some of those studies that inform us about the constraints imposed by the properties of the user's cognitive system in the integration process; in particular, we focus on the memory constraints of the user. A common concept in instructional fields as well as in cognitive psychology is the concept of working memory. It is usually thought of as a memory system that has limited capacities. When a multimedia presentation is used, the integration of information may lead to a competition for these limited capacities. Even if general concepts are shared, the theoretical grounds and the methodological approaches may differ. Two main bodies of research are explored. First, a series of studies aimed at improving the design of instructional procedures in order to maximize learning is presented. In these studies, the goal is to know whether, and if so, how multimedia systems can improve learning. A second series of recent studies is presented that have been conducted with the primary objective of understanding the cognitive processes involved in the construction of a mental representation from information presented in various media. In the final section, we examine the methodological and the theoretical implications of these two lines of research.

WORKING MEMORY CONSTRAINTS AND THE INSTRUCTIONAL APPROACH

Sweller and Chandler (1994) and Mayer (1997) gave an exhaustive review of work conducted in the domain of multimedia learning. Mayer (1997) summarized the issues raised by multimedia learning into four questions: Is multimedia effective for learning? When is multimedia effective? For whom is multimedia effective? In what format, visual or auditory, is verbal information more effective? Our objective is not to present all the evidence Mayer (1997) provided to answer each of these questions. Rather, we will present the major theories in this area and examine closely the proposals made about working memory, and describe the instructional methods used to improve multimedia learning and are focused on working memory constraints.

The Cognitive Load Theory

Numerous experiments have been conducted, mostly within the instructional field, with the primary objective of finding means to improve the design of instructional procedures and learning. In this line of research, some authors have questioned the contribution of various new technologies—computers and now multimedia systems—on learning. Sweller (1994) developed a theory, the *cognitive load theory*, which attempts to account for the outcomes of the limitations of the human information-processing system for the design of instructional procedures and learning. The ultimate goal of this approach is to generate new instructional techniques to facilitate learning. Basically, the cognitive load theory shares with classical modular theories an architecture composed of a working memory with limited capacity and a long-term memory with unlimited capacity. The limitations of working memory are thought of as limitations in the cognitive resources a learner may devote to the performance of a given task. One of the functions of long-term memory is to store automatized schemata. These schemata are complex, cognitive constructs that permit the learners to categorize information in simple, easily retrievable units. With practice and time, the cognitive processes required to complete a task become more and more automatized. Gradually, these processes may become fully automatic, freeing cognitive resources for other activities. Consequently, learning is based on two mechanisms, schema acquisition and automation (Sweller, 1994).

According to this view, many instructional techniques are superfluous because they impose unnecessary cognitive constraints, which interfere with the learning process. For Sweller and Chandler (1994), these constraints may either be intrinsic or extraneous. An intrinsic cognitive load is determined by the mental demands imposed by the nature of the material to be learned, regardless of the form in which it is presented. Any task consists of discrete elements that the learner must integrate in order to assimilate them. The cognitive load theory assumes that the intrinsic load is a function of the degree of interactivity between these elements. Depending on the task, each element may be learned either in isolation (i.e., without reference to the other elements), or in combination with another element. In the first case, the cognitive load associated with learning is low because the interactivity between elements is low. The task will eventually become difficult to perform when the number of elements the individual has to process linearly increases. Conversely, the cognitive load associated with learning is high when the amount of information that must be learned simultaneously is high. The task will also be difficult to learn when the level of interactivity between elements is high, even if the number of individual elements is small. Thus, it is not the total number of elements to learn per se that gives the source of intrinsic cognitive load, but the extent to which the elements interact.

An extraneous cognitive load is determined by the way information is structured and related to the instructional format of the task, irrespective of subject matter. The design, techniques, and procedures used for the presentation of instructional material (e.g., diagrams, written statements, etc.) are important. Sweller (1994) reported that because of the way the material is presented, most of the traditional instructional techniques impose constraints in processing such that they engage learners in cognitive activities that are irrelevant to the learning process. A cognitive activity irrelevant to learning is an activity that is not directed toward the acquisition of schemata and/or the automation of processes. Sweller and Chandler (1991) described several phenomena that could be responsible for extraneous cognitive load. For example, learners faced with a multimedia environment are subjected to several sources of information that, when presented in isolation, are often not understandable. The learners have to divide their attention between multiple sources of information in order to mentally integrate the information and to achieve understanding. This mental integration is cognitively demanding, and by increasing the load of working memory, makes use of resources and consequently reduces learning. For instance, the so-called *split-attention effect* (Mayer & Moreno, 1998) occurs when a diagram and textual statements are presented together in order to explain a problem of geometry, while the same sources of information (diagram and statements) are unintelligible in isolation. An extraneous cognitive load may also be present when multiple sources of information convey the same or similar information. If a diagram, for example, presents enough relevant information in itself for a problem to be understood, the concurrent presentation of statements becomes redundant because it gives rise to additional and unnecessary processing, therefore increasing the cognitive load. Studies conducted within the institutional field are aimed at developing techniques that may reduce both intrinsic and extraneous cognitive load.

The Generative Theory of Multimedia Learning

Mayer (1997), who has proposed a theory of multimedia learning, also supports the idea that the limited capacity of working memory could constrain the use of multimedia information. The generative theory of multimedia learning is basically concerned with how learners integrate verbal and visual information. Learners are viewed as "knowledge constructors" due to the multiple pieces of information they have to integrate. Compared to Sweller, Mayer (1997) suggested a more extensive and constructive view of multimedia learning. This theory proposes that multimedia instructions imply cognitive processes engaged by learners when visual and verbal information are to be processed together. According to Mayer (1997), three categories of processes govern multimedia learning: selection of words and pictures from the material to be learned; organization of words and pictures into verbal and visual representations, respectively; and integration of these representations into one coherent mental representation. Each process operates, at least initially, in working memory. Mayer and Moreno's (1998) conception of working memory is based on assumptions from Paivio's (1986) dual-coding theory. According to the *dual-coding theory*, working msemory in the domain of multimedia learning involves two limited capacity stores, an auditory store and a visual store, analogous to the phonological loop and the visuospatial sketchpad of Baddeley's (1992) theory. Information presented visually is processed in visual working memory, whereas information presented auditorily is processed in auditory working memory. Information is organized independently in each working memory space before being connected together.

In the selection process, the learner chooses relevant words from the verbal information for the subsequent building of a verbal representation, or a propositional representation that forms the text base. In parallel, the learner selects from the visual information the relevant pictures for the construction of the pictorial representation, which forms the image base. Thus the role of the selection process includes two procedures: First, the numerous pieces of information perceived in the multimedia environment relevant for processing are extracted; second, this information is put into verbal or visual working memory in order to elaborate the text and image bases. After selection, the organizing process is conducted to represent the selected material in a more coherent way. Both the words of the text base and the images of the image base are transformed into two separate representations: a verbal mental model of the situation described in the text and a visual mental model of the situation depicted in the pictures. This transformation takes place within verbal working memory and within visual working memory, respectively.

Once the two models have been constructed, the last step consists of establishing connections between each of them. The integration process gives rise to both the building of connections between the two representations and between these representations and other relevant knowledge structures present in memory. Integration also takes place in working memory; the verbal information must be held in the verbal store of working memory while the visual information is simultaneously held in the visual store of working memory. Integration is achieved when the learner establishes systematic connections between the verbal and the visual representations.

Thus, working memory plays a crucial role in the accomplishment of the three processes that govern multimedia learning. Working memory is involved in the maintenance of relevant information in each store, in the transformation of information of each store into a coherent representation, and in the establishment of connections between visual and auditory representations.

How to Improve Learning?

The two theories presented here, the cognitive load theory and the generative theory of multimedia learning, have given rise to a series of experimental studies that examine the theory and develop new techniques to improve learning. The results of these various studies inform us how learners circumvent the limitations imposed by working memory in order to enhance learning. The two main ways that have been explored for improving learning will be presented successively. First, we review the studies that have focused on the cognitive activities that impose a load on working memory. Second, we review those that have focused on the amount of information held in working memory at a certain time in processing.

Decreasing Cognitive Activities That Impose a Load on Working Memory. "The split-attention effect occurs when learners are required to divide their attention among and mentally integrate multiple sources of information" (Mousavi, Low & Sweller, 1995, p.319). The generality of the split-attention effect has been demonstrated with a variety of materials, including engineering (Chandler & Sweller, 1991), numerical control programming (Chandler & Sweller, 1991), psychological reports (Chandler & Sweller, 1992), physics phenomena (Mayer & Moreno, 1998), and arithmetic word problems (Mwangi & Sweller, 1998). Many experiments by Sweller and colleagues showed that the split-attention effect can be eliminated when the multiple sources of information are physically integrated. For example, Sweller, Chandler, Tierney, and Cooper (1990), using mathematics materials, showed that performance on geometry problems was substantially enhanced when written statements associated with a diagram were set in appropriate places (i.e., inside the diagram) as compared to when the statements were conventionally presented (outside the diagram). When material is combined into a unitary source of information, learners do not have to search for relations between the statements and the diagram. The load in working memory is thus reduced and more resources become available for searching and using schemata.

However, the physical integration of information sources may also have a negative effect on learning. Bobis, Sweller, and Cooper (1993) demonstrated that learning was enhanced by the elimination of textual material describing the contents of a geometric diagram. In the case of a self-contained diagram, adding redundant textual elements can engage learners in unnecessary activities. For example, learners may be forced to consider diagrammatic information, textual information, and the relations between them. In this case, the elimination rather than the integration of redundant material improves learning.

Some studies conducted by Mayer and colleagues may also be related to the work of Sweller. In most of these studies, two groups of subjects were contrasted. One group received a verbal explanation of a particular phenomenon coordinated with a visual explanation (coordinated group) and the other group received a verbal and visual explanation separate from one another (separated group). In one set of experiments (Mayer & Anderson, 1991), students viewed a computer-generated animation of how a tire pump works and listened to a narration describing the actions necessary for the functioning of the pump. The animation and the narration were presented simultaneously for the coordinated group, whereas the narration was followed by the animation for the separated group. Learning was measured using performance on transfer problems, which asked the students to draw inferences about the causes and the probable consequences of the pump dysfunction. The results showed that the coordinated group generated more correct solutions on the transfer problems than did the separated group. This so-called "contiguity effect" has been demonstrated with animation and narration on other subject matters, such as a car's hydraulic braking system (Mayer & Anderson, 1992) and the human respiratory system (Mayer & Sims, 1994). This effect has also been demonstrated with text and static illustrations. For instance, in Mayer, Steinhoff, Bower, and Mars (1995), students were asked to learn how lightning storms develop. The material was composed of a long, written passage on lightning and five captioned illustrations depicting the five central events in the formation of lightning. In the coordinated group, the illustrations were placed near the corresponding paragraphs, whereas in the separated group, the illustrations were presented after the text. Once again, students who received a coordinated presentation of text and illustrations produced more solutions on transfer problems than students who received the same information in a separated manner.

Increasing the Amount of Information Held in Working Memory. Another way to facilitate learning is to increase the amount of information held in working memory. The rationale behind this idea is that separate subsystems exist in working memory and can perform in parallel. In particular, one system could be responsible for the storage of auditory information and another system could be responsible for the storage of visual information. If information is presented both in an auditory format and in a visual format, that is, if several channels are involved, the capacity of working memory could be greater. Mousavi, Low, and Sweller (1995) compared the performance of three groups of subjects who were presented geometry problems. One group was visually presented a static diagram and its associated statements, and simultaneously heard the statements (simultaneous group). A second group was presented with the static diagram and its associated statements, but did not hear the statements (visual-visual group). For the third group, diagrams were presented visually and the statements were presented only auditorily (visual-auditory group). In a series of six experiments, Mousavi et al. (1995) showed that, compared to the other modes of presentation, the presentation of the instructional material in a mixed visual–auditory mode systematically leads to a reduction in the learner's acquisition time, problem-solving time, and number of errors. This is consistent with the findings of Tindall-Ford, Chandler, and Sweller (1997), which showed that learning improves when the material is presented in a dual mode (visual diagrams and auditory statements) as compared to a conventional presentation (visual diagrams and statements).

Using a short computer-generated animation depicting the process of lightning formation or a car's braking system, Mayer and Moreno (1998) examined how students integrate animation with a text presented visually or auditorily. Students viewed the animation along with the corresponding text presented visually (same-modality presentation) or they viewed the animation along with the concurrent narration presented auditorily (different-modality presentation). Three measures of performance were considered: a memory test of the relevant steps in the process described, a matching test between the names for elements and those placed in an illustration, and a transfer test requiring the subject to apply his or her learning to new situations. Students performed better on these tests when the animation was accompanied by the text presented in an auditory rather than in a visual modality. The authors interpreted this to indicate that visual working memory is overloaded when materials are presented in the same modality, whereas cross-modal presentation of the information in effect reduces the processing overload. Because learners are not able to hold the corresponding pictorial and verbal representations in working memory at the same time, they have difficulties building connections between representations presented in the same modality.

WORKING MEMORY CONSTRAINTS AND THE
COGNITIVE PSYCHOLOGY POINT OF VIEW

In the field of cognitive psychology, studies are conducted to understand the cognitive processes involved in the construction of mental representations from information that may be presented in various media. Several models and theories have been developed. Concerning the integration of verbal and pictorial information, we first briefly present the dominant theoretical points of view and the most broadly accepted model of working memory. Some experiments are motivated by these theoretical views and involve an experimental design and procedure specific to these viewpoints, which are presented in more detail.

Comprehension of Illustrated Texts and Baddeley's Working Memory Model

Contemporary theories of language comprehension commonly assume that understanding a text requires the construction of a referential representation of the meaning of the text: a representation of the things (objects, events, processes) described in the text, not a representation of the text itself. Such a representation is also called a *situation model* (Kintsch, 1988; van Dijk & Kintsch, 1983) or a mental model (Johnson-Laird, 1980, 1983). This understanding is the product of the interaction between information provided by the text and the reader's world knowledge, including his or her goals and attitudes. Such a referential representation features the information that is implicit in the text, and adding to the literal meaning of the text by incorporating relevant world knowledge. Based on empirical evidence, several authors (Glenberg & Langston, 1992; Gyselinck, 1995; Gyselinck & Tardieu, 1999; Hegarty & Just, 1993; Kruley, Sciama & Glenberg, 1994) proposed to interpret the facilitative effect of illustrations in the framework of Johnson-Laird's (1983) theory. According to this theory, the reader constructs an internal representation, called a *mental model*, that has a structure analogous to that of the situation described in the text. Hence, illustrations depicting the content of the text they accompany should facilitate the construction of a mental model. Van Dijk and Kintsch (1983) and Johnson-Laird (1983) assumed that the mental representation built during text comprehension is temporarily stored in a memory that has limited capacities. Johnson-Laird (1983) also clearly states that these limitations may heavily tax mental model building. In the theories of text comprehension just described, however, the locus of construction, storage, and integration of the representation is not clearly defined. Nevertheless, until now, only a few studies have dealt with the question of the involvement of working memory in the construction of a mental model, especially in the case of illustrated texts.

Working memory plays a crucial role in various domains of higher level cognition. Comprehending a text, solving a problem, and reasoning all critically hinge on a person's ability to store various intermediate products of a computation while simultaneously processing new information. The model originally proposed by Baddeley and Hitch (1974) addressed simultaneous processing and storage requirements and has become a dominant conception of working memory in cognitive psychology (see the reviews of Barrouillet, 1996; Ehrlich & Delafoy, 1990; Monnier & Roulin, 1994). Working memory has been defined (Baddeley, 1986, 1992) as a system of limited capacity that ensures a double function of dealing with and temporarily holding information. In Baddeley's model, working memory comprises three components. One component, the central executive, is the system proposed to be responsible for reasoning, decision making, and coordinating the operations of subsidiary specialized "slave systems." The peripheral subsystems, currently under investigation, are the articulatory or phonological loop and the visuospatial sketchpad. The *phonological loop* has the role of maintaining active speech-based verbal information during the process of articulation. Verbal information presented visually would also be transferred into the phonological loop, via articulatory rehearsal. The *visuospatial sketchpad* is considered to be responsible for the temporary storage of spatial and visual information, thus helping to ensure the formation and manipulation of mental images. This multicomponent model of working memory has successfully accounted for a wide range of data on short-term memory and appears to account for many processes in everyday cognition outside the laboratory (Logie, 1995). Concerning text comprehension, quite a number of studies have clearly highlighted the role of the central executive in working memory (e.g., Oakhill, Yuill, & Parkin, 1986). The capacity of this central system, as measured by performance on a reading span task, is an important factor in the high-level psycholinguistic operations underlying comprehension (e.g., Just & Carpenter, 1992; also see the meta-analysis of Daneman & Merikle, 1996). Nevertheless, as Gathercole and Baddeley (1993) underlined, except for a few studies, the role of the articulatory loop and the visuospatial sketchpad in comprehension have not been adequately explored.

Hegarty, Carpenter, and Just (1996) outlined the complexities involved in the integration of texts and pictures. The processing of texts accompanied by illustrations requires the learner to use the selection and coordination processes more efficiently than when used to process just text or illustrations. The learner has to evaluate the textual information and decide when it is appropriate to explore the illustration, but also consider and maintain various pieces of information in memory during this process. According to the authors, the integration of verbal and pictorial information is restricted, not only by the imagery and spatial abilities and previous knowledge of the learner, but also by the limited capacity of working memory. In the case of verbal and pictorial information presented on a computer screen, the screen page imposes a restriction on the amount of information that can be presented simultaneously (De Bruÿn, de Mul, & van Oostendorp, 1992). Complex phenomena and information often need to be presented over several screen pages. The learner must then not only integrate the information presented simultaneously on the same screen page, but maintain the information presented on the preceding screen pages in working memory in order to be able to integrate it with the new incoming information. The capacity of the working memory and more particularly that of the visuospatial working memory plays an important role in the comprehension of illustrated texts.

**The Visuospatial Sketchpad and the Phonological Loop
in the Integration of Verbal and Pictorial Information**

Online use of visuospatial working memory during the comprehension of illustrated texts was addressed by Kruley et al. (1994). They claimed that illustrations facilitate the construction of a mental model and that this construction takes place in the visuospatial working memory. These authors used a dual-task paradigm, which is widely used in several studies aimed at demonstrating the existence of separate subsystems. Texts containing spatial descriptions of an object (e.g., a volcano), a part of an organism (e.g., a leaf) or a mechanical device were presented orally. They were or were not accompanied by one picture displaying the structural relationships between the parts of the objects described in the texts. In the first experiment, a concurrent task was used, requiring subjects to maintain a dot display in visuospatial working memory while simultaneously listening to the text. In the "preload" condition, listening was interrupted after the presentation of each sentence, and subjects had to verify whether a test configuration of dots within a 4 × 4 grid matched a similar configuration presented earlier. In the control condition, no maintenance of the visual configuration was required during comprehension; subjects had merely to judge whether the majority of dots was above the center line of the grid. Text comprehension was tested by means of multiple-choice questions presented at the end of the text. The hypothesis was that if processing the pictures involves visuospatial working memory, this processing should compete with the maintenance of the configuration (the preload material) in working memory. A decrease in the benefit of the picture in comprehension performance in the preload condition should result. Consequently, an interaction between the presence and or absence of the picture and the preload and or control condition is expected to show up in comprehension. Another possibility, not exclusive of the first one, is that performance on the concurrent task in the preload condition will be lower in the picture condition than in the no-picture condition. In fact, comprehension was facilitated by the presence of the picture, and impaired in the preload condition, but there was no interaction between the two variables. However, the interaction hypothesis was corroborated by the concurrent task data; performance was higher in the control condition than in the preload condition, and the presence of a picture decreased performance in the preload condition only. When a nonvisual concurrent task was used in another experiment involving the maintenance of digits, such an interaction was not observed. From these results, the author interpreted that the interference observed in the previous experiments was specific to visuospatial processing.

In a series of experiments, Gyselinck, Cornoldi, Ehrlich, Dubois, and de Beni (in press), and Gyselinck, Ehrlich, Cornoldi, de Beni, and Dubois (2000) investigated the involvement of visuospatial working memory and the phonological loop in the comprehension of short, scientific texts presented on a computer screen and accompanied by illustrations. The same six texts were used in three experiments, and each text reviewed six notions of physics (static electricity, electrolysis, gas pressure, etc.). Each text consisted of nine sentences that were presented successively on the computer screen. The subject had to maintain in memory and also relate the content of successive sentences in order to understand the topic. Each sentence was or was not accompanied by an illustration. Previous investigations (Gyselinck, 1995) showed that these illustrations facilitate the construction of a mental model of these physics topics described in the texts, as assessed by subjects' performance on inference questions. In the present experiments, a concurrent task paradigm was used. While reading, subjects had to perform tasks involving either the visuospatial sketchpad or the phonological loop. Their comprehension of the phenomena described was tested by means of paraphrase and inference questions. The rationale was that if the integration of verbal and iconic information involves the visuospatial sketchpad, this integration should be disrupted by a concurrent spatial task. Consequently, the beneficial effect of illustrations on comprehension should decrease. However, this decrease should not be observed with a concurrent verbal task.

In the first experiment, a concurrent visuospatial task derived from Kruley et al. (1994) was used, and a verbal concurrent task and control task were constructed on the same basis. The beneficial effect of illustrations on comprehension was preserved, despite the concurrent tasks. Also, contrary to Kruley et al. (1994), no selective interference on concurrent task performance was observed. A close examination of the material, however, suggest that because of the characteristics of the illustrations used and the sequential mode of presentation, spatial–sequential processing (Pazzaglia & Cornoldi, 1999) rather than visual processing should predominate, as in Kruley et al. (1994). Therefore, in the second and third experiment (Gyselinck et al., in press), different concurrent tasks were implemented.

In addition, some studies suggest that individual differences may affect the comprehension process and the integration of texts and pictures.

Pazzaglia and Cornoldi (1999) showed that the capacity of the visuospatial sketchpad affects the memorization of a descriptive text. Subjects with a high spatial span, measured by means of the Corsi-blocks test, recalled the description of a city better than low spatial span subjects. Both subgroups of subjects were equivalent on a digit span test. In Mayer and Sims (1994), the spatial ability of subjects as measured by rotation tests was considered. Results showed that high spatial ability subjects benefited more than low spatial ability subjects from the concurrent presentation of a text and visual animation compared to a successive presentation of each. In Gyselinck et al. (2000), the spatial span determined the ability of subjects to integrate verbal and pictorial information. Individual differences, then, appear to be an important factor to consider.

The concurrent tasks chosen by Gyselinck et al. (in press) are widely used in working memory studies (e.g., Farmer, Berman, & Fletcher, 1986). A sequential tapping task was used to produce spatial suppression. Subjects had to repeatedly press a series of buttons to form a geometrical figure. A verbal articulatory task was used to produce articulatory suppression; subjects had to repeatedly produce a series of syllables. In the control condition, subjects had no task to perform. In the second experiment (Gyselinck et al., in press), subjects performed these concurrent tasks together with the texts or with illustrated texts. Results on comprehension performance showed that the tapping concurrent task resulted in the disappearance of the beneficial effect of illustrations, while the articulatory concurrent task impaired performance similarly in both formats of presentation without decreasing the advantage due to the presence of illustrations. Second, only high spatial span subjects benefited from illustrations. These subjects were selectively disturbed by the tapping concurrent task, whereas low span subjects did not demonstrate this pattern.

These results clearly show that visuospatial working memory is selectively involved in the processing of illustrations facilitating the comprehension of scientific texts. Two sources of evidence converge to support this claim. First, the dual-task procedure produced a selective interference effect on comprehension performance. Second the capacity of spatial working memory determined the patterns of results.

In the third experiment (Gyselinck et al., in press), the focus was on the role of the phonological loop. The presentation of texts alone was contrasted with a format involving merely the illustrations with some necessary labels associated to them (thus, verbal processing was reduced). Results showed that the articulatory concurrent task selectively impaired comprehension in the text-only format. That is, an interference effect was obtained in the text-only format, but not in the illustrations-only format. This result suggests that the interference is specifically related to phonological memory and is not a general effect due to another general mechanism such as a decrease in attention. Second, the capacity of phonological memory, as measured by performance on the digit span test, determined the pattern of performance. High digit span subjects performed better in text-only format than in the illustrations-only format, whereas low digit span subjects had similar performance in the two formats. In addition, high digit span subjects were selectively disturbed by the articulatory concurrent task, whereas low digit span subjects did not show such a selective interference effect. Concerning the effect of the tapping concurrent task on the processing of illustrations presented alone, no significant selective impairment was observed in this format. However, the mean values varied in this direction. Thus, processing illustrations presented alone does not seem to involve the visuospatial working memory to the same extent as processing illustrations presented with a text.

METHODOLOGICAL AND THEORETICAL IMPLICATIONS OF THE TWO APPROACHES

Two lines of research, which differ in their objective and in their methodology, have been presented here. On the one hand, on the instructional field, studies focus on the processes that allow learners to integrate verbal and visual information in order to improve learning. For that purpose, the conditions that facilitate or prevent learning are manipulated and the constraints of human information processing (particularly that of working memory) are considered. Additionally, the studies we present here in the field of cognitive psychology focus on the construction process of a mental model in working memory. To understand the involvement of working memory in learning, subjects are required to process various sources of information while simultaneously performing several tasks. In the first set of studies, the study of processes involved in working memory is a secondary aim, whereas in the second set of studies, the investigation of these processes is the main aim. One consequence of this divergence in focus in these studies is differing methodologies. This chapter will not compare the respective interests of the instructional and the cognitive approaches concerning the integration and comprehension of information in a multimedia context (for a review, see Dixon, 1991, for a discussion about the relations between research and application; and Goldman, 1991, for a review of the contrast between the cognitive load theory and constructivist theories). As Sweller and Chandler (1991) observed:

> . . . it is one thing to accept process models and a constructivist perspective; it is another to reject complementary viewpoints arrived at by alternate means. We believe cognitive load theory and the effects and findings it has generated should be judged on their merits

and not by whether the theory and procedures accord closely with the current orthodoxy.
(p. 361)

We totally agree with this view. Indeed, one of the main interests of the theories developed by Mayer (1997) and Sweller (1988) is that they provide a good survey of the problems and ideas of the last 20 years regarding verbal and visual information processing in learning. As discussed earlier, these theories, as well as theories developed in cognitive psychology, have generated numerous experiments and reliable data. We now summarize the main findings of the studies reported and present some of the criticisms that can be made about them. We then discuss the question with which any theory concerned with processing of various sources of information is faced: How do learners perform and achieve a learning task imposing such a load on storage and processing with such a limited working memory?

The Main Findings and the Methodological Limitations and Problems

Among the various studies conducted in the instructional field, one of the main findings is that redundant material has negative effects on performance. For example, Chandler and Sweller (1991) and Bobis et al. (1993) showed that learning was enhanced by the elimination of textual material described the contents of a diagram. We think that this result is not as generalizable as the authors believe it to be. A careful analysis of Chandler and Sweller's (1991) design and material show that the redundancy effect is only present in a few and very restricted situations. Inclusionary criteria for this effect to appear are that (a) the textual material must convey exactly the same information as the diagram (i.e., the diagram must be completely understandable in isolation), (b) the text must be short (i.e., the memory should not be prompted to relate the contents of the two sources of information), and (c) learners must be explicitly instructed to study both text and diagram (i.e., they must have to divide their attention between two tasks). In conclusion, this effect seems restricted to very particular instructional situations that are not very ecological. In most of the other situations, even in the case of a high redundancy of verbal and pictorial information, the concurrent presentation, as compared to the presentation of only one form of information, tends to lead to an increase in performance on memory and comprehension (see Gyselinck & Tardieu, 1999, for a review).

Apart from that point, the studies we present provide overall robust evidence that presentation of verbal and visual information when the material is combined into unitary source of information is beneficial. The integrated presentation allows learners to (a) avoid dividing their attention between several sources of information, (b) encourages them to pay attention only to relevant aspects of information, and (c) hold more information in each working memory store, reducing the processing load for working memory.

Some comments have to be made, however, about the consequences of the methodologies used. As previously stated, studies conducted in the instructional field tend to manipulate the learning conditions and to consider working memory constraints. However, the experimental designs used in the instructional studies tend not to strictly control variables related to working memory in the tasks performed. For example, the authors ( ) do not directly control the burden of working memory. From our point of view, this control is necessary in order to validate a theory based on load in working memory. In one study only, the authors have tempted to control memory load. Kalyuga, Chandler, and Sweller (1998) asked subjects to rate the perceived level of mental effort associated with their learning. This rating is not, however, a direct measure of memory load. Additionally, it is not clear whether such a subjective measure is reliable because it is not independent of the task. In other words, a learner may have the feeling that a task requires a greater cognitive effort than another, but this effort may not be a direct reflection of the actual load in memory. The differences in effort could just as well correspond to differences in interest or motivation of the learner for each task. Mayer and Moreno (1998) also assumed that the visual working memory is overloaded when materials are presented in the same modality. However, it may be that it is released from a part of processing by the auditory working memory when materials are presented in different modalities. Nothing, however, directly indicates that the visual component of working memory is overloaded. Theirs is only one of the possible interpretations for the decrease of performance. Using a dual-task paradigm would have more directly proved involvement of visual working memory.

Such a paradigm was used in the field of cognitive psychology, and reports here tend to confirm Baddeley's (1986), Logie's (1995), or more recently, Baddeley and Logie's (1999) model of working memory. Kruley et al. (1994) provided some evidence that visuospatial working memory is involved in the processing of illustrated texts. However, these data are limited to one type of material. Specifically, they used scientific texts describing a single object presented orally, accompanied by one static illustration that shows the structural relationships between parts of the object. This does not reflect the kind of phenomenon or event that is usually presented via multimedia systems, which, as we have previously noted, often needs to be presented on several successive screens. In the last three experiments reported (Gyselinck et al., 2000, in press), results indicate that the integration of texts and illustrations involves two subsystems of working memory. The phonological memory and the visuospatial memory could thus be considered as subsystems specialized in the storage of a verbatim trace of linguistic information and of a visual trace, respectively. These representations would then be the basis for higher level processes, which could be the prerogative of the central executive. These subsystems are directly involved in comprehension, and particularly in the integration of pictorial and linguistic information. In addition, these experiments clearly show the importance of taking individual differences into consideration. The ability of subjects to integrate pictorial and verbal information and their ability to cope with dual tasks appears to be an important factor to consider in constructing efficient multimedia systems.

However, these experiments do not inform us on the precise role of the visuospatial memory in the various stages of the integration process (i.e., the exploration process, storage process, and combination process). Another limitation of these studies is that only two types of information were studied: verbal information (presented orally or visually) and static pictorial information, which is far from the range of possibilities provided by multimedia systems. In particular, we wonder if the same processes are involved when dynamic pictorial information is presented. The study of these other various forms of presenting information is still in its infancy, and working memory constraints are not the main focus in this area yet (Schnotz, Böckheler, & Grzondziel, 1999; for a review see Bétrancourt & Tversky, 2000).

A Theoretical Dilemma

As mentioned earlier, Mayer (1997) as well as Sweller (1988) adopted the classical conception of working memory having a limited capacity in both size and duration of storage. Because of this limitation, very little information can be held inside this memory store at one time. It is generally agreed on that working memory is the place where current mental activities take place, and that because it is dramatically limited in duration and in capacity, few elements can be stored in working memory much less processed at the same time. These elements must be combined, compared, or related together, and these processes use working memory resources that are limited. Then the question arises for the theories presented, and for any cognitive theory: How do learners perform and achieve a learning task with such a load on storage and processing with a limited working memory?

This question is a well-known dilemma for memory theories (Kintsch, 1998). The dilemma comes precisely from the contradiction between the numerous demands the high level cognitive processes put on a limited working memory, and the visible easiness with which learners seem to learn when they have to face these demands. A great number of cognitive tasks should exceed the capacities of working memory. To solve a problem, to understand a text, illustrated or not, to acquire new knowledge, and so on, requires from the individual temporary storage of information and execution of operations needed for the achievement of these tasks at the same time. It is difficult then to imagine that all or even a small part of this information can be held in a working memory system that is limited in space and in time.

Kintsch (1998) asked "How can people live with such a terrible memory?" (p. 215). The theory of long-term working memory (Ericsson & Kintsch, 1995) may provide a solution to this dilemma. In the classical theory of working memory, short-term working memory (STWM) can be thought of as the active part of the long-term memory, the focus of attention, containing no more than four to seven items. These items, available in STWM, could serve as retrieval cues for the subsets of long-term memory linked to those in STWM through retrieval structures. One retrieval operation from one cue in STWM could make part of long-term working memory (LTWM) connected to that cue accessible. Hence, the quantity of information that can be processed in working memory would depend both on items present in STWM and on those retrievable from LTWM. Such a view accounts for limits in the capacity of human processing, not only in terms of a strictly limited capacity of a STWM, but also in terms of limits of a LTWM, only restricted by the number and the nature of the retrieval structures available by contents of STWM.

To illustrate the distinction between STWM and LTWM, Ericsson and Kintsch (1995) referred to the work of Glanzer and colleagues concerning the effect of interrupting reading on comprehension. For example, Glanzer, Dorfman and Kaplan (1981) presented to their subjects texts containing eight sentences. After each sentence, subjects have to read another unrelated sentence, so that sentences 1, 3, 5, and 7 form a connected discourse, and sentences 2, 4, 6, and 8 are unrelated. Subjects then had to answer comprehension questions. The results showed that the interruptions had no effect on comprehension, as subjects were able to answer questions for the interrupted texts as well as for the texts without interruption. This kind of result is not easily interpretable within the classical framework of working memory. Each unrelated sentence should have eliminated from short-term memory the trace of the preceding sentences, or at least disturbed the establishment of the coherence of the text and had a detrimental effect on comprehension. The theory of LTWM may provide an explanation for this result. Sentences following each interruption provide cues in short-term memory (STM), which permit the retrieval of the long-term memory (LTM) trace of the previous part of the text from LTWM. The mental representation that the subject has constructed during comprehension works then as a retrieval structure. Each new sentence read gives the subject access to the previous trace of the text in LTM.

Such a view raises several questions. First, what is the precise definition of a *retrieval structure*? In comprehension, for example, retrieval structures for a text comprise the network of micropropositions derived from the text. The units of the network are connected both in a hierarchical macrostructure and are linked with structures of LTM (such as schema, script, frame, or knowledge-based associations). When a new proposition is constructed during comprehension, it belongs to the text base. It is then associated with other propositions because it shares with them an argument or together, they form a set of propositions depending on the same macrostructure. This new proposition is linked to other propositions in working memory that are already connected to the propositions held in LTM. This new proposition becomes a cue to retrieve propositions previously derived. The question remains as to how these retrieval structures work when the reader must process textual information in addition to pictorial information.

Another problem is that these retrieval structures depend on a rich knowledge base and automatic encoding strategies. In the case of text comprehension, of course, these encoding strategies have become standard operations, acquired with time and experience. Automatization of these operations is not the case however for all cognitive activities, especially those that require time and practice. In addition, when knowledge fails to accurately represent information, it is difficult to establish links between items held in STM and items held in LTM, and thus to generate a LTWM. The LTWM could then only operate in situations where learners have expertise and good use of encoding strategies. The applicability of this theory is therefore very constrained.

CONCLUSION

To conclude, we presented a survey of various theories and related studies concerning constraints on working memory in the integration and comprehension of information in a multimedia context. Though the range of media explored is still restricted, it is clear that working memory is an important psychological concept, which has to be considered when thinking about cognitive constraints in the use of multimedia systems. Even if the objectives, theoretical constructs, and methodologies employed in these studies differ in some regard, the studies conducted on the instructional field and those conducted on the field of cognitive psychology come to the same conclusions. Users seem able to cope with multiple sources of information; it can even be beneficial in most cases for learning, when they are presented in a way that encourages their integration. However, the characteristics of the various types of information associated with the kinds of processing they require have to be taken into consideration. A user may well be able to cope with several sources of information requiring different types of processing by making use of different components of working memory. This user may, however, become less efficient and may lose some information if part of the information requires simultaneous processing of similar material, making use of the same components of working memory. The studies reported in this chapter also emphasize the need to consider the limitations in cognitive resources available to the user. In order to be successful, systems must be adapted to the cognitive limitations of the user (Reinking & Bridwell-Bowles, 1996), and particularly those of working memory. Finally, it seems that working memory, a storage system limited in size and in duration, is a necessary component for any model or theory aimed at describing and explaining how users integrate multiple sources of information. The concept of working memory provides us, however, with a dilemma that Ericsson and Kintsch (1995) proposed to solve with the theory of LTWM. Their solution has to be further investigated to see if it applies not only to text understanding, but also to multimedia processing.

REFERENCES

Baddeley, A. (1986). *Working memory*. Oxford: Oxford University Press.
Baddeley, A. (1992). Is working memory working? The fifteenth Bartlett lecture. *The Quarterly Journal of Experimental Psychology, 44A*, 1–31.
Baddeley, A., & Hitch, G. (1974). Working memory. In G. A. Bower (Ed.), *The psychology of learning and motivation* (Vol. 8, pp. 47–89). New York: Academic Press.
Baddeley, A., & Logie, R. (1999). Working memory: The multiple-component model. In A. Miyake & P. Shah (Eds.), *Models of working memory: Mechanisms of active maintenance and executive control* (pp. 28–61). New York: Cambridge University Press.
Barrouillet, P. (1996). Ressources, capacités cognitives et mémoire de travail: Postulats, métaphores et modèles [Resources, cognitive capacities, and working memory: Postulates, metaphors, and models]. *Psychologie Française, 41*, 319–338.
Bétrancourt, M., & Tversky, B. (2000). Effect of computer animation on user's performance: A review. *Le Travail Humain, 4*(63), 311–329.
Bobis, J., Sweller, J., & Cooper, M. (1993). Cognitive load effects in a primary school geometry task. *Learning and Instruction, 3*, 1–21).
Chandler, P., & Sweller, J. (1991). Cognitive load theory and the format of instruction. *Cognition and Instruction, 8*, 293–332.
Chandler, P., & Sweller, J. (1992). The split-attention effect as a factor in the design of instruction. *British Journal of Educational Psychology, 62*, 233–246.
Daneman, M., & Merikle, P. (1996). Working memory and language comprehension: A meta-analysis. *Psychonomic Bulletin & Review, 3*, 422–433.
De Bruÿn, D., de Mul, S., & van Oostendorp, H. (1992). The influence of screensize and text layout on the study of text. *Behavior & Information Technology, 11*(2), 71–78.
Dixon, P. (1991). From research to theory to practice: Commentary on Chandler and Sweller. *Cognition and Instruction, 8*, 343–350.
Dobson, M. (1999). Learning with interactive graphical representations [Special issue]. *Learning and Instruction, 9*.
Ehrlich, M.-F., & Delafoy, M. (1990). La mémoire de travail: structure, fonctionnement, capacité [Working memory: structure, function and capacity]. *L'Année Psychologique, 90*, 403–428.

Ericsson, K. A., & Kintsch, W. (1995). Long-term working memory. *Psychological Review, 102,* 211–245.

Farmer, E. W., Berman, J. V. F., & Fletcher, Y. L. (1986). Evidence for a visuo-spatial scratchpad in working memory. *The Quarterly Journal of Experimental Psychology, 38A,* 675–688.

Gathercole, S. E., & Baddeley, A. D. (1993). *Working memory and language.* Hillsdale, NJ: Lawrence Erlbaum Associates.

Glanzer, M., Dorfman, D., & Kaplan, B. (1981). Short-term storage in the processing of text. *Journal of Verbal Learning and Verbal Behavior, 20,* 656–670.

Glenberg, A. M., & Langston, W. E. (1992). Comprehension of illustrated text: Pictures help to build mental models. *Journal of Memory and Language, 31,* 129–151.

Goldman, S. R. (1991). On the derivation of instructional applications from cognitive theories: Commentary on Chandler and Sweller. *Cognition and Instruction, 8,* 333–342.

Gyselinck, V. (1995). *Les Modèles mentaux dans la compréhension de textes: le rôle des illustrations* [Neutral models in text comprehension: The role of illustrations]. Unpublished doctoral dissertation, Université René Descartes, Paris V.

Gyselinck, V., Cornoldi, C., Ehrlich, M.-F., Dubois, V., & de Beni, R. (in press). Visuospatial memory and phonological loop in learning from multimedia. *Applied Cognitive Psychology.*

Gyselinck, V., Ehrlich, M.-F., Cornoldi, C., de Beni, R., & Dubois, V. (2000). Visuospatial working memory in learning from multimedia system. *Journal of Computer Assisted Learning, 16,* 166–176.

Gyselinck, V., & Tardieu, H. (1999). The role of illustrations in text comprehension: What, when, for whom, and why? In H. van Oostendorp & S. R. Goldman (Eds.), *The construction of mental representations during reading.* Mahwah, NJ: Lawrence Erlbaum Associates.

Hegarty, M., Carpenter, P. A., & Just, M. A. (1996). Diagrams in the comprehension of scientific texts. In R. Barr, M. L. Kamil, P. Mosenthal, & P. D. Pearson (Eds.), *Handbook of reading research* (Vol. 2, pp. 641–668). Mahwah, NJ: Lawrence Erlbaum Associates.

Johnson-Laird, P. N. (1980). Mental models in cognitive science. *Cognitive Science, 4,* 71–115.

Johnson-Laird, P. N. (1983). *Mental models.* Cambridge: Cambridge University Press.

Just, M. A., & Carpenter, P. A. (1992). A capacity theory of comprehension: Individual differences in working memory. *Psychological Review, 99,* 122–149.

Kalyuga, S., Chandler, P., & Sweller, J. (1998). Levels of expertise and instructional design. *Human Factors, 40,* 1–17.

Kintsch, W. (1988). The use of knowledge in discourse processing: A construction-integration model. *Psychological Review, 95* 163–182.

Kintsch, W. (1998). *Comprehension: A paradigm for cognition.* Cambridge: Cambridge University Press.

Kruley, P., Sciama, S. C., & Glenberg, A. M. (1994). On-line processing of textual illustrations in the visuospatial sketchpad: Evidence from dual-task studies. *Memory and Cognition, 22,* 261–272.

Logie, R. H. (1995). *Visuo-spatial working memory.* Hillsdale, NJ: Lawrence Erlbaum Associates.

Mayer, R. E. (1997). Multimedia learning: Are we asking the right question? *Educational Psychologist, 32,* 1–19.

Mayer, R. E., & Anderson, R. B. (1991). Animations need narrations: An experimental test of a dual-coding hypothesis. *Journal of Educational Psychology, 83,* 484–490.

Mayer, R. E., & Anderson, R. B. (1992). The instructive animation: Helping students build connections between words and pictures in multimedia learning. *Journal of Educational Psychology, 84,* 444–452.

Mayer, R. E., & Moreno, R. (1998). A split-attention effect in multimedia learning: Evidence for dual processing systems in working memory. *Journal of Educational Psychology, 90,* 312–320.

Mayer, R. E., & Sims, V. K. (1994). For whom is a picture worth a thousand words? Extensions of a dual-coding theory of multimedia learning. *Journal of Educational Psychology, 86,* 389–401.

Mayer, R. E., Steinhoff, K., Bower, G., & Mars, R. (1995). A generative theory of textbook design: Using annotated illustrations to foster meaningful learning of science text. *Educational Technology Research and Development, 43,* 31–44.

Monnier, C., & Roulin, J.-L. (1994). A la recherche de calepin visuo-spatial en mémoire de travail [Searching for the visuo-spatial scratchpad in working memory]. *L'Année Psychologique, 94,* 425–460.

Mousavi, S. Y., Low, R., & Sweller, J. (1995). Reducing cognitive load by mixing auditory and visual presentation modes. *Journal of Educational Psychology, 87,* 319–334.

Mwangi, W., & Sweller, J. (1998). Learning to solve compare word problems: The effect of example format and generating self-explanations. *Cognition and Instruction, 16,* 173–199.

Oakhill, J. V., Yuill, N., & Parkin, A. J. (1986). On the nature of the difference between skilled and less-skilled comprehenders. *Journal of Research in Reading, 9,* 80–91.

Paivio, A. (1986). *Mental representations: A dual coding approach.* New York: Oxford University Press.

Pazzaglia, F., & Cornoldi, C. (1999). The role of distinct components of visuo-spatial working memory in the processing of texts. *Memory, 7,* 19–41.

Reinking, D., & Bridwell-Bowles, L. (1996). Computers in reading and writing. In R. Barr, M. L. Kamil, P. Mosenthal, & P. D. Pearson (Eds.), *Handbook of reading research* (Vol. 2, pp. 310–340). Mahwah, NJ: Lawrence Erlbaum Associates.

Schnotz, W. (1999a). Introduction [Special issue]. *European Journal of Psychology of Education, 14,* 163–165.

Schnotz, W. (1999b). Visual Learning with new technologies [Special issue]. *European Journal of Psychology of Education, 14.*

Schnotz, W., Böckheler, J., & Grzondziel, H. (1999). Individual and co-operative learning with interactive animated pictures. *European Journal of Psychology of Education, 14,* 245–265.

Sweller, J. (1988). Cognitive load during problem solving: Effects on learning. *Cognitive Science, 12,* 257–285.

Sweller, J. (1994). Cognitive load theory, learning difficulty and instructional design. *Learning and Instruction, 4,* 295–312.

Sweller, J., & Chandler, P. (1991). Evidence for cognitive load theory. *Cognition and Instruction, 8,* 351–362.

Sweller, J., & Chandler, P. (1994). Why some material is difficult to learn. *Cognition and Instruction, 12,* 185–233.

Sweller, J., Chandler, P., Tierney, P., & Cooper, M. (1990). Cognitive load and selective attention as factors in the structuring of technical material. *Journal of Experimental Psychology: General, 119,* 176–192.

Tindall-Ford, S., Chandler, P., & Sweller, J. (1997). When two sensory modes are better than one. *Journal of Experimental Psychology: Applied, 3,* 257–287.

van Dijk, T. A., & Kintsch, W. (1983). *Strategies of discourse comprehension.* New York: Academic Press.

Chapter 2

People @ Play: Electronic Games

Jeffrey Goldstein
University of Utrecht, The Netherlands

In the summer of 1997, Senator Lauch Faircloth of North Carolina led the charge in Congress to ban games from computers used by civil servants. "We don't condone the loafing that goes on," he said, citing the diabolical 'boss key,' a tool included with some games that allows a guilty player to quickly shift his screen to a convincing-looking spreadsheet the moment a supervisor appears. Other businesses also banned computer games on the job, fearing that they interfered with job performance (*New York Times*, 1997; *International Herald Tribune*, 1997). Does work suffer as a result of electronic games? Do the contents of games, for example, violent themes or sexual stereotypes, have deleterious consequences on players? Have computer games no redeeming value? If they do not, why are they played by nearly all children and a growing percent of the adult population?

This chapter summarizes selected research on the effects of electronic games. No attempt has been made to review the 300 or so studies on computer games (Federman, Carbone, Chen, & Munn, 1996), but rather to examine some of the issues surrounding their uses, effects, and applications. The chapter examines the demographics of electronic game play, discusses the effects and appeal of violent games, and considers the uses of computer games in educational and therapeutic settings.

There is substantial research, in terms of quantity anyway, on console video games (those played on such systems as Nintendo, Sega, and SONY Play Station) and arcade video games (those played on dedicated game machines in commercial spaces). These games form the basis of this review. Differences between console, arcade, CD-ROM and online games may be crucial to their effects. Just as television violence and the violence in video games may have different effects (Goldstein, 1995), so too may differences between platform and online games be of importance in determining their effects on players. Online games can involve many players simultaneously, whereas platform games tend to be limited to four players. Online gamers are not subject to the same kind of social cues as platform players, who often play with others looking on or competing. Cognitions also differ between online and platform players: knowledge that one plays in real time, and with many others around the world can add to the excitement, immediacy, and intensity of play. When it is necessary to distinguish video games, CD-ROM games for personal computers, or online games downloadable or playable through the Internet, this is done. Otherwise, the terms *computer game*, *video game* and *electronic game* are used to include computer, CD-ROM, platform/console, and online games.

THIRD-PERSON EFFECTS IN MEDIA RESEARCH

The media do not affect me, and perhaps they do not affect you, but you and I can agree that they have undesirable effects on other people. This line of reasoning is known as the *third-person effect* in media research—the belief that the media affect unknown others more than they affect oneself (Perloff, 1999).

With the introduction of nearly every new entertainment medium, questions are raised about its possible harm. Will it displace reading, studying, sports? Is it addictive? Will it turn good children bad? Neither the concerns nor the arguments about computer games differ from those raised by earlier media, including the belief that "this time, it's different."

According to a survey of more than 6,300 individuals online by PC Data (1999), an independent research firm that tracks hardware and software sales in North America, "The group with the highest negative feelings about games are older people and they are also the ones least likely to actually have a computer or video game." This confirms what other studies also report—that those who are least familiar with video games are most likely to believe that they pose a threat (e.g., Ferreira & Ribeiro, 2001; Holm Sorensen & Jessen, 2000; Sneed & Runco, 1992). Eighty-five percent of teenagers in a Canadian survey said that games had some harmful influence on kids who played them (Kline, 2000). About 33% felt that violent games had a bad influence on some kids, and 27% believed violent games have a negative effect on many players. Only 15% thought violent games had no harmful consequences at all. Girls were significantly more likely than boys to believe that video games are harmful, and tended to be much harsher critics of video games than boys. The majority of teenagers believe that video games can be addictive, but heavy players viewed video games less negatively than light players.

WHO PLAYS COMPUTER GAMES?

A survey of 346 Dutch children in 7th and 8th grades (mean age 11.5 yrs.) found that 35% of boys and 9% of girls spent more than 30 min per day playing video games (van Schie & Wiegman, 1997). The Dutch children kept a diary for 1 week in which they recorded their out-of-school activities. About 70% of the children had played video games in a given week (75% of boys, 63% of girls). Comparable results have been found throughout Europe and North America (Goldstein, 1994).

Social isolation, loneliness, popularity, social status, and intelligence were measured with standardized questionnaires. School performance was rated by the child's teacher. Playing video games did not appear to take place at the expense of children's other leisure activities, social integration, or school performance. "Children who spent more time on video games seem to be more active overall" (van Schie & Wiegman, 1997, p. 1189). A positive relationship was found between time spent on video games and a child's intelligence. The only social behavior measured by van Schie and Wiegman (1997) related to playing video games was prosocial behavior (that is, offering help to another person), but even this was weak ($r=-.12$).

Although children and adolescents are the predominant platform video game players, online and PC gamers tend to be adults. Nearly ¾ of PC entertainment software users are over age 18. Thirty-nine percent of those using PCs to run entertainment software are age 36 and over; 31% are between the ages of 18 and 35. Seventy percent of online gamers are between ages 25 and 55. Ninety percent of all purchasers of video and or PC game software are over 18 years of age.

People play electronic games for many different reasons and with varying patterns of play. Some play to experience excitement, some to become experts and to impress their friends, and others because computer games are challenging or educational. Some even play widely vilified games in order to elicit predictable, if negative, reactions from teachers, parents, or girls. Males and females enjoy different kinds of games and enjoy play for different reasons (Goldstein, 1994; Kline, 2000; Nikken, 2000; PC Data, 1999).

Based on his observations of behavior of multiuser dungeons, text-based virtual reality environments (MUDs), Bartle (1996) described four types of player in multiplayer games. *Achievers* who focus on the game-related goals, such as accumulating treasure, mastering puzzles, or increasing skills. *Explorers* appear to enjoy mapping the topology of the game, learning about its secrets, and gathering esoteric knowledge about how the game actually works. *Socializers* join a MUD primarily to interact with others. Finally, there is a small group of people known as *killers* who harass others online, often using the tools provided by the game itself to do so. According to Wallace

(1999), "Intergroup tension develops routinely among some of the player types because their motives for participating are quite distinct. Socializers and killers, for example, have the most fractious relationship because their motives for participating are, for all practical purposes, mutually exclusive" (pp. 97–98).

Addiction to Video Games

Are electronic games addictive? Surveys in North America, Europe, and Japan estimate that from 6% to 20% of boys who play computer games may be characterized as "excessive" players (Ng, 1990; Saxe, 1994). Cumberbatch and colleagues in England interviewed 100 young people ages 7 to 16 years (Cumberbatch, Maguire, & Woods, 1993). When the children were asked directly whether they thought that young people could become addicted to computer games, 97% thought that this was possible. However, just 29% knew anyone who was addicted to electronic games. It was clear from the interviews that *addiction* was interpreted generously to include playing for prolonged periods of time. Few children reported any feelings of compulsion to play. Nearly 40% of interviewees reported that they had experienced addiction at some time. "From the interviews, it was evident that children were clearly interpreting the term addiction in terms of short-term, transitory fascination with a newly acquired game or equipment" (Cumberbatch et al., 1993).

The term addiction is often used imprecisely. In the past few years, psychologists have modified the American Psychiatric Association's Diagnostic and Statistical Manual, 4th Edition for maladaptive gambling and applied it to video game play. According to Fisher (1994), the modified dimensions of video game addiction include the following: (a) Preoccupation with video game playing, (b) playing video games as a way to escape from problems, (c) trying for an increasingly high score, and (d) borrowing money to play video games. Anyone who answered *yes* to these (or any) four items was regarded as a "pathological player" according to Fisher (1994). Even by these relaxed criteria, only 6% of Fisher's sample of 460 school children met the definition of pathological players.

Studies that consider addiction to electronic games offer us snapshots in time rather than dynamic pictures of play over a period of weeks or months. At any given moment, there are players deeply immersed in the gaming experience, but should this temporary obsession be regarded as addiction? In a Canadian survey, Kline (2000) found that electronic game play did not dominate the leisure activity even of the heavy players, who preferred hanging around with friends, going out in town, and watching TV. The majority of teens said they were *sort of interested* (46%) or *not at all interested* (37%) in playing video games. Only 14% considered themselves to be *really into*

games. Most of these enthusiasts were boys (22% of male respondents), although there were a number of girls (6%) who were also deeply "into"
games.

Will the growth of online gaming alter this picture? Concerns about Internet addiction have been expressed lately (Kraut et al., 1998; see also
Shapiro, 1999).

The "holding power" of electronic games for frequent players reflects a
certain degree of *attentional inertia.* The term was used by Anderson and colleagues to describe the fact that the longer a child watches TV, the more
difficult it is to distract him from the screen (Anderson, Choi & Lorch,
1987). A similar effect may occur with computer games; the more one plays,
the more one wants to play.

"Heavy" Players

Some studies compare the players who play computer games most frequently with those who play less often (e.g., Griffiths & Hunt, 1998; Roe &
Muijs, 1998). Heavy video game players are sometimes found to be less aca-
demically successful, more aggressive, or less sociable than those who play
less often. Such findings are particularly likely when the focus of research is
on video arcade games, rather than home personal computers (PCs) or
video game systems. These studies typically suffer from a serious flaw: By
comparing heavy users of video games with less frequent players, they end
up comparing (mostly) boys, the most frequent players, to a group
composed mainly of girls, the least frequent players. Of course the former
will exhibit more "masculine" traits: more aggression, less interest in book-
ish activities, poorer grades. This has everything to do with differences between boys and girls and little or nothing to do with electronic games. However, even among boys, there is a correlation between amount of time spent
playing video games and poorer school performance. There is no reason to
think that games are the cause of poor school performance. Indeed, according to Roe and Muijs (1998) poor performance in school drives some
boys to achieve success in the world of video games.

Physiological Effects of Electronic Games

Arousal can be influenced by the contents of electronic games (their excitement, emotional content, tempo), the act of playing, and the circumstances
in which play takes place. Indeed, Winkel, Novak, and Hopson (1987) attributed the effects of violent video games not to their violent content, but
to their arousing nature. There are large individual differences in tonic
arousal level and arousability (see Scott, 1995; Winkel et al., 1987).

Segal and Dietz (1991) assessed metabolic and cardiovascular responses of 32 males and females, ages 16 to 25 years, while playing video games. Heart rate, blood pressure, and oxygen consumption were measured over a 30-min period while playing *Ms. Pac-Man*™, and compared with measurements taken in a standing, inactive position. Playing the video game significantly increased heart rate, systolic and diastolic blood pressure, and oxygen consumption in both males and females.

However, in other circumstances, playing electronic games can result in just the opposite effects. In one study (Vasterling, Jenkins, Tope, & Burish, 1993), cancer patients undergoing chemotherapy were assigned to one of three groups: a no-treatment control, relaxation, or cognitive distraction, which involved playing video games during chemotherapy. Distraction and relaxation patients reported less nausea prior to chemotherapy and lower systolic blood pressure following chemotherapy than no-treatment controls.

Positron emission tomography (PET) scans were taken while healthy men played a computer game. The neurotransmitter dopamine, thought to be involved in learning, reinforcement of behavior, attention, and sensorimotor coordination, was released during computer game play (Koepp et al., 1998). *Neurotransmitters* are substances that facilitate communication between neurons. Eight healthy men, ages 36 to 46, underwent two 50 min PET scans, one while playing a computer game and one while looking at an empty screen. The computer game involved using a mouse to move a tank through a battlefield on a screen. Subjects had to collect flags with the tank while destroying enemy tanks. If subjects collected all flags, they progressed to the next level, which required more flags to be collected. A $10 reward was given for each level achieved. Playing computer games resulted in an increase and binding of dopamine to its receptors. This was positively related to performance level during play. These results show *in situ* behavioral conditions under which dopamine is released in humans.

Video Games and Seizures

Controversy has revolved around the possible inducement of paroxysmal discharges (seizures) as a result of playing certain video games. Badinand-Hubert and colleagues (1998) studied whether video games induce paroxysmal discharges in different groups of patients. One hundred fifteen subjects ages 7 to 30 from five different French laboratories were studied; 33 had had seizures exclusively under visual stimuli, 42 had both photogenic seizures and spontaneous seizures occurring independently, and 40 had nonphotosensitve seizures. The research protocol included one television sequence, three sequences of video games (one with a high-speed, flickering pattern, one with a stroboscopic effect, and one with an emotional battle scene), presented at different distances from the screen at 50 and 100 Hz. The following factors were crucial in relation to seizures: the 100 Hz screen was significantly safer than 50 Hz, the distance from the screen (1 m was safer than 50 cm), and, for the 50 Hz screen, the pattern of images. Video games did not provoke seizures in subjects who had nonphotosensitive epilepsy, but may induce seizures in photosensitive subjects, a result also reported by Fylan, Harding, Edson, and Webb (1999). However, even among photosensitive subjects, a hand-held game module failed to induce seizures. For those who are photosensitive, a 100 Hz screen may offer significant protection against seizures.

Conclusion

Under appropriate conditions, electronic games are capable both of increasing and decreasing sympathetic nervous system activity, and altering heart, blood pressure, and respiration rates. We can speculate that whether games have the effect of heightening or lowering sympathetic activity levels depends on the players' cognitions, on their beliefs about why they are playing, and what they hope to accomplish by playing.

VIOLENCE IN VIDEO GAMES

Recent incidents of horrendous violence by young people have resurrected concern about a culture of violence. Interactive electronic games figure into this equation. Video and computer games are indicted along with television, films, and pop music, with no meaningful distinctions made among them.

Several studies report that playing violent games is correlated with lower school performance, more aggression, delinquency, and behavioral and emotional problems (Dill & Dill, 1998; Funk, Germann, & Buchman, 1997). Those who prefer violent video games are most likely to be above average in aggression, and to show other characteristics of aggressive people; namely, poorer school performance, more delinquency, and so on (Roe & Muijs, 1998).

Matters of Definition and Measurement

There is much confusion about the definition of *violence* and terms like *media violence* and *violent video games*. Psychologists define violence and aggression as the intentional injury of another person. However, there is neither intent to injure, nor a living victim in a video game. When critics refer to violence in the media or violent video games, they rarely distinguish between real violence—people hurting one another as in warfare or a slap in the face—and symbolic or fantasy violence, in which characters engage in mock battle. Nor do they distinguish in their body counts between cartoon characters, fantasy figures in video games, dramatic violence portrayed by human actors, and real violence in news and documentary programs.

On the question of measurement, studies of violent video games typically fail to distinguish *aggressive play* from *aggressive behavior*. What appears to a researcher to be an increase in aggression may be an increase in aggressive *play*, where there is no intent to injure anyone. Media violence research is clouded by such ambiguities.

An article by K. E. Dill and J. C. Dill (1998) serves as an illustration of this confusion. They wrote that video games should have the same negative effects as television violence, namely,

> priming of aggressive thoughts, weakening of inhibitions against antisocial behavior, modeling, reinforcement, decreased empathy for others, and the creation of a more violent world view.

> "Repeated exposure to aggressive video games could make aggressive cognitions and affect chronically available, thus increasing the likelihood of aggressive responses. In the long term, this would mean that chronic exposure to violent video games would lead to increases in the tendency of an individual to act aggressively and that this effect would be pervasive. . . . If violent video game play indeed depicts victims as deserving attacks, and if these video games tend to portray other humans as "targets," then reduced empathy is likely to be a consequence of violent video game play, thus putting the player at risk for becoming a more violent individual.

The Dills write that perhaps video games would have stronger effects than TV because of the active involvement of players. They argue that players must act aggressively and are then reinforced for this aggression. Dill and Dill (1998) wrote that

> In violent video games, aggression is often the main goal, and killing adversaries means winning the game and reaping the benefits. While in real life, murder is a crime, in a violent video game, murder is the most reinforced behavior. . . . The violent video game player is an active aggressor and the players' behavioral repertoire is expanded to include new and varied aggressive alternatives.

Dill and Dill (1998) noted that

> "Much of what has been done has focused on very young children and has examined aggressive free play as the main behavioral dependent measure." According to Griffiths (1999), in a review of research on violence and video games, "the majority of studies on very young children tend to show that children become more aggressive after playing or watching a violent video game, but *these were all based on the observation of free play*."

This is precisely the problem that leads to fuzzy conclusions, confusing aggressive play with aggressive behavior. In the rare studies that measure both aggressive play and aggressive behavior (e.g., Cooper & Mackie, 1986; Hellendoorn & Harinck, 1997), violent games affect the former and not the latter. The strongest effects of video games are found with the weakest, most ambiguous measures of aggression, those most removed from real violence (see, e.g., Anderson & Dill, 2000).

In part because of these ambiguities, those who review the existing research on violent electronic games arrive at different conclusions. Among recent reviews, some conclude that violent video games are a cause of violent behavior (Anderson & Bushman, 2001; Anderson & K. E. Dill, 2000; K. E. Dill & J. C. Dill, 1998), whereas others conclude that there is insufficient evidence to draw a conclusion (Bensley & Van Eenwyk, 2001; Durkin, 1995; Federal Trade Commission, 2000; Funk et al., 1997; Griffiths, 1999; Gunter, 1998; Saxe, 1994).

The Attractions of Violent Video Games

No one is forced to play Mortal Kombat or Doom. The attraction of violent entertainment is best explained by analyzing its portrayal, its audience, and the context in which it is consumed.

The makers of violent entertainment are sometimes accused of marketing "violence for violence's sake" (Federal Trade Commission, 2000; Grossman, 1995). But that is not what people seek. Violence, if it is to be entertaining, must fulfill certain requirements: It must have a moral story in which good triumphs over evil, and it must carry cues to its unreality—music, sound effects, a fantasy storyline, or cartoon-like characters. People are highly selective in the violence they seek or tolerate (Goldstein, 1998, 1999). Nearly everyone likes some form of violent entertainment, but they do not appreciate the violent entertainment preferred by other people.

The Audience

Violent entertainment offers something for nearly everyone. For some boys and men, violence is the thing. But for the majority of consumers, violence is a means to an end, a device valued more for what it does than for what it is. The consumers of violent entertainment do not share a single motive; some seek excitement, others seek companionship or social acceptance through shared experience, and still others wish to see justice enacted. Immersion in a fantasy world is also conducive to the pleasant transcendental experience known as "flow" (Csikszentmihalyi, 1990).

People can choose the degree of emotional content and frenzy with which they are most comfortable, just as they do when selecting the music to which they listen. An undeniable characteristic of violent imagery is its emotional wallop; it gives most people a jolt. Not everyone finds this kind of stimulation pleasant, but some do, namely, those who have a strong need for sensation. Even if players find the violence repugnant, they can fine tune their involvement in the game by focusing on its graphics, technique, or on their score, in order to control their degree of engagement.

Researchers who fail to acknowledge the importance of social life for adolescents are unlikely to offer us much insight into the world of computer games. Almost no studies of the presumed harmful effects of computer games have considered how and why people play them, or why people play at all. This is surprising given that research on video games is often conducted by social psychologists. Kline (2000) and Holm Sorensen and Jessen (2000) are among the few researchers who place video games in a social context. Holm Sorensen and Jessen (2000) noted, "The social aspect of playing computer games is another essential reason for the children's interest . . . Computer games generate friendship and social events, and computer games can be cultivated as a common interest—an interest that often goes beyond the playing itself" (p. 120).

Youngsters, like researchers who study violence, are willing to expose themselves to unpleasant images because the benefits of doing so outweigh the costs. Thus, players have overriding reasons for engaging with violent themes.

Social Identity

Violent entertainment appeals primarily to males, and it appeals to them mostly in groups. These are social occasions, particularly suitable for "male bonding" and communicating a masculine identity to friends. Boys may play violent video games alone in their rooms, but they are almost certain to talk about them with their friends. Zillmann (1998) described the process: "Boys must prove to their peers, and ultimately to themselves, that they are unperturbed, calm and collected in the face of terror; and girls must similarly demonstrate their sensitivity by being appropriately disturbed, dismayed and disgusted" (pp. 197–198). For the rebellious young, the mere fact that the topic is taboo is reason enough for engagement.

Young people bring their entertainment choices and experiences to bear on their intense concerns with questions of identity, belonging, and independence. Nearly all their public behavior—the clothes they wear, the music they listen to, and the games they play—has a social purpose. How else are we to understand the fads of body piercing and tattooing except in reference to social behavior? Or the popularity of horror films or violent video games? We are more likely to come to terms with our entertainment media when we regard the audience as members of social groups. A laboratory experiment with isolated individuals forced to play a video game for 15 min is unlikely to provide any insight into our entertainment choices or their effects.

When Violence Is Not Attractive

The premise that portrayals of violence are inherently appealing is untenable. Depending on personality and social context, these portrayals are capable of evoking fear, disgust, or elation. Why don't the gruesome images make for an unpleasant experience? Feelings of control moderate the effect. With a joystick or remote control in their hands, players can control not only what happens on screen, but indirectly what physical and emotional effects it will have on them.

The Importance of Context

Both the context of violent images and the circumstances in which they are experienced play a crucial role in their appeal. In order to experience pleasure from exposure to violent images, the players must feel relatively safe and secure in their surroundings. Furthermore, there must be cues that the violent images are produced for purposes of entertainment and consumption. Bloody images lose their appeal when there are few cues to their unreality (McCauley, 1998). If the violent imagery does not itself reveal its unreality, the physical environment may do so. We are aware of holding a joystick or remote control, of playing a game on a console or computer screen. Without background music, special effects, or fantasy characters, images of violence are unattractive to both males and females. In one study, preschool children typically showed facial expressions of joy while watching cartoon violence, but displayed negative emotions while watching realistic physical violence (Lagerspetz, Wahlroos, & Wendelin, 1978). Similarly, boys who played video games with aggressive themes showed the same positive facial expressions, quality of peer interaction, and enjoyment as those who played "neutral" games (Holmes & Pellegrini, 1999).

Summary

Video games with violent themes appeal to a mostly male audience, above average in sensation-seeking and aggressiveness, who use their gaming experience to satisfy social and personal needs.

Do violent electronic games result in more aggressive behavior among players? Two kinds of research have been conducted to answer this question: studies that examine the correlates of game playing, and experiments that manipulate the play experience. The majority of correlational studies report that experience with video games, especially video games with violent themes, is related to poor school performance, heightened juvenile delinquency, and aggression. This does not necessarily imply that playing video games causes any of these phenomena. One analysis suggested that boys may become video game experts to find the status that they cannot so easily attain by other means.

Experimental studies of the effects of video games are mired in ambiguity. On one hand, there is no sense in which subjects in psychological experiments "play" video games. Instead, they are required to play a game, not of their choosing, for a brief period of time. How much this resembles the experience of play, which is always voluntary, is not known. On the other hand, we have few ways of measuring aggressive behavior in the laboratory and are required to use indirect, often dubious measures, such as the willingness to use blasts of white noise as punishment in a learning task. A few studies have observed children on the playground after playing a violent video game or with a violent toy. These studies rarely distinguish between fantasy play aggression (pretending to fight) and aggressive behavior (trying to harm someone). Those studies that do make this distinction typically fail to find any effects of playing video games on aggressive behavior. No wonder that reviews of the research on this topic come to such widely different conclusions.

EDUCATIONAL AND THERAPEUTIC USES OF ELECTRONIC GAMES

In the book, *Playing With Power*, Kinder (1991) noted that video games

> have considerable educational and therapeutic value for a diverse range of groups—including adolescents, athletes, would-be pilots, the elderly in old-age homes, cancer patients undergoing chemotherapy, stroke victims, quadriplegics, and young children suffering from palsy, brain damage, and Down's syndrome. (p. 112)

Electronic games are used to teach and reinforce skills in education, science, and medicine. Games are used increasingly to study learning (Blumberg, 1998; Rieber, 1996), memory (Shewokis, 1997), motivation (Wong, 1996), cognitive processes (Kappas & Pecchinenda, 1999), attention and attention deficits (Pope & Bogart, 1999), and spatial abilities (Subrahmanyam & Greenfield, 1994; Tkacz & LaForce, 1998). There are games specifically designed to help students in virtually any subject—art, history, language, mathematics, and science. Games have for years proved useful in training motor skills, such as driving, navigation, and air traffic control (Brown, Brown, & Reid, 1992; Dorval & Pepin, 1986; Lowery & Knirk, 1983). Video games have been developed to promote health (Bosworth, 1994), to teach safe sexual practices to adolescents (Thomas, Cahill, & Santilli, 1997), and to help diabetic children better manage their illness (Lieberman, 1998).

Games as Research Tools

Commercial video games have much to recommend them as psychological tests. The equipment is robust, inexpensive, small, light, and portable. Scoring is completely objective and, because the rules for any given game are the same for every player, the games are standardized. Jones (1984) described an American mountaineering expedition to the 7,700 m high Tirich Mir, the highest peak in the Hindu Kush range in Afghanistan. Two games were used to measure performance, Simon Says to measure short-term memory, and Split Second to measure pattern recognition and reaction time. The expedition placed four men on the summit of Tirich Mir. The games operated normally even at 7,000 m under the extreme conditions of the climb (but the batteries had to be warmed by the climbers). Performance did not degrade until a very high altitude. When it did deteriorate, it did so mainly on *Simon Says*. It took the climbers considerable effort to play this game on the mountain. "The problem seems to have been more a matter of maintaining attention than of impaired short-term memory" (Jones, 1984). "What seems beyond doubt is the possibility of testing performance under extreme conditions by means of electronic games" (Jones, 1984).

Games and Learning

Four pertinent features of electronic games make them attractive as educational tools: instantaneous feedback, continual improvement, high response rates, and an unlimited ceiling on performance (Wong, 1996). Knowledge learned while playing enables the player to move from one level to another, and is transferred to other games. Instantaneous feedback "lets players know immediately what they have done wrong; they don't become annoyed and frustrated, but can play the game again and correct their mistakes. Because they can repeat the game and correct the mistakes, students can learn without the fear of making errors" (Wong, 1996).

The attractiveness of video games offers guidance for designing computer-assisted learning systems. Rieber (1996) stressed the value of play in providing a healthy learning climate. The microworlds created by software designers can be enhanced in their ability to maintain the interest of users, whether they are children or adults, if they offer clear and simple goals with uncertain outcomes and new challenges to keep users on their toes. Gradually increasing layers of complexity serve to stretch users to an optimal degree, so that once they have reached one level of competence they are pushed toward another, higher level. Each successive level of complexity, however, is not so far removed from the preceding one that it runs the risk of causing disillusionment, because for some users it proves to be excessively difficult to achieve. Once achieved, feedback on the user's success is immediate, allowing users to evaluate their progress quickly. These are basic features of computer games but they have relevance to other computer interface applications.

Blumberg (1998) investigated developmental differences in children's performance on a popular video game (Sega's Sonic the Hedgehog 2). Forty-three girls and 61 boys ages 7 to 12 played the video game for 10 min and then were questioned about the game features they paid attention to while playing, and about specific game and attention strategies that they would recommend to a novice player. Older children and children identified as frequent players showed better performance. There were developmental differences regarding game features, strategies, and evaluative assessments. Younger children focused more on evaluative assessments, emphasizing whether they liked the game or not. By comparison, older children focused more on specific goals for game play, explaining what one must do to attain a high score; such a focus was correlated with better performance on the game. This study aims to throw light on how intrinsically motivating tasks like playing electronic games can be used to motivate attention and performance.

Spatial Abilities

Electronic games have been among the most successful means for reducing the typically reported sex differences in spatial abilities. Subrahmanyam and Greenfield (1994) found that practice with a video game improved the spatial scores of both fifth grade boys and girls. Furthermore, the improvements transferred from video games to other spatial activities. Boys and girls ages 10 to 12 were randomly assigned to play an action video game (Marble Madness) or a computerized word game (Conjecture). Measures of spatial abilities were taken before and after approximately 2 hr of play. Video game practice was significantly more effective than the word game in improving spatial performance. Video game practice was most effective for children who started out with relatively poor spatial skills.

Tkacz and LaForce (1998) enlisted 18 men and 13 women undergraduates to play the videogame Snakebyte for about 1 hr a day for 4 days. The game involves both simple and complex skills under time pressure, including the ability to maneuver, plan routes, and select targets. As in all such studies, men initially scored higher than women on the game. Game score improved for both sexes with practice. Men and women improved in spatial abilities at the same pace. According to the authors, video games and virtual reality might be useful for training in geographic information systems. Games can be used "to examine how digital displays in vehicles should provide 'you are here' information. Should digital maps be geocentric or egocentric? Should north always be 'up' regardless of the direction of movement?" (Tkacz & LaForce, 1998, pp. 1403–1404).

Greenfield, Brannon and Lohr (1994) found a strong relationship between video game expertise and ability in spatial tasks. Study 1 examined the relationship between skill in the arcade game, The Empire Strikes Back, and ability to do a difficult spatial representation task (a mental paper-folding test). Among the 24 male university students studied, those with expertise in the video game also scored highest in the spatial task. Study 2 considered whether this was a causal relationship by having some students reach a certain level of proficiency in The Empire Strikes Back and comparing their spatial abilities with nonplayers. Study 2 did not find a short-term practice effect of video game play. Those who had played the video game did not perform better on the spatial task. However, further statistical analysis did provide strong evidence that videogame expertise, developed over the long term, had a beneficial effect on the spatial task.

Video Games in Therapy

Electronic games are used increasingly in psychotherapy with children and adolescents (Delfos, 1992; Spence, 1988; Margalit, Weisel & Shulman, 1987).

Attention deficit disorder (ADD) is a behavioral disorder characterized by the inability to sustain attention long enough to perform activities such as schoolwork or organized play. Treatments include medication and brain-wave biofeedback training, in which feedback information shows trainees how well they are producing the brainwave patterns that indicate attention. Pope and Bogart (1996) developed an electronic game that expands this concept by becoming more difficult as the player's brainwaves indicate that attention is waning. The trainee can succeed at the game only by maintaining an adequate level of attention. The game is a modification of a biocybernetic system used to assess automated maintenance of pilot engagement.

Gardner (1991) claimed that the use of computer games provide common ground between himself and his client. Gardner observes the following while children are playing video games:

• The child's problem-solving strategies:

- ability to perceive and recall subtle cues as well as foresee consequences of behavior:
- eye–hand coordination:
- the release of aggression and control:
- the ability to deal with victory and frustration:
- recall of information:
- the enjoyment of mutually coordinating activities with another in the spirit of cooperation.

Video Games and the Elderly

There is evidence from studies of the noninstitutionalized elderly that electronic games can speed reaction time, and may have cognitive and emotional benefits. Dustman, Emmerson, Steinhaus, Shearer, and Dustman (1992) found faster reaction times among men and women 60 to 79 years of age who played video games 3 hr per week for 11 weeks. Goldstein et al. (1997) found similar effects within 5 weeks. Cognitive effects of video games have not been consistently obtained in studies of the elderly. Improved knowledge acquisition and retention among videogame-playing adults was reported by Ricci, Salas and Cannon-Bowers (1996), while Drew and Waters (1986) found higher WAIS IQ scores among the elderly after playing video games for 8-9 hours over a two-month period.

In 1997 we (Goldstein et al., 1997) asked noninstitutionalized elderly people aged 69 to 90 yrs. to play a video game (SuperTetris) for 5 hr per week for 5 weeks. We measured reaction time (computerized Sternberg test, 1969), cognitive flexibility (Stroop Color Word Test, 1935), and emotional well-being before and after this play period, and administered the same tests to a random half of the sample who did not play video games during this period. Some of the results are portrayed in Table 2.1. Playing video games was related to a significant improvement in reaction time and to a relative increase in feelings of well-being. Those who played video games had faster reaction times and felt better compared to their nonplaying counterparts.

CONCLUSION

Research on a new entertainment medium typically begins with the question: How bad is it? If the medium survives long enough, the youngsters that grew up with it will ask a different set of questions. How is it used? How can it be applied to the resolution of problems?

TABLE 2.1
Effects of Video Games on the Elderly (from Goldstein et al., 1997)

	Experimental Group	Control Group
Reaction time (msec)		
Before	1287.5	1269.1
After	940.5	1158.1
Change	347.0	111.0
Stroop Color Word Test[a]		
Before	52.2	47.7
After	38.4	41.5
Change	13.8	6.2
Emotional well-being[b]		
Before	2.11	2.18
After	1.89	.63
Change	.22	1.55

[a] Interference score, in secs.
[b] Range −5 to +5.

What Is Missing From Computer Game Research?

Missing from this research is any acknowledgment that video game players freely engage in play and are always free to terminate it. They enter with a playful frame of mind, something entirely missing from laboratory studies of video games, but a feature that may be crucial to the effects of games.

Future games will be faster, more complex, and more realistic, and will give players greater control over the story and structure of the game. If we are to better understand the cognitive and social effects and uses of electronic games, researchers will profit from longitudinal, prospective studies, with a broader range of outcome measures than is currently the case.

Computer games have been banished from most schools, and many workplaces seek to prohibit play on company computers. If research on the potential uses and benefits of play were attempted with the same zeal as that which seeks to demonstrate their harmful nature, we would know how and when games could be used to advantage.

REFERENCES

Anderson, C. A., & Bushman, B. J. (2001). Effects of violent video games on aggressive behavior, aggressive cognition, aggressive affect, physiological arousal, and prosocial behavior: A meta-analytic review of the scientific literature. *Psychological Science, 12*, 353–359.

Anderson, C. A., & Dill, K. E. (2000). Video game violence and trait aggressiveness. *Journal of Personality and Social Psychology, 78,* 772–790.

Anderson, D. R., Choi, H., & Lorch, E. P. (1987). Attentional inertia reduces distractibility during young children's television viewing. *Child Development, 58,* 798–806.

Badinand-Hubert, N., Bureau, M., Hirsch, E., Masnou, P., Nahum, L., Parain, D., & Naquet, R. (1998). Epilepsies and video games: Results of a multicentric study. *Electroencephalography and Clinical Neurophysiology, 107,* 422–427.

Bartle, R. (1996). Hearts, clubs, diamonds, spades: Players who suit MUDs. *Journal of MUD Research, 1.* Available: http://journal.penmush.org

Bensley, L., & Van Eenwyk, J. (2001). Video games and real-life aggression: Review of the literature. *Journal of Adolescent Health, 29,* 244–257.

Blumberg, F. C. (1998). Developmental differences at play: Children's selective attention and performance in video games. *Journal of Applied Developmental Psychology, 19,* 615–624.

Bosworth, K. (1994). Computer games and simulations as tools to reach and engage adolescents in health promotion activities. *Computers in Human Services, 11,* 109–119.

Brown, R. M., Brown, N. L., & Reid, K. (1992). Evidence for a player's position advantage in a video game. *Perceptual and Motor Skills, 74,* 547–554.

Clark, J. E., Lanphear, A. K., & Riddick, C. (1987). The effects of video game playing on the response selection processing of elderly adults. *Journal of Gerontology, 42,* 82–85.

Cooper, J., & Mackie, D. (1986). Video games and aggression in children. *Journal of Applied Social Psychology, 16,* 726–744.

Csikszentmihalyi, C. (1990). *The Flow Experience.* San Francisco: Jossey-Bass.

Cumberbatch, G., Maguire, A., & Woods, S. (1993). *Children and video games: An exploratory study.* Aston University. Birmingham, England: Communications Research Group.

Delfos, M. F. (1992). De computer als hulpmiddel in de spelkamer. [The computer as aide in the play room.] *Nederlands Tijdschrift voor Opvoeding, Vorming en Onderwijs* [Netherlands Journal of Child Care, Development & Education], *8,* 388–394.

Dill, K. E., & Dill, J. C. (1998). Video game violence: A review of the empirical literature. *Aggression and Violent Behavior, 3,* 407–428.

Dorval, M., & Pepin, M. (1986). Effect of playing a video game on a measure of spatial visualization. *Perceptual & Motor Skills, 62,* 159–162.

Durkin, K. (1995). *Computer Games Their Effects on Young People: A Review.* Sydney, Australia: Office of Film & Literature Classification.

Dustman, R. E., Emmerson, R., Steinhaus, L. A., Shearer, D. E., & Dustman, T. J. (1992). The effects of video game playing on neuropsychological performance of elderly individuals. *Journal of Gerontology, 47,* 168–171.

Federal Trade Commission. (2000). *Marketing violent entertainment to children.* Washington, DC: Federal Trade Commission.

Federman, J., Carbone, S., Chen, H., & Munn, W. (1996). *The social effects of electronic interactive games: An annotated bibliography.* Studio City, CA: Mediascope.

Ferreira, P. A., & Ribeiro, J. L. (2001). The relationship between violent electronic games and aggression in adolescents. *Aggressive Behavior, 27,* 166–167.

Fisher, S. (1994). Identifying video game addiction in children and adolescents. *Addictive Behaviors, 19,* 545–553.

Funk, J. B., Germann, J. N., & Buchman, D. D. (1997). Children and electronic games in the United States. *Trends in Communication, 2,* 111–126.

Fylan, F., Harding, G. F., Edson, A. S., & Webb, R. M. (1999). Mechanisms of video-game epilepsy [Suppl. 4]. *Epilepsia, 40,* 28–30.

Gardner, J. E. (1991). Can the Mario Bros. help? Nintendo games as an adjunct in psychotherapy with children. *Psychotherapy, 28,* 667–670.

Goldstein, J. H. (1994). Sex differences in toy preference and video game play. In J. Goldstein (Ed.), *Toys, play, and child development* (pp. 110–129). New York: Cambridge University Press.

Goldstein, J. H. (1995). Aggressive toy play. In A. D. Pellegrini (Ed.), *The future of play theory* (pp. 127–147). Albany, NY: SUNY Press.

Goldstein, J. H. (1998). Immortal Kombat: War toys and violent video games. In J. Goldstein (Ed.), *Why we watch: The attractions of violent entertainment* (pp. 53–68). New York: Oxford University Press.

Goldstein, J. H. (1999). The attractions of violent entertainment. *Media Psychology, 1,* 271–282.

Goldstein, J. H., Cajko, L., Oosterbroek, M., Michielsen, M., van Houten, O., & Salverda, F. (1997). Video games and the elderly. *Social Behavior and Personality, 25,* 345–352.

Greenfield, P. M., Brannon, C., & Lohr, D. (1994). Two-dimensional representation of movement through three-dimensional space: The role of video game expertise. *Journal of Applied Developmental Psychology, 15,* 87–103.

Griffiths, M. (1999). Violent video games and aggression: A review of the literature. *Aggression and Violent Behavior, 4,* 203–212.

Griffiths, M., & Hunt, N. (1998). Dependence on computer games by adolescents. *Psychological Reports, 82,* 475–480.

Grossman, D. (1995). *On killing.* New York: Little, Brown.

Gunter, B. (1998). *The effects of video games on children: The myth unmasked.* Sheffield, England: Sheffield Academic Press.

Hellendoorn, J., & Harinck, F. (1997). War toy play and aggression in Dutch kindergarten children. *Social Development, 6,* 340–354.

Holm Sorensen, B., & Jessen, C. (2000). It isn't real: Children, computer games, violence and reality. In C. von Feilitzen & U. Carlsson (Eds.), *Children in the new media landscape: Games, pornography, perceptions* (pp. 119–122). Goteborg, Sweden: UNESCO International Clearinghouse on Children and Violence on the Screen.

Holmes, R. M., & Pellegrini, A. D. (1999, June). Children's social behavior during video game play with aggressive and non-aggressive themes. Paper presented at International Toy Research Conference, Halmstad, Sweden.

Jones, M. B. (1984). Video games as psychological tests. *Simulation & Gaming, 15,* 131–157.

Kappas, A., & Pecchinenda, A. (1999). Don't wait for the monsters to get you: A video game task to manipulate appraisals in real-time. *Cognition & Emotion, 13,* 119–124.

Kinder, M. (1991). *Playing with power in movies, television and video games.* Berkeley: University of California Press.

Kline, S. (2000). Killing time? A Canadian meditation on video game culture. In C. von Feilitzen & U. Carlsson (Eds.), *Children in the new media landscape: Games, pornography, perceptions* (pp. 35–60). Goteborg, Sweden: UNESCO International Clearinghouse on Children and Violence on the Screen.

Koepp, M. J., Gunn, R. N., Lawrence, A. D., Cunningham, V. J., Dagher, A., Jones, T., Brooks, D. J., Bench, C. J., & Grasby, P. M. (1998). Evidence for striatal dopamine release during a video game. *Nature, 393,* 266–268.

Kraut, R., Patterson, M., Lundmark, V., Kiesler, S., Mukhopadhyay, T., & Scherlis, W. (1998). Internet paradox: A social technology that reduces social involvement and psychological well-being? *American Psychologist, 53,* 1017–1031.

Lagerspetz, K., Wahlroos, C., & Wendelin, C. (1978). Facial expressions of preschool children while watching televised violence. *Scandinavian Journal of Psychology, 19,* 213–222.

Lieberman, D. A. (1998). Health education video games for children and adolescents: Theory, design, and research findings. Paper presented at the annual meeting of the International Communication Association, Jerusalem. (available online at *www.clickhealth.com/lieb98/diabetes.htm*)

Lowery, B. R., & Knirk, F. G. (1983). Micro-computer video games and spatial visual acquisition. *Journal of Educational Technology Systems, 11,* 155–166.

Margalit, M., Weisel, A., & Shulman, S. (1987). The facilitation of information processing in learning disabled children using computer games. *Educational Psychology, 7,* 47–54.

McCauley, R. C. (1998). When violence is not attractive. In J. Goldstein (Ed.), *Why we watch: The attractions of violent entertainment* (pp. 144–162). New York: Oxford University Press.

Ng, D. (1990). Exciting play: Arcade video gaming and youth. Proceedings of the International Play Association, Tokyo.

Nikken, P. (2000). Boys, girls and violent video games: The views of Dutch children. In C. von Feilitzen & U. Carlsson (Eds.), *Children in the new media landscape: Games, pornography, perceptions* (pp. 93–102). Goteborg, Sweden: UNESCO International Clearinghouse on Children and Violence on the Screen.

PC Data. (1999). PC Data survey on violent games. *http://www.gamecenter.com*

Perloff, R. M. (1999). The third person effect in mass media research. *Media Psychology, 1,* 353–378.

Pope, A. T., & Bogart, E. H. (1996). Extended attention span training system: Video game neurotherapy for attention deficit disorder. *Child Study Journal, 26,* 39–50.

Ricci, K. E., Salas, E., & Cannon-Bowers, J. A. (1996). Do computer-based games facilitate knowledge acquisition and retention? *Military Psychology, 8,* 295–307.

Rieber, L. P. (1996). Seriously considering play: Designing interactive learning environments based on the blending of microworlds, simulations and games. *Educational Technology Research and Development, 44* (No. 2), 43–58.

Roe, K., & Muijs, D. (1998). Children and computer games: A profile of the heavy user. *European Journal of Communication, 13,* 181–200.

Saxe, J. (1994). Violence in video games: What are the pleasures? Paper presented at International Conference on Violence in the Media, St. John's University, New York.

Scott, D. (1995). The effect of video games on feelings of aggression. *Journal of Psychology, 129,* 121–132.

Segal, K. R., & Dietz, W. H. (1991). Physiologic responses to playing a video game. *American Journal of Diseases of Children, 145,* 1034–1036.

Shapiro, J. S. (1999). Loneliness: Paradox or artifact? *American Psychologist, 54,* 782–783.

Shewokis, P. A. (1997). Is the contextual interference effect generalizable to computer games? *Perceptual and Motor Skills, 84,* 3–15.

Sneed, C., & Runco, M. A. (1992). The beliefs adults and children hold about television and video games. *Journal of Psychology, 126,* 273–284.

Spence, J. (1988). The use of computer arcade games in behavioral management. *Maladjustment and Therapeutic Education, 6,* 64–68.

Sternberg, S. (1969). Memory scanning: Mental processes revealed by reaction-time experiments. *American Scientist, 57,* 421–457.

Stroop, J. R. (1935). Studies of interference in serial verbal reactions. *Journal of Experimental Psychology, 18,* 643–661.

Subrahmanyam, K., & Greenfield, P. M. (1994). Effect of video game practice on spatial skills in girls and boys. *Journal of Applied Developmental Psychology, 15,* 13–32.

Thomas, R., Cahill, J., & Santilli, L. (1997). Using an interactive computer game to increase skill and self-efficacy regarding safer sex negotiation: Field test results. *Health Education & Behavior, 24,* 71–86.

Tkacz, S., & LaForce, P. (1998). Sex of player and practice in lateral discrimination and videogame performance. *Perceptual and Motor Skills, 84,* 3–15.

van Schie, E. G. M., & Wiegman, O. (1997). Children and video games: Leisure activities, aggression, social integration, and school performance. *Journal of Applied Social Psychology, 27,* 1175–1194.

Vasterling, J., Jenkins, R. A., Tope, D. M., & Burish, T. G. (1993). Cognitive distraction and relaxation training for the control of side effects due to cancer chemotherapy. *Journal of Behavioral Medicine, 16*, 65–80.

Wallace, P. M. (1999). *The psychology of the Internet.* New York: Cambridge University Press.

Winkel, M., Novak, D. M., & Hopson, H. (1987). Personality factors, subject gender, and the effects of aggressive video games on aggression in adolescents. *Journal of Research in Personality, 21*, 211–223.

Wong, K. K. (1996). Video game effect on computer-based learning design. *British Journal of Educational Technology, 27*, 230–232.

Zillmann, D. (1998). The psychology of the appeal of portrayals of violence. In J. Goldstein (Ed.), *Why we watch: The attractions of violent entertainment* (pp. 179–211). New York: Oxford University Press.

Chapter 3

Integration of Specialist Tasks in the Digital Image Archive

Ed S. Tan
Free University Amsterdam (NL)

Heimo Müller
Fachhochschule Technikum Joanneum, Graz[1]
Joanneum Polytechnic, Graz (AU)

RESHUFFLING OF TASKS IN THE DIGITAL WORKFLOW

In a digital world, the division of labor across persons is very different from traditional role divisions in most areas of production. Driving forces behind the reshuffling are two developments that are part of the digital revolution. First, digitization of products, services, and communication results removes spatial constraints on production. There is much less necessity to transport goods and people physically from one place to another as part of the regular work flow if goods are digital and people can manipulate these online. As an example, compare the way a newspaper article is written today with how it was produced yesterday. The journalist sends an electronic copy of an article from anywhere in the world to a store that can be accessed by editors who finish a final version. Only this version has to assume the form of a hard copy; all previous manipulations have been carried out on digital proxies. Neither is there any physical product until the press release of the paper containing the article, nor has any physical transport of the would-be product taken place. Digital copies and remote access, then, have rendered separation and distribution of tasks obsolete.

Second, separate tasks within one domain can be combined and integrated through software that facilitates new ways of collaboration, includ-

---

[1]At the time of the research reported Müller was a research fellow at the Faculty of Arts, Vrije Universiteit, supported by a grant from the TMR programme, "Marie Curie," of the European Commission.

ing alternative distribution of tasks across specialists. For instance, the journalist may use the same word processor to conceive, write, and edit the article, finalizing it to the point of deciding on the ultimate layout. One person produces newspapers published on the Web that way, collapsing traditional roles of reporting journalist, editor, corrector, and typographer into a single set of integrated tasks. Alternatively, the journalist may hand in a rough draft, to be elaborated on by other journalists specialized in editing and finalizing the article for inclusion into a database from which it is transferred to various editions of a newspaper. In both cases, there may be some redefinition of traditional tasks, with software playing a key role in the definition and distribution of these over various roles.

It is not clear how the novel distribution of tasks and roles will look like in any domain of production in the digital world, and whether general trends can be observed. But some main issues do seem clear that are of interest not only to management researchers, but also to students of applied human cognition, especially Human–Computer Interaction. Does digitization of production enable despecialization, that is, an integration of tasks that have traditionally been in the hands of experts delivering separate contributions to the product? If so, how far do we want despecialization to go? Do we want to share all specialist knowledge and skills among as many persons possible? Do all persons become generalists? And does the latter mean that they are proficient in all specialties or that they know something about everything?

In this chapter, we present an exploratory design study that may serve as an elaborate example of the relevance of these questions for the development of systems supporting the core of a traditional workflow in the digital age. Our example derives from a study of a number of European national television archives that are in the process of transforming into digital video archives. We describe the effects of the two developments, and present the design of an integrated software system for archiving and production that attempts to meet some anticipated redistribution of current specialist tasks.

THE TELEVISION ARCHIVE GOES DIGITAL

Current Workflow in Television Archives

National broadcast networks in Europe have maintained archives keeping stock of large parts of all broadcast materials. Collection of materials may or may not be a legal deposit obligation, depending on national legislation. In either case, the archives' main objectives are typically (a) preserving the national cultural heritage, and (b) enabling and stimulating reuse of audiovisual content for purposes of consultation or study, and especially incorporation into newly produced television, video, or multimedia programs. In recent years, television production has increased rapidly, giving rise to ever larger supplies of archived materials as well as to a growth in demand for these materials, for example, "stock shots." This has resulted in an increased distribution of tasks across specialists.

The workflow in current archive practice consists of archiving properly and supporting reuse of archived video materials. The latter group of tasks is part of the production of new television programs. Production is a process that is not a regular part of the archive's activities. It is carried out by external production agencies that function as end users of archive contents. Because digitization affects both archiving and archive use in production, we briefly describe both workflows. (For other, more extensive accounts of the workflows involved, see, for exampel, Green & Klasén, 1993).

Tasks and Roles in Archiving. The work in an image archive is largely comparable to other forms of information storage and retrieval. The following account is based on research in four middle-sized European television archives (Tan, 1998). Archiving consists of all the work that is necessary to render video sound and images reusable. Apart from proper storage, content needs cataloguing in order to be retrieved. An overview of cataloguing tasks is given in Fig. 3.1.

Cataloguing involves formal description and content description. *Formal cataloguing* consists of adding formal information to an archived item such as names of maker, crew, and other details of production, date of transmission, and so forth. These are derived from other information systems that receive data from television production units. *Content cataloguing* consists of classification of programs and describing their contents using key words, also called index terms. Selected program segments are indexed, that is, described at a more fine-grained level by key words and annotations. Keywords are attached to time-coded shots and sequences, and free text annotations may be added concerning technical details, such as quality and content information not covered by the index terms. In general, within program indexing requires viewing materials, whereas program level cataloguing and formal cataloguing can often be done using data that were made available in producing the footage. Completeness and detail of indexing and annotation vary according to the nature of the materials and the anticipated reuse. In TV archives, high quality and rare materials such as footage from documentaries are being meticulously indexed at shot level, because these are wanted for reuse as stock shots of a certain object, scene, or person, and have to meet high technical and aesthetic standards. Precision viewing takes up to about ten times the playing duration of materials. Abundantly available programs, on the other hand, such as quiz shows, are indexed coarsely at the level of the program as a whole. The results of cataloguing and indexing are stored in a database that covers the archive's collection and that is, in fact, the archive's catalogue.

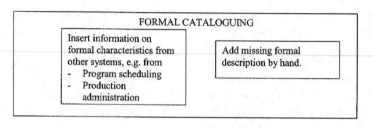

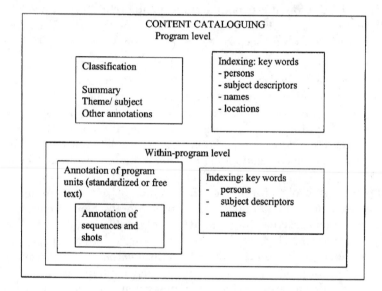

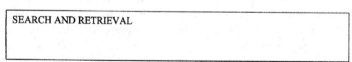

FIG. 3.1.   Overview of the typical cataloguing processes in a television archive.

Search and retrieval are tasks initiated and carried out by producers that use archive materials. These are discussed in the next section on production tasks. They are mentioned here also because the archive enables and supports search and carries out retrieval, and they can only be performed where the archive is located. Assistance of producers in searching for materials is often considerable, because for an external user, it may take lots of time to know the cataloguing system and the best ways to search items of interest. In other words, there exists an asymmetry between archive staff members on one hand, and producing journalists or image researchers on the other, as to their knowledge of cataloguing rules and procedures, and of archived materials. Archive staff members may have considerable knowledge about production due to the fact that they have to index productions all the time.

Specialization in Archiving Tasks. It stands to reason that cataloguing and indexing images is a critical job. Errors may result in an impossibility to retrieve materials that cannot always be detected and repaired later. Apart from the risk of simple errors being made, classification, indexing and annotation may be insufficient or inadequate to retrieve materials. Therefore archive professionals consider cataloguing as a delicate matter, requiring considerable skills. Cataloguing is a highly standardized task. Use is made of lists of authorized terms, names, and description formats. Because of its specialized nature, experts, mostly called *documentalists*, have traditionally done cataloguing. They receive training and supervision, geared toward molding the large amount and diversity of the image supply into standardized descriptions. Further specialization among documentalists concerns genre identification and level of responsibility. Documentalists may be members of groups dealing with news, sports, and other genres. Some documentalists check others' work as to consistency with rules, are involved in training novices, and in revision of catalogue systems. Finally, some documentalists are only involved in cataloguing; others are for support of external users in search and retrieval.

Tasks and Roles in Production. We do not give an account of television production at large, but focus on those productions that make use of archive materials. Obviously, live broadcasts are underrepresented among these, except for news shows, whereas documentary types of productions are overrepresented. Figure 3.2a offers an overview of tasks in production; Fig. 3.2b expands on the search and retrieval tasks.

Writing. Production staff are generally journalists involved in producing a TV program. In most cases, they have conceived at least some rough script for the production; sometimes they have available a complete story board with texts and image descriptions. They may also have written out or shot original materials in a final version to be completed by archive footage. In searching and collecting materials, they have a context for the reuse of archive materials in mind that may differ enormously from the footage's original context.

Shooting original materials may be the major task in production. However, in some program types, such as historical documentaries, archive materials are predominant.

Search and retrieval of images necessarily starts with consulting the catalogue, because no direct viewing access to images is allowed by any larger professional archive. Results of cataloguing and indexing are available as

---

a. Production Reusing Archive Materials in Short

1. Write treatment, scenario and script;
2. shoot original imagery;
3. collect archive materials: search, retrieval and first selection;
4. final selection of archive materials;
5. assemble program;
6. final editing and post-production;
7. documentation and information for broadcasting.

---

b. Search, Retrieval and Selection in Steps

1. Enter query terms (with or without using Boolean operators, e.g. "and", "or", "not");

2. browse through result-screens;

3. predict the reuse value of the as yet unseen materials from the descriptions by:
   - length of story
   - kind of story (news, documentary)
   - content of story / context of story
        Example: if the content of a story is on policematters, pictures of
        policemen are generally reusable (quality, length) and more
        representative than police-pictures in a story on nonpolice matters.
   - are there any other pictures, originally not searched for, that could be
   used from the same story?
   - copyright details

   If necessary, repeat from step 1;

4. order and borrow materials;

5. preview and select shots because of their:
   - representativeness
   - atmosphere
   - color brilliance and focus
   - composition / aesthetic considerations
   - appropriate length
   - sound (no voice over)

   If necessary, repeat step 1.

FIG. 3.2.   (a) Overview of tasks in production of television programs incorporating archive materials and (b) steps in search, retrieval and selection. Description of search steps was adapted from ORF, Documentation and Archives Department, Vienna, in Tan (1997).

index terms and formal data to be used in filling queries. As in all database use, queries can be composed and refined in various cycles. It is important to stress that retrieval is generally an expensive process from the perspective of the archive. This is because it takes a lot of handling of image carriers. Film reels and video tapes require a lot of handling, including transport from and to shelves and transcription to viewing formats. From the producing journalist's point of view, retrieval is no less expensive, for at least two reasons. First, it should be noted that the immediate query result is merely a list of identification numbers of tapes and films with their complete catalogue data. Without having a copy of the images themselves (or low quality resolution copies that can be used, it is usually impossible to carry out the last step of the search process, identifying best matching items (see Fig. 3.2b, Step 3) and finally selecting one or more images. In order to do this, the journalist has to order the carriers and inspect all items. If the first queries are as specific to include proper names of people (e.g., Nixon), places (e.g., Hanoi), events (e.g., the cease fire of 1972), and especially combinations of these, query results will have high relevance and the number may be manageable. But if the production leaves a lot to be chosen by inspecting a larger set of images, the user needs a lot of time to order long lists of candidate tapes. Second, journalists sometimes want footage satisfying criteria that are hard to match with index terms (see also Armitage & Enser, 1997; Enser, 1995). Atmosphere images, images illustrating a concept, and even many images portraying an object without a proper name are impossible or difficult to find using the database's key terms. An example of the latter is finding a "big red sports car," as the main object in a video sequence. In order to succeed, you have to know that certain cars with brand names, are likely to be among the index terms, and to infer that some of the names, for example, Ferrari, are associated with the kind of car that is sought. In some cases, the production requires a prototype or indication of a generic concept or class rather than a particular instance. The use of a thesaurus may be helpful in many cases, as it may bridge the gap between terms that the user has available and index terms. However, thesauri that can be used to search for images are rare and not in use in the archives.[2]

Once all or most materials have been gathered, a crude version of the program is *assembled.* A final version is *edited,* and effects, such as titles and graphics, as well as music may be added in postproduction. A finalized television program is *documented* in various information databases, such as the broadcast schedule and rights management systems.

Specialization in Production.   For each of the tasks listed in Fig. 3.2a there is usually a specialist on the production team. All work under the supervision of the producing journalist in charge. For our purposes, it is necessary to discuss the distribution of tasks in collecting and integrating archive materials in more detail. The final selection of materials for adoption in a production (Fig. 3.2a, Step 4, and Fig. 3.2b, Step 5) is in many cases done by another person than the one who did the searching and first selections (Fig. 3.2a, Step 3, and Fig. 3.2b, Steps 1–4). In our own research, we have observed this distribution of tasks in TV archives and film archives. Markkula and Sormunen (1998) reported the same role distribution in photo ar-

---

[2]An example of a semantically based thesaurus that can be used for classification of images is ICONCLASS (see van den Berg, 1995).

chives. Collection and first selection of materials is possibly taken care of by an image research assistant who has a fair knowledge of the production at hand. The assistant may have other tasks that contribute to the reuse of the selected materials, like clearing copyrights and defining formats and conditions for the copies to be delivered by the archive for production. The final selection, followed by assembling archive images with other production materials (texts, original shots) is done by the producing journalist, often assisted by a professional editor. Of course the film and video editor's expertise is matching shots' cinematographic properties with surrounding materials (Fig. 3.2b, Step 5). The journalist in charge of production, in turn, decides on the basis of his or her ideas on the content of the production, in particular the theme, and local and global coherence considerations (does the image fit in the article as a whole, and does it fit in exactly this or that position?). The function of the image for the journalist is to *represent* a concept, scene, object, and so on in a precise context. Final selection of an image is therefore never determined by the character of the retrieved sequence alone, but also by what the user wants to express, and this is often very hard to describe. For example, producers are often faced with the question whether a given shot is a good example or a fair representation of some state of affairs in the world (see, e.g., Goodman, 1978; Zillmann, 1999). This general question is of course inherent to any television production, but reuse of archive materials renders this problem more glaringly, as the number of options is more limited than in shooting new materials. Relations between image and text are among the prime constituents of context (e.g., see Barkin, 1989; Bentele, 1985; Graber, 1989; van Oostendorp & Peeters, 1996). Image research assistants cannot take into consideration all the factors that are relevant for selection, and even if they could, not all producing journalists in charge can or want to leave final selection to an assistant. Nevertheless, it is considered cost effective that the journalist in charge delegates the search and retrieval to a specialized assistant because (a) search and retrieval is extremely time consuming, as we have seen; and (b) the archive is mostly remote from the cutting room or the office where a program is being assembled and edited.

The Digital Archive in a World of Digital Production

Changes Within Archive and Production Tasks. Television archives all over the world are faced with a growth of television production and broadcasting. The availability of digital technology and especially the sharp decrease in costs of digital storage are additional driving forces behind the transition from analogue to digital archiving. Publications on the transition process are still scarce at present. Our account is based on Tan (1998), Galliano (1998), and Buscher (1998).

It is expected that television archives will preserve large parts of their entire collections in a digital format. It is also anticipated that archives will play an important role as major content providers in the future Internet economy. Digital preservation solves the problem of signal decay due to transferring content from one analogue image carrier to another. Analogue carriers have a limited lifetime, and therefore video contents have to be written to fresh tapes every now and then. Each analogue transcription involves considerable signal loss.[3] Solution of some major preservation problems brings along other positive things as well. Once digitized, items of the archive's collection can be catalogued, searched, and retrieved through direct access. The crucial difference with current archiving practice is that there is no barrier any more between the catalogue as a system of image identification and description and the physically stored video materials. The image itself is in the catalogue, next to its formal data and textual indexes; the programs in store are data, and the catalogue entries are "metadata" of one and the same digital archive system.

A second difference is remote and direct access to digital copies of stored video, which solves some spatial and physical constraints on the workflow discussed earlier. Producers no longer need to travel to the archive location for searching content. Queries result in viewing copies of the image, reducing the number of copies that need to be retrieved for inspection. Also, retrieving digital copies from some mass storage device involves less carrier handling (see Fig. 3.3).

A third difference with current practice (see Fig. 3.3a) is that archiving and production tasks can be integrated. In the most far-reaching conception, the borders between production and archiving are completely wiped out. The archive extends into the production unit (see Fig. 3.3b), which has a twofold implication. Archiving after transmission of a program has changed into archiving from the source. That is, automatic tools take care of raw cataloguing and indexing when images are being produced; that is, first, when shot on the spot (indexing in the camera), and, second, in the editing room or production office. In addition to this, the metadata generated manually or automatically are handed over from step to step and enriched throughout the production chain from shooting to postproduction and eventually transmission. After production, the archive receives the materials together with all these metadata and applies the finishing touches. Production tasks in a proper sense are directly supported by the archive; production staff have the complete contents of the archive, that is, both catalogue and images, in their hands, ready to retrieve at any moment. The best example is the concept of the *digital news room*, where editors receive roughly labeled texts and imagery online from everywhere in the world for

---

[3]However, digitization does not definitely solve any preservation problems. See McKenzie-Owen (1996).

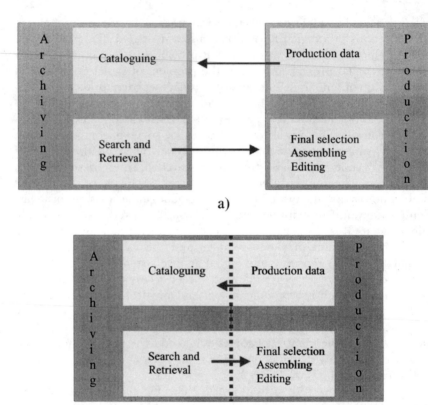

FIG. 3.3.   Integration of archiving and production tasks. (a) Current situation and (b) integration enabled by digital archiving.

production of a news show or journal article. Television news bulletins and newspaper articles can be conceived, collected, assembled, and edited by combining newly arrived videos and texts with related pictures from the archive. Automated routines pass the footage on to the digital information system, ready for instant reuse and for further elaboration of indexes and annotations. Archiving and indexing may also be done in the news room, rendering the production more valuable by extending its range and future accessibility.

Distribution of Tasks in the Digital Archive and Designing Software Tools.   If it is clear that television archiving and production will be integrated, it is still to be decided what tasks will be combined and how they will be distributed across persons, or better, roles. Looking at Fig. 3.3 we can ask, for instance, whether a video editor should take care of indexing and annotation on the spot by adding rough indexes and annotations to Editing Decision Lists (EDL files). A journalist in charge of the production may also do the job, combining it with writing bulletins for the publicity department that he or she is to do all the same. These solutions look like the newspaper journalist who, in addition to writing an article, also does its typographical layout. Alternatively, an archiving specialist may be added to the production team. Documentalists may be working in a news room-like production environment. In contrast to production specialists, the documentalists do more than just make rough and tentative classifications and indexes. In this case, the task is not new to the specialist, and they can finalize it, adding data individually in the catalogue according to standards. An advantage would be that the documentalist, as a catalogue expert, can collect archive materials for reuse in the production, having queries and selections interacting directly with the journalist in charge and the editor.

In many work places that are about to enter the digital world, we do not yet know how tasks will be combined. Optimal integration can take many shapes depending on the perspective one assumes. What is more, it is particularly difficult to predict the specialists' willingness to accept new tasks and share existing ones with others. The need for and feasibility of integrating tasks differs from one production to another, as budgets and circumstances vary.

Software tools are necessary for performing currently existing tasks once the archive's collection has been digitized, in order to perpetuate the archives' main functions. In contrast to human factors and efficiency considerations, the software for archiving and production tasks poses relatively few constraints on distribution of tasks. For instance, there is no need at all from a software engineering point of view to reproduce existing specialties, say, for editing and cataloguing sport programs. Therefore, one way to design tools that integrate tasks in a way users can work with and that is also efficient in light of other requirements would be to develop general purpose software, and observe how users fulfilling various roles in the current nondigital world deal with it. Subsequently, various specialized versions of the general system can be implemented, adapted to the combinations of tasks discovered and favored by test users. This approach seems especially fit when it is difficult for specialists to imagine how tasks will be performed using new applications. In the case of archiving and television production this has turned out to be the case (Tan, 1998). Various so-called multimedia asset management systems are currently being developed by the large broadcasting hardware companies in collaboration with manufacturers of large information systems, based on the same idea that all existing tasks in a media archive and production environment should be supported by one integrated system.

In our research, Heimo Müller designed to this end a multipurpose system for use in an integrated archive-production environment, in collaboration with Joanneum Research in Graz. It is at present being tested as a prototype.

VINE (VIDEO NAVIGATOR AND EDITOR)

Backgrounds and Functions of the System

VINE (Müller, 1999) is based on two assumptions. One is that immediate viewing, enabled by direct access to content, improves current practices of cataloguing and retrieval; the other is that archiving and production tasks will be combined. In a digital environment, archiving and production tasks require fast browsing and inspection. The documentalist needs to switch easily from judging a program or a set of programs as a whole, for example, for classification, to viewing sequences shot by shot. The producing journalist likewise has to browse through larger result sets, consisting of whole programs, whereas in selection, sequences and shots have to be carefully inspected. The major asset of the digital archive, direct viewing access, can only be exploited if browsing and inspection functions are fast and intuitive.

Navigating and browsing through large amounts of video materials, ranging from 20 to hundreds of hours, then, is VINE's core function. Various other functions have been added to this that enable manipulation of video files and content descriptions required as part of the current archive's main tasks. The main tasks that can all be performed using VINE are cataloguing, search and retrieval, and assembly and editing. Thus, VINE supports archiving as well as production. The system allows the user to perform any of the main tasks without leaving the system. In this respect VINE is more general than current video information management systems on the market (Matzken, 2000; see also Christel et al., 1995; a good overview is to be found in Multimedia Tools and Applications, 1998). Besides supporting the main tasks, VINE was designed if possible, to improve current task performance.

We cannot go into any details of VINE's system architecture. It will suffice to say that its data structures draw on research into the structure of film and digital video (see Müller & Rehatschek, 1999). Instead we review VINE as it has been designed. Not all functions have been implemented yet, but users have tested most parts of the prototype, and it is this prototype that we present here. A full implementation would require integrating VINE with (a) a mass video storage device, (b) existing catalogue relational database management systems, and (c) a quality online editing system, such as AVID (by Avid Technology. For documentation see, e.g., Bayes, 2000).

Cataloguing and Indexing. VINE assists the user in cataloguing and indexing (see Fig. 3.1), by three functions: automatic preliminary processing, an annotation editor, and grouping facilities. A screen shot of the system is shown in Fig. 3.4, displaying a scene of *Pulp Fiction.* The example shows an analysis of a feature film or movie. Typically, however, a television program is analyzed, which can be a movie but more often represents another genre, such as a live sports broadcast or a news show. The "scenes" of a movie correspond to program items, movie parts to program parts; these are program segments of arbitrary length and nature.

Some selection of materials, generally a larger number of programs is imported as a collection of MPEG-files in the system, acting as a "temporary collection." MPEG (for "Moving Picture Experts Group") is the most common compression format for video data. The top three items of the leftmost column in the screen shot show the contents of the temporary collection, for example, three movies, *Sissy, Jackie Brown* and *Pulp Fiction,* and two others near the bottom of the leftmost column, *Reservoir Dogs* and *From Dusk Till Dawn.* One or more items from the temporary collection, for example, a television program, can be selected for automated preprocessing by the system that prepares for actual cataloguing and indexing. It consists of shot detection and key frame generation. A time code is assigned to the beginning and end of each shot, which saves the effort of manually finding shot boundaries while viewing. For every shot, one or more key frames best representing its visual content are extracted, according to a number of choices the user makes beforehand (e.g., the key frame may be the first, the middle, or the last frame of the shot, or it may represent a change of the image in terms of parameters such as colour distribution, motion, and the like). Furthermore, various forms of motion in the shot can be analyzed automatically, for example, "pan (L–R)" and "zoom (In–Out)." Preliminary processing results in a shot identification list (see Fig. 3.4, Column "Shot ID") with technical details (see Fig. 3.4, Column "Camera/ Movement"), that acts as a basis for indexing and annotation. (Shot size detection, e.g., Extreme Close-Up (ECU), has not yet been implemented.) The same modules involved in shot detection can be used for finding footage that is identical to a given video shot or sequence, that is for *identity matching,* a function that can be called from the upper menu bar.

VINE has an annotation editor that can be connected to the archive's catalogue system. (It is an entry of the "Tools" menu). This allows the user to catalogue programs in the usual manner. In addition, other indexes can be added that are useful for later content access, but not supported by current nondigital archiving practice. They include technical characteristics such as color and content descriptions of objects, persons, scenes, and actions. To this end, modules for automated content recognition (i.e., extraction and classification), such as VICAR's can be connected to VINE. (For a presentation of VICAR, see Den Uyl, Tan, Müller-Seelich, & Uray, 1998).

60

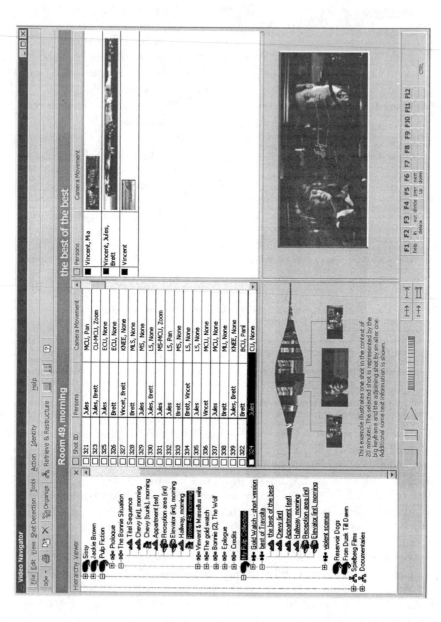

FIG. 3.4. Screen shot of VINE. *Note.* the annotations in the example shown do not conform to standard archiving rules for indexing and annotation.

For alternative content recognition systems see Golshani and Dimitrova (1998), Ratley (1999), and Wilf (1999). It should be noted in passing that annotating movement is also an innovation of current indexing practice.

Figure 3.4 shows a "Person" column. Cataloguing, indexing, and annotation are supported by an MPEG-player, visible in the bottom bar of the screen. Shots can be grouped at will. They can be taken out of chronological order and sorted on the basis of similarity, using the "Organize" function, located in the second menu bar. For instance, if in a documentary on wild life in Africa, there are frequent shots of zebras, interspersed with shots of a presenter, it is easy to form groups of the shots containing zebras and those showing the presenter and assign the proper key word to all shots of one group through one single action. In Fig. 3.4, "My Pulp Collection" is an example of a group—obviously not made for indexing purposes. It has subgroups, including "the best of the best," shown in the upper half of the rightmost column. Catalogue data, indexes, and annotations produced by the user are stored in the catalogue system. Retrieval functions, to be discussed next, may also be used by documentalists; for example, when they need an annotation example of unusual images, they can perform a query by image example and view the annotations assigned to a similar image.

Search and Retrieval. VINE is suited for use in the last step of the search and retrieval process. The result, sets of traditional key words or free text queries from the entire archive catalogue, can be imported as a Temporary Collection. It can then be browsed and viewed for preliminary or final selection. Direct access to videos rather than catalogue information means that much larger result sets can be managed in this stage than usual in current retrieval practice. Viewing fifty videotapes is too cumbersome, whereas browsing through fifty titles is feasible. Selection is supported by fast navigation through the whole video set. The user imports the titles in the Temporary Collection and can then apply shot analysis to all the materials. Existing annotations are a first means for searching through the Temporary Collection. Primary groups can be made on the basis of existing catalogue and index metadata that are imported into VINE along with the video data. Query and grouping by similarity is done using modules for automated support, like VICAR (Den Uyl et al., 1998). VICAR's VIP finder can be used to index persons automatically. It is also the engine for identity matching of shots and sequences. Browsing and inspection are possible at various levels of detail, as can be seen from Fig. 3.4. The user can zoom in on materials to get higher temporal and spatial resolutions. The far left column shows whole movies and parts or scenes, and is called the Hierarchy Viewer. Formal catalogue and content indexing at this coarse level of detail can be made visible and guide selection of relevant materials. The upper part of the second column from the left shows shots of a selected part, with indexes

and annotations. There is as yet no automated device for generating
macrosegmentation (see, e.g., Aigrain, Joly, & Longueville, 1997; Rui,
Huang, & Mehrotra, 1999). A selected shot can be viewed by playing it on
the screen at the lower half of the third column. Below the annotated shot
list, the selected shot is visualized together with its immediate neighbors.
(This function has not yet been presented to test users.) By moving the cur-
sor in the shot list from one shot to the next, the central key frame of the shot
changes; also the two smaller key frames of neighboring shots. The user has
additional support for keeping track of the wider context of the shot by using
the eye-shaped window above the key frames. It consists of Y sections of each
consecutive frame, that is, single pixel columns taken from each frame, that
have been arranged tightly together from left to right. The array of consecutive Y-sections forms the so called O(bject +) M(ovement) images; OM.
Müller-Seelich & Tan, 1999). It is possible to visualize any stretch of video this
way. An object moving from left to right through the shot will pass through
the consecutive Y sections of all frames and be displayed as a static object in
the OM image. In contrast, static objects show as horizontal bars. For instance, the shots of Vincent and Mia and of Vincent, Jules, and Brett in the
Best of the Best, upper right column, contain recognizable objects, due to camera movement, whereas the bars in the shot of Vincent indicate that neither
the camera nor the person moved. A complete movie or program can be visualized in a few pages using OM images. The OM image representation allows the user to inspect large parts of a film in order to judge selected dynamic abstract qualities such as unfolding of color schemas (the shots of
parts of say 10 to 20 minutes length can be seen to have their own particular
colors), and movement patterns (e.g., distribution of motion vs. no motion,
camera motion vs. object motion). In some cases this saves viewing, in others it helps in selecting parts that are worthwhile to view.

Assembly and Editing.   The assembly function is geared toward production, using archived and other images as raw materials. In this respect, it is
less general than interactive authoring systems (e.g. Ahanger & Little, 1998;
Song, Ramalingam, Miller, & Yi, 1999). Cataloguing and search do not per-
manently add new video footage to the archive collection. VINE's assembly
functions (see "Retrieve and Restructure," second menu bar) do serve this
purpose.

   1. *New group.* As we have seen, existing shots can be combined to form
new groups. But scenes and parts can also be members of a group. Saving
and exporting groups is the most elementary form of assembly for production.

   2. *New virtual movie.* A completely new program can be assembled in the
user interface. Selected components of programs in the Temporary Collec-

tion, that is shots or sequences or whole program items (e.g., a sequence of shots with one object), an interview, animation, or chart can be part of a virtual movie or program. Shots and sequences in the Temporary Collection are defined as *video objects*, and a virtual movie or program consists of a chronologically ordered and time coded set of links to these objects. If a virtual movie is complete, it can be rendered and exported.

3. *New virtual parts and shots*. In the same way, the user can create new virtual parts and shots by selecting parts of existing parts and shots from the Temporary Collection. The user interface enables drag and drop functionality in composing virtual video objects, i.e., using the mouse to select and move shots and parts. In particular, moving and copying shots and other objects is done by drag-and-drop actions. Although the operations are performed on links in the first place, the effect of the final rendering is editing the video materials.

Taken together, the assembly functions help the user in building hierarchical structures, with the movie at the root, and shots in the leaves, with parts and scenes in between. However, the group clusters elements cut across layers of the hierarchy.

Search and assembly can also be done with no special program in mind, but for *potential* programs. Hierarchically structured sets of thematically related materials may serve as a pool for future programs.

User Studies in the Digital Archive–Production Environment

Before moving to its effectiveness in inviting test users to perform new tasks, and especially ones that belong to roles other than their own, we first discuss VINE's appropriateness for executing existing tasks, or in other words, its usability for standard archiving and production tasks. The reason for this is that it is necessary to know how well the system does in performing current tasks before judging whether it has the potential to invite the user to go beyond any well-known tasks.

Usability Tests of VINE. Unfortunately, there has been no test of VINE in a fully implemented form. In the studies that we draw on, test users were presented with two or more, but not all of the functions that are part of VINE. It should be stressed that in all cases, the user interface presented differed from the one just discussed, in fact being simpler in most cases. The studies have been reported in detail in Buscher, Frykholm, Kraus, Haitz, and Oomen (2000), Matzken (2000), Oomen (2000). Matzken (2000) performed an evaluation study of a somewhat limited version of VINE that included the following functions: basic video analyser (i.e., shot detection and key frame generation), identity matcher, motion detection, setting classification, car detection, face finding, and a search engine. Matzken performed tests of the system starting from two different use cases. The documentalist case was a test of the use value of the key frame function, focusing on the question of whether this function renders the description of footage more efficient. When a video is input into the system, it detects shots and generates key frames for every shot, returning these in the form of a storyboard. A 5 min sequence from a news bulletin was subjected to the system and subsequently Matzken checked to what degree annotations to the same sequence that had in reality been made as part of normal archiving routines could be made on the basis of the automatically generated storyboard. The annotations included only standard description categories, such as a story, major events, persons, location, and content subjects corresponding to key word categories. Matzken (2000) concluded that a rough annotation could be based on the key frames, and that especially the major events were covered when key frames were used. However, for annotations to conform to the specificity that is currently required, it would be necessary for the documentalist to view and listen in detail to larger parts of the video.

The production journalist case consisted of finding an equivalent video sequence of French president Jacques Chirac standing beside a French flag. The system returned no more than 40% of the relevant shots that were in stock, and it also returned a large amount of completely irrelevant materials. In other words, *recall* and *precision* left a lot to be desired. However, some of the recognition modules, that is, the car finder and face finder, performed a lot better, and also better than competing object recognition packages (E. van Huis, personal communication, December, 2000). Furthermore, the amount and variety of retrieved examples would be sufficient for many production purposes.

Test Users' Adherence to Current Tasks and Roles Versus Willingness to Consider Integration. *Cataloguing.* End user tests were held at the Netherlands Audiovisual Archive (NAA), the Swedish Television Archive (SVT) and the archive of the German Südwest Funk (SWR). End users were documentalists in charge of formal cataloguing and indexing television programs. Tests were reported in Buscher et al. (2000). It would not be informative to report the tests in detail, but they all were more or less similar to the following study conducted by NAA. Seven documentalists were presented with a prototype of VINE. The main screen contained four panels, exhibiting:

- Program functions, that is, file handling and video analysis;
- key frames. This panel allowed for key frame and shot manipulation;
- an MPEG video player, presenting a screen as usual, plus a window showing an array of OM images for the present and neighboring shots;
- the annotation editor.

Documentalists were satisfied with the visual support that key frames offered in distinguishing subsequent shots. They enjoyed the navigation potential offered by the generation and presentation of key frames. They also liked the shot-grouping feature, especially the facility for creating folders, enabling them to personalize their working collections. They felt that efficiency of indexing was enhanced by first grouping shots or sequences that are similar as to content, and then index these all together. Likewise, SVT video editors felt that having key frames instead of the unstructured video right from the start and being able to play the video starting from any key frame was the functionality that they always had wanted to have. However, in other tests, carried out by the SWR archive, the differences between VINE and the usual environment for cataloguing and indexing were emphasized and in part resented. Tested documentalists tend to judge details of the user interface with the current instruments for existing tasks in mind. For instance, differences between the MPEG-player and common analog video players were reported by documentalists to be irritating. Also, deviations from Windows GUI style, i.e., the usual windows screen layout, icons, bars and buttons, were noted as unpleasant (Buscher et al., 2000). Some prefer visualization of a chronological time line to a hierarchical folder structure of a complete program as offered in VINE's user interface. And finally, most of them prefer a user interface geared exclusively to cataloguing tasks, rather than a possibility to choose among cataloguing, search and assembly (E. van Huis, personal communication, Sept., 1999). It would seem, then, that many though not all documentalists would favor a specialist team scenario, remaining as close to existing practice as possible.

The added viewing function representing a shot as an array of OM images, was found confusing and unnecessary in all tests (Buscher et al. 2000). We do not know yet whether producing journalists who have to browse and search through larger amounts of videos will have a more favorable opinion on this function. A group of academic film scholars, professionally involved in detailed film analysis and comparison did recognize a use for this way of visualizing film. They also indicated that using it would require a significant amount of training in order to interpret this "movie map" correctly.

Data just referred to are based on some 20 tested documentalists, and in a situation where they did not have access to larger sets of video. Neither were they invited to experiment with tasks that they were not used to perform, which would constitute by far a better test for the feasibility of any integration scenarios.

Search and retrieval. Oomen (2000) described another test at NAA of only the search functions of the VINE system, in which users were expressly challenged to envision new uses of these. They were presented with working examples of searches resulting in key frame displays, and of query by image. They received search assignments and were interviewed immediately after having completed each of the assignments. The tested user interface looked like the online intranet search interface to the catalogue in use at the archive. Assignments included (a) query by image, (b) inspecting key frames attached to an entire news bulletin, (c) comparing textual indexes and annotations with key frames, and (d) imagining possible uses of query by image supported by modules for recognition of camera and object movement, persons, objects, and settings. Test users were 10 professional journalists, either producers or research specialists, and 4 in-house archive staff members, documentalists at the cataloguing department. Both the nature of the assignments and the composition of the group of informants allowed us to explore the willingness to integrate new tasks into one's current role. All interviews were written out verbatim and summaries were made for every test person.

Key frame delivery. All test users exhibited very positive opinions about the use of key frames in search results, because they do away with the need to retrieve and view video tapes, and because they allow immediate selection of features that are underrepresented or ambiguous in textual indexes and annotations. Atmosphere, visual looks, setting, whether persons are in the shot ("an image of X"), or are the invisible subject of a dialogue ("an image about X"), are examples of features that cannot be "read" from textual indexes and annotations. Tests of the same functions at the Austrian Broadcast Archive (ORF) indicated that key frames are a tremendous help in selecting materials. Users suggested that series of key frames be available online as Hypertext Markup Language (HTML) pages linked to the catalogue record of a given program, and this envisioned use has been made a reality by the archive.

NAA test users could also indicate when textual descriptions were superior to key frames, as when a person is sought whose name is known, but whose looks are unfamiliar to the searching person, and when the name of locations matters.

Various test users mentioned the possibility of using a key frame search to establish identity of different materials, although this function was not available in the test interface. For instance, raw materials, such as "camera rushes" (i.e., unedited footage of a television production), are usually not indexed and catalogued, due to lack of time. These raw materials can lend themselves excellently for reuse, and when reused, produce higher returns in terms of license fees. In addition, there may be a wealth of them, as the ratio of materials shot to ones used in a program may be as low as 1:6 or less, rendering systematic indexing and cataloguing of these unfeasible for most archives (Buscher et al., 2000). For these reasons, it would be worthwhile to know for any shot in the final version of a production whether or not it is a copy of parts of nonindexed raw materials available in the archive. Subsequently, query-by-image search can be used to trace equivalent but nonidentical shots. Identity matching has by now become a standard task in the ORF archive (G. Stanz, personal communication, June 14, 2001).

Query-by-image. Most test users found it difficult to imagine a sensible and concrete use of the query-by-image function because they feel content targets that can be labeled as text almost exclusively guide that search. About half of the test users mentioned the use of search using form or color qualities for programs that contain artistic images or otherwise hinge on image qualities rather than semantic content. It proved the most difficult to conceive of useful applications of object recognition. Faces of VIPs do not have to be recognized as their names are already available in the program information that is generated in the shooting phase; the same goes for relevant objects. And camera and object motion is only rarely a criterion used in a search, according to four test users that mentioned the subject. However, various persons specialized in archive research for productions felt that they could check whether materials selected from the catalogue as featuring a VIP did indeed show the target person, rather than merely mentioning him or her in a voiceover, or involving the person off-screen, or showing images related to the person but not presenting him or her. (Buscher et al., 2000).

CONCLUSIONS AND DISCUSSION

From the studies discussed, we can conclude that the exploration of new access functions results at best in a limited reconceptualization of one's current task repertory. New functions are judged as to their fitness for tasks with which the user is already familiar. This was the ostensibly clear reason why documentalists in charge of cataloguing and indexing denounced the use of new functions such as query by image and automated motion classification. It was also the reason why producers and documentalists were unanimous in acclaiming the use of key frames.

The task assigned to the test user may also result in the persons's sticking to the familiar. Inviting the user to envision new uses of presented functions helped users to imagine a task that was not part of the current repertoire (e.g., identity matching). The same goes for the task environment. Recognizing familiar instruments distracts from envisioning new tasks or another combination of current tasks. The degree to which minor deviations from the familiar task environment are accepted seemed related to perceived efficiency gains, with the current task conceptualization as the criterion. Efficiency gains seemed to motivate integration of new tasks in one's role in that documentalists were willing to add identity matching to their job in order to index materials that had to be omitted for want of automated assistance. Finally, we observed that documentalists had no trouble at all in identifying themselves with producers searching for suited materials, whereas no producer or producer's research assistant indicated any interest in performing indexing or cataloguing tasks, even if they could profit from reuse of materials that they make available. This observation is in perfect accordance with current archive practice, that is based on the idea of service lent by a provider who has to adapt to the end user's perspective. In other words, for archive staff, it is already natural to cross the archiving–production divide, whereas this does not apply to production staff.

Test users did not mention any implications of new functions for their own role, if they have considered these at all. For instance, in spite of the acceptance of the key frame facility, virtually all respondents leave the answer to the question of whether adoption of key frame functionality would implicitly change their own tasks. Only two test users seemed to point at a more immediate control of image selection by producing journalists than is usual at present, at the cost of their own roles. They suggested that, in general, producing journalists consciously or unconsciously have certain images and looks of target materials in mind, that they can recognize immediately at their own desk top. They match this internal image with key frames in order to accept or reject materials at first sight and without the mediation of a researcher, either from the production staff or the archive. The conspicuous fact that no one user mentioned the possibility of automated indexing based on machine recognition of persons, objects, places and so on, as suggested by the query-by-image facilities, may result from an awareness of a threat to the current role of the documentalist. However, a completely legitimate doubt on the present efficacy of the technology underlying the functioning of these modules would have influenced this apparent omission just as much.

Additional Evidence on Integration of Tasks and Roles.   We discuss in brief a number of further informal observations made by archive researchers on the use of newly installed online cataloguing and search functions comparable to VINEs. Part of the online catalogue at the archive of the ORF has been extended to include direct access to compressed video, and facilities for browsing the retrieved materials. It has been observed that researchers working on productions and searching for suitable materials in this part of the catalogue have changed their habits of collecting materials. Before the introduction of the browsing facility, they used to gather written notes on content and formal catalogue details of suited materials from query outputs. These would be handed over, together with archive tapes, to the producer journalist and to the editor. At present, they create Edit Decision Lists, that is, lists of time codes for entering and exiting a tape sequence in editing a source tape to a target tape. In other words, they have adopted a task that is usually part of the role of the editor, crossing the divide between archiving and production just discussed (G. Stanz, personal communication, June 16, 2001).

Future Developments

The design of VINE and the experiences of its test users offer a basis for speculating about forms of integration of tasks in a digital archive—production environment. We mention two distributions of tasks that seem a priori. The *composer/director scenario* hinges on one generalist role, the producing journalist carrying out all production tasks. In this scenario, an integrated set of tools such as VINE's is played like a one-man orchestra. The journalist has absolute control over the content and looks of the program, and the more so if he or she is also in charge of shooting original materials. In the realm of newspaper production, such a scenario is almost a reality already. Franssen (1998) described an automated authoring system for newspaper journalists that allows them to enter articles into a web newspaper, defining to a large extent the layout by choosing one from a larger number of templates. According to the researcher, a logical next step would be to allow the journalists to design their own templates. As a most general illustration of the one-person-creates-all scenario, we can mention the development of authoring environments meant to be used by one person only for the production of entire products, such as information systems, user interfaces, specialized texts, music, video, games, and so on that are currently offered.

At the other extreme, we have the *specialist team scenario*, in which each production task is taken care of by one specialist, thus reproducing current production practice. Of course, variants of this scenario involve combinations of two or more tasks in one role. Awaiting further test results, it is unknown which tasks can be integrated to form role clusters, both in terms of the current staff's willingness and more objective feasibility, that is, physical and logistic efficiency. However, the combination of search and assembly may be the most obvious integration compared to current practice. From informal research with small groups of producers with very limited test set sizes—up to about 4 hours of video—(Buscher et al., 2000), it has become clear that the producing journalists recognize the potential of the system to handle massive amounts of video in assembly and selection. It would seem that at least these producing journalists would like to gain control over search and preliminary collection that is now delegated to an assistant, and thus move in the direction of the composer/director scenario.

We may also think of a new role in the production of programs. A search and assembly specialist, who may be a journalist or a documentalist, may collect archive materials with no special program in mind. Hierarchically structured sets of related materials may serve as a pool for future programs. Such pools may contain video contents that are difficult to find using the catalogue or through query by image, such as footage associated with atmosphere, historical periods, and abstract themes. This possibility has also been underscored by tested producers (Buscher et al., 2000). An even broader conception of the "general cultural content expert" circulates in archive management circles. This should be a highly qualified person who has a profound understanding of the uses of archived video materials, both actual and potential, and is fluent in the use of various content management software, from authoring tools to information systems. This role is as broad and flexible to encompass both the composer–director scenario and the traditional specialized disciplines, in some form (G. Stanz, personal communication, June 16, 2001).

It has turned out in interviews with archive staff that they are concerned about losing grip on both the collection of archived images and the catalogued data (Buscher et al., 2000). This fear is due to one real implication of crossing the archive-production divide, which is that systems like VINE, enhanced by automatic search functions, help in creating copies and new versions of both archive footage and catalogue descriptions. A small group of documentalists indicated that they found the possibility of grouping similar content in order to index all these at once a useless and confusing add-on.

CONCLUSIONS: QUESTIONS FOR COGNITIVE SCIENCE

What does our exploratory design study mean for research into cognition in a digital world? The developments within television archives that were reviewed are exemplary of changes taking place in other archives, cultural institutions, and entertainment industries that are transforming into content providers in the electronic market. The digitization of audio, photography, film and other cultural and entertainment fare will introduce an integration of production, storage, distribution, and access comparable to those in television archives. More generally, the digitization of parts of production processes in all areas of industry brings along a reshuffling of tasks and roles on a very large scale. Moreover, in a digital world, people will work with computer systems that are constantly changing, and every major change may open up possibilities for another definition of tasks and roles. A first conclusion regarding software development for the digital world, then, is that we need task analysis at the supraindividual level. We do not only need to know how tasks are performed by skilled persons, but also how they are distributed across various individuals at present, and what mutual dependencies exist among them. In addition, we need to figure out how they can be combined or redefined so as to fit within novel roles that are both manageable and recognizable to the performing persons. The example of documentalists that are hesitant to assume production tasks can be generalized to most situations where task and roles are subject to redistribution and redefinition. It is likely that combination of specialized tasks is not only limited by compatibility in a physical and logistic sense; performing persons have to be able to subsume the tasks under one abstract *action identity*. Action identity is the description of an activity as a person experiences it (Vallacher & Wegner, 1987). It is related to larger concerns than the success in finishing subtasks, like higher order goals and values of the person and the organization. Exploratory design, as proposed here, is of course just one approach to investigating subjective limits to novel combination of tasks, and more approaches are required.

We also need to know what the limits of task integration are in terms of the development of expertise. Younger generations are visibly more and more willing and capable not only to switch from one job to another, but also to rotate over tasks and roles. Many people wonder whether the nature of expertise in skilled professionals is changing. This raises more fundamental questions about the elasticity of expertise. If expertise requires considerable experience of, say, 10 years of learning by doing (e.g., Hayes, 1985), does this put limits on the combination of professional skills during a career of, say 40 years? When does expertise in one area transfer to or hinder developing expertise in another? Is it possible to be a generalist expert? These are questions posed by the digital world that may challenge students of human cognition.

ACKNOWLEDGMENTS

The authors are indebted to the end user group of the VICAR Consortium for their collaboration and comments: Istar Buscher (SWR), Sten Frykholm (SVT), Eva-Lis Green (SVT), Herbert Hayduk (ORF), Connie Herben (NAA), Annemiek de Jong (NAA), Johannes Kraus (ORF), Johan Oomen (NAA), and Gerhard Stanz (ORF).

REFERENCES

Ahanger, G., & Little, T. D. C. (1998). Automatic composition techniques for video production. *IEEE Transactions on Knowledge and Data Engineering, 10*, 967–987.

Aigrain, P., Joly, P., & Longueville, (1997). Medium knowledge-based macro-segmentation of video into sequences. In M.T. Maybury (Ed.), *Intelligent multimedia information retrieval* (pp. 159–173). Menlo Park, CA: AAAI Press/MIT Press.

Armitage, L.-H., & Enser, P.-G. (1997). Analysis of user needs in image archives. *Journal of Information Science, 23*, 287–299.

Barkin, S. M. (1989). Coping with the duality of television news. *American Behavioral Scientist,* *33,* 153–156.

Bayes, S. (2000). *The AVID Handbook.* New York: Focal Press.

Bentele, G. (1985). Audio-visual analysis and a grammar of presentation forms in news programs: Some mediasemiotic considerations. In T. A. van Dijk (Ed.), *Discourse and communication* (pp. 159–184). Berlin: De Gruyter.

Buscher, I. (1998). Going digital at SWR TV archives. In D. Hiemstra, F. de Jong, & K. Netter (Eds.), *Language technology in multimedia information retrieval. Proceedings of Twente Workshop on Language Technology, 14,* 99–106.

Buscher, I., Frykholm, S., Kraus, J., Haitz, H. J., & Oomen, J. (2000). Final evaluation report [*Tech. rep. VICAR-T4.6-SWR-xxx.05.01.2000*]. Baden-Baden, Germany: Südwest Rundfunk.

Christel, M., Kanade, T., Mauldin, M., Reddy, R., Sirbu, M., Stevens, S., & Wactlar, H. (1995). Informedia digital library. *Communications of the ACM, 38,* 57–58.

Den Uyl, M., Tan, E., Müller-Seelich, H., & Uray, P. (1998). Towards automatic indexing and retrieval of video content: The VICAR system. In D. Hiemstra, F. de Jong, & K. Netter (Eds.), *Proceedings of Twente Workshop on Language Technology, 14, Language technology in multimedia information retrieval* (pp. 177–181). Enschede: Universiteit Twente.

Enser, P.-G. (1995). Pictorial information retrieval. *Journal of Documentation, 51,* 126–170.

Franssen, M. (1998). Electronic newspaper case study. *Trends in Communication, 4,* 37–64.

Galliano, F. (1998, May). The BBC Digital Media Asset Management Centre Project. Paper presented at the FIAT/IFTA seminar, Digital Workflow Through Production and Documentation, London.

Goodman, N. (1978). On rightness of rendering. In N. Goodman, *Ways of worldmaking* (pp. 1–22). Indianapolis, IN: Hackett Press.

Graber, D. A. (1989). Content and meaning: What's it all about? *American Behavioral Scientist, 33,* 144–152.

Green, E.-L., & Klasén, L. (1993). Indexing and information retrieval of moving images—experiences form a large television information database. *Proceedings of On-line Information 93,* December 7–9, 1993.

Hayes, J. (1985). Three problems in teaching general skills. In S. Chipman, J. Segal, & R. Glaser (Eds.), *Thinking and learning skills* (pp. 391–406). Hillsdale, NJ: Lawrence Erlbaum Associates.

Markkula, M., & Sormunen, E. (1998, August). *The photo needs, searching behaviour and photo selection criteria of journalists.* Report of the Working Group on Evaluation methods for content-based photo-rerieval, University of Tampere, Tampere, Finland.

Matzken, I. (2000). *Evaluation of the Vicar Video Navigator* [Tech. rep.]. Leyden University, Netherlands.

McKenzie-Owen, J. S. (1996). Preservation of digital materials for libraries. *LIBER Quarterly,* 6(4), 35–451.

Multimedia Tools and Applications (1998). *Multimedia Tools and Applications, 7,* 1–2, July 1998, W. S. Subrahmanian & S. K. Tripathi (Guest Eds.). Special issue on Multimedia Information Management Sytems.

Müller, H. (1999). *VINE: Video Navigator & Editor* [Tech. rep.] Amsterdam: Faculteit der Letteren, Vrije Universiteit.

Müller H., Rehatschek H. (1999). A generic annotation model for video databases. In N. Huijsmans & A. W. M. Smeulders (Eds.), *Visual information and information systems* (pp. 383–390). Berlin and New York: Springer.

Müller-Seelich, H., & Tan, E. S. (1999). *Movie maps.* In Banissi, E., Khoshrowshahi, F., Sarfraz, M., Tatham, E., & Ursyn, A. (Eds.), Proceedings of the 1999 IEEE International Conference on Information Visualization – IV99, London, 1999, pp. 348–353. Los Alamitos: IEEE Computer Society.

Oomen, J. (2000). *Evaluatie NAA-Pilot.* [Evaluation of NAA Pilot pilot project]. The Netherlands: National Audiovisual Archive, in collaboration with the VICAR Consortium.

van den Berg, J. (1995). *Subject retrieval in pictorial information systems. Electronic filing, registration, and communication of visual historical data.* Abstracts for Round Table No. 34 of the 18th International Congress of Historical Sciences, Montreal, Aug.–Sept. 1995.

van Oostendorp, H., & Peeters, A. L. (1996). De verwerking van nieuws: Waarom vinden mensen nieuws leuk en waarom onthouden ze er weinig van? Een onderzoeksoverzicht. [News processing: Why do people like news and why do they remember so little? A research survey]. *Taalbeheersing, 18,* 133–160.

Ratley, M. (1999, October). Searchable video is the key to success in the digital frontier. *Broadcast Hardware International,* 48–49.

Rui, Y., Huang, T. S., & Mehrotra, S. (1999). Constructing table-of-content for videos. *Multimedia Systems, 7,* 369–384.

Song, J., Ramalingam, G., Miller, R., & Yi, B.-K. (1999). Interactive authoring of multimedia documents in a constraint-based authoring system. *Multimedia Systems, 7,* 424–437.

Tan, E. (Ed.) (1998). *End user requirements. Current practice, current use and envisioned use of television archive content* [Tech. rep. No. VICAR-T1.2-VUA-002.04-25098]. Amsterdam: Vrije Universiteit.

Vallacher, R. R., & Wegner, D. M. (1987). What do people think they're doing: Action identification and human behavior. *Psychological Review, 94,* 3–15.

Wilf, I. (1999, October). Excalibur sharpens video archive material. *Broadcast Hardware International,* 53–54.

Zillmann, D. (1999). Exemplification theory. Judging a whole by some of its parts. *Media Psychology, 1,* 69–94.

Part II

SOCIO-PSYCHOLOGICAL CHARACTERISTICS OF INFORMATION USAGE ON THE WORLD WIDE WEB

The Levels of Web-Based Discussions: Using Perspective-Taking Theory as an Analytical Tool

Sanna Järvelä
University of Oulu, Finland

Päivi Häkkinen
University of Jyväskylä, Finland

Considerable promises have been made for the use of the World Wide Web for this millennium's educational purposes. Various Web-based learning environments have been developed and different Web courses have been designed for higher education and continuing education. Recently, virtual universities have been actively planned. There has been an optimistic view that global networks and the use of computers for intellectual communication will further enhance and expand how humans connect, communicate, and create a sense of community (Bonk & King, 1998; Fetterman, 1998; Harasim, 1993; Owsten, 1997). The strongest argument for Web-based learning has been access: learning can be made available to students for whom distance or time is the primary impediment to certain studies. Learners can, for example, access virtual classrooms, online collaborative groups, learning circles, peer networks, and online libraries in a shared space.

Also, pessimistic views about the quality of web-based learning have been presented (Cothrel & Williams, 1999; Järvelä & Häkkinen, 2002; Schlager, Fusco, & Schank, 2000). Roschelle and Pea (1999) indicated several difficulties for using today's Web as a medium for productive interaction: (a) Interactive communication on the Web is very much dependent on text. Thus, it is much easier to passively read and view information than to actively create it; (b) Collaborative processes are overemphasized, generalized, and their Web-specific features are not explicated; (c) Asynchroneous communication is very different than face-to-face communication. Some of the most important processes in human communication, like creation of mutual understanding or shared values and goals, are hard to reproduce in the Web environment.

The ideas presented in this article are especially challenged by the critical questions focused on Web-based interaction. Are the students able to reach out in such an interaction, leading them to educationally relevant, higher level Web-based asynchronous discussion? For analysing the level of Web-based discussion, we developed a theory-based tool following the ideas of Selman's (Selman, 1980) sociocognitive construct of perspective taking. The model and its theoretical basis are introduced and the practical stages for data analysis are demonstrated in an empirical study of Web-based learning in teacher education.

IS WEB-BASED DISCUSSION EDUCATIONALLY VALUABLE?

There is growing documentation regarding the differences in communication patterns, teacher roles, and student performances when using Web-based learning environments in college or higher education settings (e.g. Khan, 1997; Lehtinen, Hakkarainen, Rahikainen, Lipponen, & Muukkonen, 1999). It is, however, very difficult to evaluate the educational relevance of Web-based learning because most research on the use of different Web-based communication tools still lacks theoretical grounding in contemporary learning theory (Koschmann, 1994). Too often, research on technologies for learning emphasises things like tool features, attractive intercultural designs, and technological procedures, and much of the published work concerning the use of Internet has been anecdotal descriptions of the activities performed.

More depth and quality in electronically networked communication is needed. Studies report how networked interaction in many learning projects results in superficial and experience-based discussion, but does not reach the level of theory-based reflection and argument. Yet, theory-based discussions and expert knowledge are crucial for high-quality knowledge construction and learning (Bereiter & Scardamalia, 1993). The nature of computer mediated discussion differs from face-to-face communication. In written communication, the main medium of communication in the Internet, the reference relations of text should be explicated, and the context created. In face-to-face communication, in contrast, they are usually known by participants or are easily checked. However, in many cases, students do not explicate such referential relations in networked discussions. In this respect, their written activity resembles oral discourse (Lipponen, 2000).

THE PROPERTIES OF SOCIAL INTERACTION
AND RECIPROCAL UNDERSTANDING
IN ASYNCHRONOUS DISCUSSION

Asynchronous interaction without immediate social interaction has many challenges to overcome because communicating parties are faced continuously with the task of constructing their common cognitive environment. A great deal of information conveyed by face-to-face interaction is derived from such things as tone of voice, facial expressions and appearance.

The absence of visual information (e.g., missing facial expressions and nonverbal cues) reduces the richness of the social cues available to the participants, increasing the social distance. For people to communicate effectively, they must solve the mutual knowledge problem (Graumann, 1995; Krauss & Fussell, 1990; Nystrand, 1986). According to the researchers in the field of sociolinguistics, the mutual knowledge problem derives from the assumption that to be understood, speakers must formulate their contributions with an awareness of their addressees' knowledge bases. That is, they must develop some idea of what their communication partners know and do not know in order to formulate what they have to say to them. Research on collaborative learning also calls for reciprocity in social interaction (Crook, 1994). Nystrand (1986) defined reciprocity as a principle that governs how people share knowledge. It rules their determination of what knowledge they will exchange when they communicate and how they choose to present this knowledge in discourse. Evidently, people acquire knowledge and patterns of reasoning from one another but for some kinds of shared knowledge, individually rooted processes play a central role. Regarding collaborative learning, in the grounding phase of coordinated problem solving, the participants negotiate common goals, which means that they do not only develop shared goals but they also become mutually aware of their shared goals (Guy & Lentini, 1995). The question arises how can we better enable participants to find each other and form collaborative teams around mutual goals, skills, and work processes in technology-based environments. There is a need to find variables in communication processes that mediate discussions in the Web environment, and also new ways to characterize discussions in categories related to quality.

FROM RECIPROCAL UNDERSTANDING
TO PERSPECTIVE-TAKING—DEVELOPING
A THEORY-BASED ANALYSIS TOOL

Our earlier empirical studies on students' interactions in the computer environment gave evidence that reciprocal understanding is a typical phenomenon in technology based interactions (e.g. Arvaja, Häkkinen,

Eteläpelto, & Rasku-Puttonen, 2000; Järvelä, 1998; Roschelle & Teasley, 1995). In a study by Järvelä, Bonk, Lehtinen, and Lehti (1999), detailed qualitative data—videotapings, tape recordings and interviews—related to students' working processes and teaching–learning interactions were collected during three experiments. The results of the analysis point to the ways in which technology can improve task-related social interaction and provide multiple opportunities for students to negotiate meanings. Reciprocal understanding seems to be connected with students' social interaction by the computer. Instead, virtual, networked interaction, as in Web-based asynchronous interaction, is a phenomenon of reciprocity that has not yet been analysed. As in face-to-face interaction, in asynchronous interaction, reciprocal understanding can play an important role.

Conditions for social interaction have been analysed by many researchers in different theoretical traditions, for example, human development based on Piagetian and Vygotskian tradition (Newman, Griffin, & Cole, 1989), social psychology (Mead, 1934) and communications (Markova, Graumann & Foppa, 1995).

In social psychology, Mead (1934) argued that human capacity to coordinate roles is both the source of a sense of the self and the core of social intelligence. Hence, in Mead's sense, without social interaction, there could not be a psychological self. Selman (1980) spoke about social perspective taking, which includes developing an understanding of how human points of view are related and coordinated with one another. Similar to this view is Flavell, Botkin, Fry, Wright, and Jarvis's (1968) focus on role taking, characterizing social or psychological information from another individual's perspective. These perspectives coalesce in pointing to the importance of social cognition or perspective taking in the building of common spaces or shared worlds between the interactors.

Perspective taking skills are critical to successful human functioning and involvement in everyday social interaction. We suppose that global networked technologies can influence student perspective taking and raise interpersonal understanding. We also assume that if Web-based interaction is aimed at educationally valuable higher level discussion among the students, the level of perspective taking will correspond to the improved quality of discussion. As the grade of perspective taking in electronic asynchronous discussion improves, so the interaction and learning among the students advances. We also believe that the coordination of different perspectives and mutual negotiation produces reasoning on a more general level (cf. Schwartz, 1995).

For example, in asynchronous Web-based discussion in preservice teacher education, as reported in this chapter, students from different countries create cases on problems encountered in schools. In such an electronic discussion, perspectives can be shared at the level of superficial information, common interests, or deeper theoretical or societal levels. Selman's (Selman, 1980) model of sociocognitive perspective-taking includes developing understanding of how human points of view are related and coordinated with one another. Although the theoretical approach is a strongly structural–developmental construct following Piagetian tradition and originally developed in studies of social and moral reasoning (Selman, 1971), its basic model gives a theoretical insight of the level of interaction in other contexts, such as in negotiations and shared experiences (DeVries & Zan, 1996).

Because Web-based interaction basically involves the essential features of reciprocity, Selman's (Selman, 1990) theory can give a theoretical insight for developing a model for analysing the deeper meaning of Web-based interaction features and for analysing the level of interactors' perspective-taking. Adopting Selman's ideas for Web-based interaction analysis does not follow its original research tradition but rather allows this interaction to be used as a theory-based analysis tool. In the next section, the theory of perspective taking is introduced and the way it has been applied to the Web-based interaction analysis is explained.

A THEORY OF PERSPECTIVE TAKING

Based on Piaget's (1963) cognitive developmental theory, Selman (1980) suggested that educators need to devise new ways for students to progress beyond their egocentric views of the world, that is, grow interpersonally. Selman's developmental construct of social cognition and perspective taking is the ability to see the world from another person's perspective or to infer another's capabilities, attributions, expectations, feelings, and potential reactions. Following Piaget's cognitive developmental theory, Selman (1980) outlined a social cognitive developmental model of five distinct stages with increasing abilities to take into account alternative viewpoints.

In our study, Selman's (1980) developmental theory of social cognitive skills offered a theoretical basis to develop a tool for exploring the level of electronic discussion. Selman and colleagues have studied the ontogenesis of interpersonal conceptions as a function of developmental levels of social perspective taking. They have defined it as the ontogenetic process by which a child comes to understand the way psychological points of view between self and the other are coordinated (Gurucharri & Selman, 1982; Selman, Beardslee, Schultz, Krupa, & Podorefsky, 1986). As a result of these studies, five developmental levels of the coordination of social perspectives are defined:

Stage 0: Undifferentiated and egocentric;
Stage 1: differentiated and subjective role-taking;

Stage 2: self-reflective/second person and reciprocal perspective;

Stage 3: third-person and mutual perspective taking;

Stage 4: in-depth and societal-symbolic perspective taking.

Descriptions of concepts at each level are divided into sections on persons and on relations. The former concept describes a person's notions of how an individual functions psychologically. The latter concept describes the closely related notions of how these individual perspectives are related and concepts of how viewpoints are mutually understood and coordinated (Selman, 1980). In other words, in his structural description of categories, Selman describes each level with two different conceptions: the conceptions of persons and conceptions of relations.

A SYSTEM OF CATEGORY FOR ANALYSING
THE LEVEL OF WEB-BASED DISCUSSION

Selman's original category descriptions (Selman, 1980) were used for developing a system of categories for analysing the level of discussion in asynchronous electronic discussion, but the categories were adapted to the new context. It was created so that after studying the theoretical basis of perspective-taking, the researchers made the first draft of a category system on the most typical elements of electronic discussion and, in particular, on the different perspective-taking stages. The category system was revised after becoming familiar with the data of students' Web-based discussions and the contextual features of the electronic discussion were added. The system of categories for analysing the level of discussion is as follows:

Stage 0: Egocentric

Students present very subjective and egocentric opinions and expressions. They do not pay attention to the point that the other students may or may have interpreted the same situation or experience differently. Conceptions of relations of perspectives are very limited. Because most of the students present their own egocentric opinions and experiences, the electronic discussion does not progress, and the postings remain very scattered.

Stage 1: Subjective Role Taking

The subjective perspectives and other students' perspectives are clearly differentiated. Students' opinions, experiences and feelings are subjective. The discussion is constructed of a one-way conception of relating perspectives and students' responses to postings are very much alike.

Stage 2: Reciprocal Perspective Taking

Students recognize and value the uniqueness of each person's opinions and expressions in discussion. A two-way reciprocity of thoughts and feelings, not merely actions, is typical. Students consider the case of an electronic discussion from variety of different viewpoints and the discussion progresses, but still, different perspectives are not taken enough into account.

Stage 3: Mutual Perspective Taking

Students coordinate the perspectives of self and others, and thus, the topic in discussion is seen from the third person or generalised-other perspective. Each one has his or her own experience about the topic under discussion. Relations are viewed as ongoing systems in which thoughts and experiences are mutually shared. The electronic discussion progresses from mutual experiences to more elaborative argumentation and develops toward discussions on more general views in education or society.

Stage 4: Societal–Symbolic Perspective

The students conceptualise subjective perspectives of persons toward each other at existing, not only on multidimensional or higher levels of communication. In discussion, they can abstract multiple mutual perspectives to societal, conventional, legal, or moral perspectives that all the individuals can share.

Even though finding the relevant theory and creating a theory-based system of categories for analysing Web-based discussion are the most important phases, there are certain other important steps to be done in data analysis before the category system can be used. Web-based data are usually very rich and multidimensional. There may be hundreds of postings or tens of discussions, the amount of participating subjects may vary from tens to hundreds of students; also the discussions are typically unstructured and multidimensional. Following the main ideas of content analysis (Miles & Huberman, 1994), it is very important to develop different ways to reduce and organize data. For analysing the levels of Web-based discussion, a graph model for characterizing the progress and dynamics of a discussion was developed. The following study demonstrates how the theory-based method was used for analysing the levels of web-based discussion.

A STUDY OF THE LEVELS OF A WEB-BASED DISCUSSION

A case-based model for Web conferencing was used in a preservice teacher education course (see Bonk, Malikowski, Angeli, & East, 1998; Järvelä & Häkkinen, 2002; Saarenkunnas et al., 2000). The subjects were preservice teachers in the United States, University of Indiana, (n = 40) and Finland, Universities of Jyväskylä and Oulu (n = 30) who used an asynchronous Web-based tool called Conferencing on the Web (COW) to collaborate in creating joint, case-based descriptions in different areas of teaching and learning. The aim of the study was to examine the level of Web-based discussion, especially focusing on the level of perspective taking between the interactors.

Procedure

The students constructed case-based descriptions (see Bonk et al., 1998) in the areas such as motivation, multicultural education, or technology in education as well as the change these practices impose on traditional teaching and learning. Different levels of expertise in peer and mentor collaboration were provided during the learning process in order to apprentice student learning. Mentoring was organized by senior students in other countries as well as by in-service teachers and faculty members from other universities.

An asynchronous Web-based tool (COW) was applied for the learning environment. COW is a shareware program, which allows users to read, browse, and add to multiple discussions asynchronously by using a Web browser anywhere in the world at any time. In order to strengthen the feeling of a virtual community, the Web-work was supported by two international videoconferences between the two Finnish sites and the American counterpart (see Saarenkunnas et al., 2000). The web-based learning project proceeded in the following way:

1. The students read a selection of articles in the areas of learning and teaching;
2. ISDN video conference meeting between Finland and the United States was organized for introducing the students;
3. The students wrote cases in COW. Each case created an electronic discussion;
4. Different levels of mentoring (peer, experienced teacher, researcher, local, and global) were provided;
5. The students summarized the discussions and the Web work was closed;
6. Final video conference meeting between Finland and the United States was organized for reflection.

Data Collection and Analysis

Transcript data of students' postings was collected. Following the principles of qualitative content analysis, three successive phases were formulated for the analysis. First, in order to organize the data, it was grouped for different types of postings (an analysis focused on individual postings). Second, a graph model was developed for structuring the detailed information received from the data and making a complete interpretation for different levels of discussions (an analysis focused on each discussion). Third, the previous two phases were exploited in classifying the data according to the system of categories developed. The second and third analyses helped us consider the connection in between the level of discussion and the quality of discussion; that is, how the perspective-taking stage contributes to the level of discussion.

PRELIMINARY ANALYSIS OF EACH DISCUSSION: THE TYPE OF POSTINGS

During the 2-month period, the students produced 25 different discussions involving 10 to 30 postings in each discussion. First, the category of the type of postings was determined in order to organize the data. The types of postings were grouped into the following categorizations: *theory, new point, question, experience, suggestion,* and *comment.* The categories were formulated from transcript data from the researchers. Second, cross-references between the student postings within discussions and mentors' postings were marked. Third, quantifications were made such as the number of postings by mentors, the number of each type of posting, and the number of cross-references.

ANALYSIS OF THE INTERACTION: THE LEVEL OF DISCUSSIONS

Preliminary analysis provided the necessary detailed information needed for analysing the levels of discussions. Graphs were drawn (see Fig. 4.1), which demonstrate the progress of a discussion, dynamics of different types of postings, postings created by a case presenter, mentors' postings, and type of postings. The ingoing and outgoing arrows describe the amount and direction of cross-referring between the postings. The Fig. 4.1 demonstrates the graph used as a tool to organize the detailed data in the discussion, "Do computers replace teachers?," which included 17 postings. This particular graph describes a progressive discussion.

Because each graph organizes multiple information, such as posting types, mentors' scaffolding, and overall cross-referencing, it was possible to see the dynamics of different pieces of information and to take them into consideration when evaluating the level of discussion. The graphs were the researchers' tools, which facilitated formulation of three groups of 25 dis-

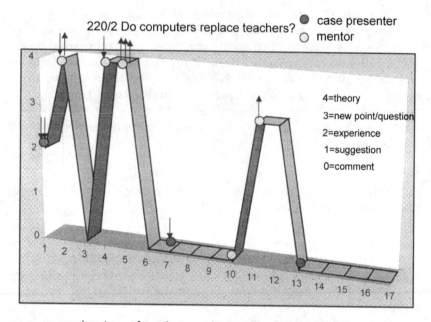

x-axis = type of posting, y-axis = rank-order of posting

FIG. 4.1. An example of a graph used for organizing the detailed data.

cussions: high-level discussions, progressive discussions and low-level discussions.

High-level discussions can be characterised as shared, theory-based discussions. The discussions maintain high-level postings, such as theory-based postings and postings involving a new point or question. Comments do not degrade the quality of discussion, but support the construction of a topic to be discussed. Rich cross-referring is typical.

Progressive discussions involve some cross-references, generalizations, and joint knowledge-building (see Fig. 4.1.). They have plenty of comments, but also experience-based postings and postings with new points or questions. In the course of the discussions, the students' postings are constructed on the previous, mainly experience-based postings, but in the end of the discussion, general thoughts and ideas are usually voiced. No theory-based discussion occurs. A typical feature of the discussions is a rich dynamic in conversation: cross-references and variety in types of postings.

Low-level discussions involve mainly separate comments and opinions. Students' comments do not take into consideration the earlier discussion but rather represent each student's independent and often unilateral comments. The amount of other type of postings other than comments is minor.

For confirming the validity of the analysis, two researchers made independent estimates of levels of discussions. Their classifications matched perfectly with 90% of the coding. The 10% of contradictory analyses (3 discussions) were negotiated until uniform estimation was reached.

SPECIFIC ANALYSIS OF THE QUALITY OF INTERACTION: PERSPECTIVE-TAKING STAGE IN DISCUSSIONS

The particular attempt was to find out what stage of perspective taking occurs among the students in an asynchronous discussion. For classifying the data according to the system of categories based on perspective-taking, each of three levels, high-level, progressive level, and low-level discussions were analysed in detail in order to understand the reciprocal understanding and perspective taking stage of each level of discussion. The idea was to better understand the characteristics of each discussion level, whether perspective taking is observable in electronic discussion, and what is the possible contribution of electronic discussion to quality of discussion. Again, two researchers made independent estimates for coding and this time classification matched perfectly in 80% of the coding. The 20% of contradictory analyses were discussed until uniform estimation was reached.

RESULTS

Three different levels of discussions were found in the qualitative analysis. Six discussions were found that belong to the high-level discussions, ten discussions to progressive discussions and nine discussions, to low-level discussions. This is illustrated in Fig. 4.2.

Because we were interested in the quality of discussions in terms of their educational value, a more specific analysis was conducted based on social cognitive theory of perspective taking (see the category system described earlier). From all 25 discussions, none of the discussions reached the highest Stage 4 (Societal-Symbolic Perspective Taking). Five discussions (20%) were in Stage 3 (Mutual Perspective Taking), 9 discussions (36%) in Stage 2 (Reciprocal Perspective Taking), 9 discussions (36%) in Stage 1 (Subjective Role-Taking), and 2 (8%) discussions in Stage 0 (Egocentric; see Fig. 4.3).

High-level discussions were either in Stage 3 or in Stage 2. In these discussions, mutual or reciprocal perspective taking was apparent. Students recognized the value of other students' opinions and considered the topic of discussion from a variety of different viewpoints. The communication

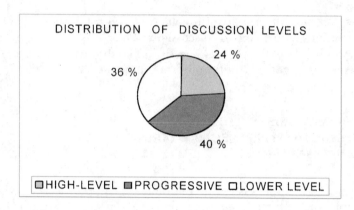

FIG. 4.2.   Distribution of discussions according to different levels.

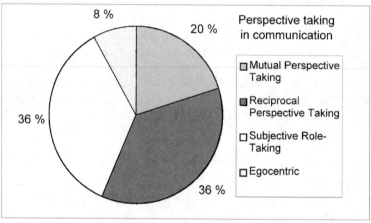

FIG. 4.3.   Distribution of discussions between categories of perspective taking.

progressed from mutual understanding to more general argumentation and conclusions.

Excerpt 1 describes mutual perspective taking (Stage 3) in asynchronous discussion. We use Excerpt 1 also to demonstrate the COW discussion. Because of space limits, only the most illustrative parts of the discussion have been chosen to demonstrate the level of perspective taking.

EXCERPT 1. of discussion 204/1 "Prerequisites for successful co-operative learning?".

1. Case -author: Mervi (Finnish student) Date: Mar. 13 9:43 AM 1998

Dear COW participants, I'm an english student doing my teacher training this year. I've tried many different approaches to studying a new text in the classroom, one of which is co-operative learning. I've had two kinds of experiences about co-operative learning. One class was very enthusiastic about it, they worked hard, they supported each other and they took responsibility of their work. They also told me that they enjoyed working that way and that they felt they really learned something. The teacher of this class has a learner-centered teaching style, so they are used to working independently.

I also tried co-operative learning in another class where the students were of same age as the ones I talked about before. This time it didn't work. The students felt very insecure about their skills, they seemed unable to work together without continuous guidance and they said they wanted to do some "real studying" (whatever that is . . .)

I don't know what kind of teaching style they are used to, because I was a substitute teacher and didn't get a chance to observe the class with their own teacher. Do you think that the teaching style that the students were used to was one reason for this? Can you think of any other reasons? (I know that group dynamics is one very important factor..)

waiting for your comments,
Mervi

2. Author: Carolyn (American student) Date: Mar. 17 9:01 PM 1998

It could be that they were used to one teaching style and when you tried to implement co-operative learning they felt intimidated. They may have felt that it wouldn't help them without giving it a fair chance. I personally think that co-operative learning methods are great and can be very beneficial to students. I also wonder if possibly some of the students felt intimidated by other students who they perceive to be smarter then themselves. Maybe when they were placed in these groups they felt as if they would be made fun of for not being as smart as another student. I would have thought that the children who weren't used to this kind of method would have really enjoyed the change. I'm glad that you had one successful experience with co-operative learning rather than two negative experiences. I am truly surprised that they didn't feel that they were "really studying" in groups with their peers. This was an interesting study!

3. Author: Minna (Finnish mentor, researcher and teacher educator) Date: Mar. 18 5:43 AM 1998

What really surprises me in School today, is that teachers and students rarely talk about learning. For example the text books we use in English courses hardly mention the topic of language learning. I think that raising learning awareness should be one important goal of all learning activity at school. I guess in Finnish schools (at least in secondary shools) we have left this topic for student councellors alone. If the topic of learning was addressed frequently in connection with different subjects, and if the students had opportunities to guide their own learning procesess, I guess they would be more flexible when it comes to alternative learning/teaching styles.

- - Minna

4. Author: Mari (Finnish mentor, researcher and teacher educator) Date: Mar. 20 6:32 AM 1998

An interesting case, Mervi! I think this is a tough one when we talk about change in education and in educational practices. Young students are willing and able to try out new methods but it doesn't take that long a time for them to get accustomed to fixed ways of doing things. This fact lays a heavy responsibility on the teacher and also the educational system. If new approaches to learning are not incorporated in the classroom practices from the very early stages on, it takes time and effort to change and "outlearn" from the old ways of doing things in the classroom and also getting a new perspective on what learning really is about. Do you think that our teacher education system takes this issue seriously when educating becoming teachers? Do they realize the long term effects of being too stuck in the "old ways"?

- - - Mari

5. Author: Hanna (Finnish student) Date: Mar. 25 7:38 AM 1998

I wonder if it's ever possible to incorporate practice on all sorts of learning methods into our teacher training system since the amount of lessons you get to keep is factually next to nothing. However, I don't think it's such a disaster as long as during the teacher training you learn to be open to all new ideas and practices. Isn't that after all what keeps wheels turning -- not the fact that you learn new things per se during the training, but the aptitude and willingness to improve yourself throughout your career (ah, and life time, indeed.)

As I think someone said(wrote) earlier on, I also think you have to play it by the ear when in contact with various classes. Only last week did I use a lot of co-operative learning, but realised later on that due to a composition of a number of weaker students, they felt all issues had been left hanging in the air as the teacher didn't provide them with the "correct" answers. Actually I understand their concern as this was grammar what they were dealing with, they need to know whether what they did is accurate or not.

It was my fault not taking care I could provide everyone with the help they felt they needed, but on the other hand it was the pupils' fault for not telling me about it until when it was too late! What are we teachers -- gods who are not to be distrubed???

6. Author: Mervi (case author, Finnish student) Date: Mar. 27 6:43 AM 1998

Hello everybody,

Thanks for your replies. You pointed out to me some things that I didn´t think of - or at least I didn´t place much importance on - when writing this case.

Feeling secure in the group where you work is of course very important. But how to create an atmosphere where everyone feels secure . . . that´s another thing.

Raising the students´ awareness about learning - I agree that it´s not happening in Finnish schools. Maybe the students have one course that deals with these things when they start high school, but that´s about it. These things should definitely be included in teaching throughout the school year.

And then, something that I found very important:the teacher being open to new ideas. After all, you can´t expect the students to be open to new approaches to learning if you yourself are stuck with the old ways.

So, once again: thanks for your thoughts. I plan to use co-operative learning methods in the future as well, keeping these things in mind.

The quality of communication in progressive discussions was mainly in Stage 2 (except one Stage 3 and two Stage 1 discussions). The discussions were characterized with reciprocal perspectives, so that thoughts and feelings were considered especially from a variety of viewpoints contributing to the progressive quality of discussion. For instance, *"I agree with Anne's comment that you can not motivate anyone. I have been to many leadership workshops, and from them I have learned that..."*. However, in these discussions, general conclusions, evaluations, or suggestions were rare.

Low-level discussions were all in Stage 1, but two discussions were in Stage 0. The discussions were restricted to subjective perspectives so that students either produced very egocentric, usually feeling-based opinions or responded to earlier postings with *"I agree ..."*—like postings without paying attention to the point that the other students may have interpreted the same situation in a different way. In these discussions, the postings remained very scattered and, actually, there was no progressive discussion at all.

In conclusion, the results of this study point out different levels of Web-based discussions. The results also show that the stage of perspective taking in electronic discussion was generally rather low. None of the discussions reached the highest stage, societal-symbolic perspective taking, but most of the discussions indicated mutual or reciprocal perspective taking or even subjective role-taking. Furthermore, high-level discussions involved communication with the highest stage of perspective taking and constructive discussion, whereas lower level discussions were mostly egocentric and superficial. Because the analysis of the level of discussion, such as high, progressive, or low-level describes the nature of discussion in a whole Web-based learning course, we may suppose that it reflects the quality of students' learning. We may conclude that the higher the level of perspective taking reached, the better the learning.

EVALUATING THE THEORY-BASED ANALYSIS TOOL FOR ANALYZING THE LEVEL OF WEB-BASED DISCUSSION

The theoretical insight of reciprocal understanding, in general, and Selman's (Selman, 1980) perspective taking theory, in particular, helped us to develop a model for analyzing Web-based interaction. The theory gave us a useful framework to explore possible cognitive growth or developing perspectives on Web-based learning. This theoretical "tool" was important because our data did not allow us to consider students' thought processes or social interaction processes where two or more students negotiate meaning during Web-based learning (cf. Reed et al., 1998). We thought that Selman's (Selman, 1980) theoretical model on conceptions of relations offers a useful tool for analyzing the quality of asynchronous discussion on a deeper level than merely focusing on linguistic structures or forms of discussion because we did not have simultaneous access on students' thoughts (cf. Howell-Richardson & Mellar, 1996).

Selman's (Selman, 1980) theory is strongly tied to children's development. In our study, we did not focus on the development of individual students, rather the development of discussion created by them in asynchronous discussion. It must be noticed that we were not measuring students' social cognitive skills or their development during networked interaction, nor did we pay attention to their developmental level of perspective taking skills.

The same categories of social perspective taking, as the five stages in the original theory, might not always be applicable to the analysis of Web-based discussion. Therefore, it is necessary to evaluate how well the original categories could be applied to the Web-based discussion or how the original categories needed to be revised in order to apply to other contexts. The researcher needs to have a strong theoretical understanding of the theory of perspective taking, which demands continuous interaction between the theory and the contextual features of the data. Because the origin of perspective taking theory comes from a very different tradition than Web-based learning, there is a danger that the model of analysis will be used in a superficial and mechanical way. In order to avoid superficial interpretation, a "graph tool" was developed to enhance the data structuring and facilitating deeper understanding of it. Multidimensional information is easier to visualize in a graphical form than in a transcribed text.

It is, however, typical that Web-based discussions are analyzed mainly using the transcribed texts or counting frequencies of different details. Because Web-based learning and interaction processes are not inherently situated in a Web environment, nor is knowledge construction derived exclusively from writings or notes on the Web, it is urgent to develop ways to organize and analyse the data so that the dynamics of different factors in Web-based learning can be taken into consideration. Different contextual social resources, such as peers, collaborative partners, or mentors are important contributors in creating shared understand. Web-based learning should not be considered only in global networks, but should be seen in a broader social context.

HOW TO FURTHER DEVELOP THE MODEL FOR ANALYSING WEB-BASED DISCUSSION?

One of the weaknesses of using the perspective-taking theory as a model for analyzing the Web-based interaction is that it is very difficult to evaluate the real perspective-taking level on the basis of a written Web-based discussion. We need to find methods for receiving data of students' own interpretations and of the social context. A relevant method could be videotaping, stimulated recall interviews, reflective group discussions, or classroom observations. In the future, our aim is to examine the strategies people employ in an effort to establish common ground in situations where students are collaboratively working with Web-based environments. Important questions will be: How do virtual social groups emerge as a result of Web-based communication? What is the quality of collaboration and how is collaboration formed? Are there certain pedagogical factors that contribute on the development of different levels of discussions? What are the possible contextual and pedagogical contributors for high-quality conversations?

It is important to further elaborate the phenomena of reciprocal understanding and the theory of perspective taking in virtual, networked environments in general. For example, current knowledge intensive organizations in modern industry have practical problems concerning the extent to which knowledge is actually shared, especially among teams of experts at different locations (Allee, 1997). A large part of the experience remains individual tacit knowledge, it is not shared explicitly, and is lost when experts leave the company. A deeper insight into the phenomena of reciprocal understanding and perspective taking could help find answers to such questions as: How do we support the building of a virtual community between these experts? How do we pedagogically support virtual work? How do we support individual participation in an expert community? As we have proposed (Häkkinen, Järvelä, & Dillenbourg, 2000), by utilizing the theoretical knowledge on perspective-taking and reciprocal understanding, it may be possible in the future to develop innovative technological ways that help to identify and share tacit knowledge by making collaborative processes visible through concrete representations of these processes.

REFERENCES

Allee, V. (1997). *The knowledge evolution: Expanding organizational intelligence.* Boston: Butterworth-Heinemann.
Arvaja, M., Häkkinen, P., Eteläpelto, A., & Rasku-Puttonen, H. (2000). Collaborative processes during report writing of a science learning project: The nature of discourse as a function of task requirements. *European Journal of Psychology of Education, 15*(4), 457–462.

Bereiter, C., & Scardamalia, M. (1993). *Surpassing ourselves. An inquiry into the nature and implications of expertise.* Chicago, IL: Open Court.

Bonk, C. J., & King, K. S. (Eds.). (1998). *Electronic collaborators: Learner-centered technologies for literacy, apprenticeship, and discourse.* Mahwah, NJ: Lawrence Erlbaum Associates.

Bonk, C. J., Malikowski, S., Angeli, C., & East, J. (1998). Web-based case conferencing for preservice teacher education: Electronic discourse from the field. *Journal of Educational Computing Research, 19*(1), 267–304.

Cothrel, J., & Williams, R. L. (1999). On-line communities: Helping them form and grow. *Journal of Knowledge Management, 3*(1), 54–60.

Crook, C. (1994). *Computers and the collaborative experience of learning.* London: Routledge.

De Vries, M., & Zan, X. (1996). Assessing interpersonal understanding in the classroom context. *Childhood Education, 72*(5), 265–268.

Fetterman, D. N. (1998). Webs of meaning: Computer and Internet resources for educational research and instruction. *Educational Researcher, 27*(3), 22–30.

Flavell, J. H., Botkin, P. I., Fry, C. L., Jr., Wright, J. W., & Jarvis, P. E. (Eds.). (1968). *The development of role-taking and communication skills in children.* New York: Wiley.

Graumann, C. F. (1995). Commonality, mutuality, reciprocity: A conceptual introduction. In I. Markova, C. Graumann, & K. Foppa (Eds.), *Mutualities in dialogue* (pp. 1–24). New York: Cambridge University Press.

Gurucharri, C., & Selman, R. L. (1982). The development of interpersonal understanding during childhood, preadolescence, and adolescense: A longitudinal follow-up study. *Child Development, 53,* 924–927.

Guy, G., & Lentini, M. (1995). Use of collaborative resources in a networked collaborative design environment. *Journal of Computer-Mediated Communication, 1,* 1–12.

Häkkinen, P., Järvela, S., & Dillenbourg, P. (2000). Group reflection tools for virtual expert community—REFLEX project. In B. Fishman & S. O'Connor-Divelbiss (Eds.), *Proceedings of the Fourth International Conference of the Learning Sciences* (pp. 203–204). Mahwah, NJ: Lawrence Erlbaum Associates.

Harasim, L. M. (1993). *Global networks.* Cambridge, MA: MIT Press.

Howell-Richardson, C., & Mellar, H. (1996). A methodology for the analysis of patterns of participation within computer mediated communication courses. *Instructional Science, 24,* 47–69.

Järvelä, S. (1998). Socioemotional aspects of students' learning in cognitive-apprenticeship environment. *Instructional Science 26,* 439–471.

Järvelä, S., Bonk, C. J., Lehtinen, E. & Lehti, S. (1999). A theoretical analysis of social interactions in computer-based learning environments: Evidence for reciprocal understandings. *Journal of Educational Computing Research, 21* (3) 359–384.

Järvelä, S., & Häkkinen, P. (2002). Web-based cases in teaching and learning—the quality of discussions and a stage of perspective taking in asynchronous communication. *Interactive Learning Environments, 10*(1), 1–22.

Khan, B. H. (Ed.). (1997). *Web-based instruction.* Englewood Cliffs, NJ: Educational Technology Publications.

Koschmann, T. D. (1994). Toward a theory of computer support for collaborative learning. *Journal of Learning Sciences, 3*(3), 219–225.

Krauss, R. M., & Fussell, S. R. (1990). Mutual knowledge and communicative effectiveness. In J. Galegher, R. E. Kraut, & C. Egido (Eds.), *Intellectual teamwork* (pp. 111–145). Hillsdale, NJ: Lawrence Erlbaum Associates.

Lehtinen, E., Hakkarainen, K., Lipponen, L., Rahikainen, M., & Muukkonen, H. (1999). Computer supported collaborative learning: A review of research and development. *The J.H.G.I Giesbers Reports on Education, 10.* The Netherlands: Department of Educational Sciences, University of Nijmegen.

Lipponen, L. (2000). Towards knowledge building discourse: From facts toexplanations in primary students' computer mediated discourse. *LearningEnvironments Research, 3,* 179–199.

Markova, I., Graumann, C., & Foppa, I. (Ed.). (1995). *Mutualities in dialogue.* Cambridge, UK: Cambridge University Press.

Mead, G. H. (1934). *Mind, self, and society.* Chicago: University of Chicago Press.

Miles, M. B., & Huberman, A. M. (1994). *Qualitative data analysis* (2nd ed.). Thousand Oaks, CA: SAGE.

Newman, D., Griffin, P., & Cole, M. (1989). *The construction zone: Working for cognitive change in school.* New York: Cambridge University Press.

Nystrand, M. (1986). *The structure of written communication: Studies of reciprocity between writers and readers.* London: Academic Press.

Owsten, R. D. (1997). The World Wide Web: A technology to enhance teaching and learning? *Educational Researcher, 26*(2), 27–33.

Piaget, J. (1963). *The child's conception of the world.* Paterson, NJ: Littlefield, Adams.

Reed, J. H., Schallert, D. L., Benton, R. E., Dodson, M. M., Lissi, M., & Amador, N. (1998, April). *Methodological issues in studying computer mediated conversation.* Paper presented at the Annual Meeting of American Educational Research Association, San Diego.

Roschelle, J., & Pea, R. (1999). Trajectories from today's WWW to a powerful educational infrastructure. *Educational Researcher, 43,* 22–25.

Roschelle, J., & Teasley, S. (1995). The construction of shared knowledge in collaborative problem solving. In C. E. O'Malley (Ed.), *Computer supported collaborative learning.* Heidelberg: Springer-Verlag.

Saarenkunnas, M., Järvelä, S., Häkkinen, P., Kuure, L., Taalas, P., & Kunelius, E. (2000). NINTER—Networked Interaction: Theory-based casesin teaching and learning. *Learning Environments Research 3,* 35–50.

Schlager, M. S., Fusco, J., & Schank, P. (2000). Evolution of an on-line education community of practice. In K. A. Renniger & W. Shumar (Eds.), *Building virtual communities: Learning and change in cyberspace.* New York: Cambridge University Press.

Schwartz, D. L. (1995). The emergence of abstract representations in dyad problem solving. *The Journal of the Learning Sciences, 4*(3), 321–354.

Selman, R. L. (1971). The relation of role taking to the development ofmoral judgement in children. *Child Development, 42,* 79–91.

Selman, R. L. (1980). *The growth of interpersonal understanding.* New York: Academic Press.

Selman, R. L., Beardslee, W., Schultz, L. H., Krupa, M., & Podorefsky, D. (1986). Assessing adolescent interpersonal negotiation strategies: Toward the integration of structural and functional model. *Developmental Psychology, 22*(4), 450–459.

Chapter 5

The World Wide Web
as a Social Infrastructure
for Knowledge-Oriented Work

Kerstin Severinson Eklundh
Kristina Groth
Anders Hedman
Ann Lantz
Henry Rodriguez
Eva-Lotta Sallnäs
Royal Institute of Technology, Stockholm

The World Wide Web (WWW) has implied an explosion in network-mediated information exchange. Its ubiquitous nature and technical strengths, in particular, the flexible hypermedia document format and the general communication protocol, have given users a powerful infrastructure for sharing knowledge and for interactive communication. This has created new research questions with respect to how people conceptualize the Web, and how the use of this medium is embedded in their professional activities.

This chapter investigates implications of Web-based information exchange for people within knowledge-oriented professions. Our point of departure is a current project on knowledge, communication, and context in electronic networks (KnowHow). People in knowledge-intensive professions, such as researchers, technical developers, teachers, and librarians typically have a continuous need for updated knowledge within their area of expertise, which necessitates contacts with others both inside and outside their local organization. Furthermore, workers in such areas are often responsible for their own competence development. This has been found in an interview study that preceded the present project (Lantz & Severinson Eklundh, 1999). These observations motivated investigation of their use of the Web as a medium for self-selected knowledge development.

Among the unique characteristics of the Web is the fact that it enables fast and global communication among its users. A range of new contact patterns and special collaboration forms have been developed on the basis of the Web infrastructure. The open question is how these increased possibilities of contact affect individuals' strategies of information exchange, both with respect to providing and acquiring information.

Our focus in this chapter is therefore: What are the implications of the "social Web" for the daily information exchange of knowledge workers? In particular, how has the Web's potential for communication and its accessible information infrastructure affected strategies for acquiring and spreading professional information? We deal with the following aspects of Web use: (a) sharing knowledge on the global network, (b) sharing knowledge within an organization, and (c) active collaboration within work groups.

These three aspects are not independent, because the Web's global character affects its use also for organizational and group purposes. However, we attempt to maintain the distinction between them as far as possible. We review research that we have come across, and describe some of our own studies in relation to these areas.[1]

THE NEED FOR RESEARCH ABOUT WEB USE

The WWW as a research area is still new. Most of the work published so far concerns technical issues (e.g., different communication protocols, document formats, and Web programming tools), or issues about the design of Websites from a usability perspective (see, e.g., Buckingham Shum & McKnight, 1997). In a workshop on the topic, "HCI and the Web" (Instone, 1996), the following research areas were mentioned as important: users' models of the Web, navigation in large amounts of information, and document design for the Web. More recently, there has been a growing interest in the design of Web-based collaborative environments; generally, the social potential of the Web is increasingly recognized and used (see e.g., Munro, Höök, & Benyon, 1999b).

In the growing literature on the Internet and the Web, there is a notable lack of empirical research about how people actually use these media in their daily work activities. Many of the existing studies of Web use are based on automatically gathered usage data, which is relatively easy to collect by adding registration functionality to Websites, or on large surveys about navigational patterns. For example, studies have been made focusing on how users revisit Web pages (Tauscher & Greenberg, 1997), and of the use of bookmarks when navigating the Web (Abrams, Baecker, & Chignell, 1998).

---

[1]As we are focusing on professional communication, many issues concerning Web and Internet usage are not covered in this chapter. For example, the area of online commerce is mainly outside the scope of this chapter. Furthermore, computer-mediated communication is only dealt with insofar as it occurs as part of Web-based activity.

In contrast to such quantitative studies of Web usage patterns, qualitative studies involving interviews or observations related to a specific work context are hard to find. (See, however, Järvelä & Häkkinen, chap. 4, this volume.) In fact, there are many challenges in studying the use of Internet technology in this way. The Web is growing rapidly and new technical solutions are developing continuously, as well as new usage forms. This makes qualitative, longitudinal studies necessary for an understanding of the research issues in which we are interested.

SHARING KNOWLEDGE ON THE GLOBAL NETWORK

In many ways, the Web is unlike any other previously existing medium, and it is natural that research about the use of the Web has touched on many different areas. In fact, the view of the Web itself is subject to constant change, as both the contexts of its uses and the technology itself develop further. We review some implications of these perspectives for Web use among knowledge professionals.

The Web as a New, Interactive Reading Medium

The dominating view of the Web has been as a medium for presenting and retrieving information. As such, it differs from traditional screen-based media in many ways. In addition to just locating and reading particular documents, users can navigate in a world of interlinked information. In fact, the vision of the global hypertext formulated by Bush (1945) is quite close to the Web as it works today.

Computer screens are well known for providing a less optimal reading environment. In this respect, Web use cannot be expected to bring new research findings, at least from an ergonomic perspective. In fact, it is unclear to what extent people actually read lengthy Web pages on screen, compared to just browsing through relevant parts, printing out the document and reading it offline.

The Web can be seen as a more social, interactive reading environment than traditional, paper-based media. Because both authors and readers are online, they can potentially communicate in a fast and interactive manner. Also, other users are visible through their personal home pages, where their interests and activities are often described explicitly. One may ask: Can the social nature of the Web outweigh the negative aspects of reading information on screens? Is the interactive nature of the Web as a reading medium sometimes felt as a burden, so that people need to protect themselves against unwanted communication?

Carleson, Lundberg, and Nässla (1997) presented a study of the introduction of a Web-based information channel to a local intranet for a telecommunications company. A survey and interviews were made to assess the
acceptance of the channel and to compare it with an existing, paper-based,
workplace magazine. With respect to design and readability of the material,
the paper-based magazine was found to be superior. It was also seen as
more flexible by encouraging reading at home, which was not possible for
the Web channel. However, the authors argued that a Web channel could
be more attractive in other aspects, especially by offering a more interactive
relationship between writer and reader.

A similar result was found in a study by Balsvik (1999), who interviewed a
group of journalists about their experience of Web publishing. E-mail was
the communication tool used most frequently by these journalists, and was
used for interviews, information exchange, and making a first contact. The
results indicated that Web-published papers could foster a closer relationship between the journalist and the reader. The journalists reported a feeling of having gotten a more extended, well-rounded education through the
use of the Internet, although it seems that they had to develop their ability
to sift information due to the use of the Internet.

However, the advantages of paper as a reading medium prevail, even in
contexts where both original text input and final reading are online. Bellotti
and Rogers (1997) found in a study of Web-publishing journals that the paper medium had an important role as a form of intermediate representation
during the production process, for example, for overview of the current state
of a page, coordination of activities, and passing information in a newsroom.
Similar results have been obtained in other studies focused on management
of documents in organizations (see, e.g., Sellen & Harper, 1997).

**Searching for Information on the Web: From Individual
to Social Navigation**

Among the main problems in the use of the Web are orientation and overview of the information available on the net (see, e.g., Instone, 1996). This
applies both to searching and navigation through hypermedia links.

In the background is the threat of information overflow by the multitude
of hits that are often rendered by ordinary search engines. A related aspect
is "lost in hyperspace," pertaining to the lack of orientation and overview of
users navigating via hypermedia links on the Web. These problems have led
researchers and developers to investigate alternative metaphors for describing parts of the Web, and to design various techniques of visualization to facilitate navigation and overview (cf. *The Web Book and Web Forager*; Card,
Robertson, & York, 1996). However, these alternative models for navigation
do not seem to have reached widespread use.

A more recent development in Web navigation emphasizes the social nature of people's information-seeking activities (Dourish, 1999; Munro, Höök, & Benyon, 1999a). The general idea is to provide possibilities for users to keep track of the activities of other users with whom they may have common interests in order to find their way through the immense space of hypermedia information. The term *social navigation* was originally introduced by Dourish and Chalmers (1994), to describe how users'navigation through an information space is guided and structured by the activities of others within that space. According to Erickson (1996), using other people's home pages as sources of information is a kind of social navigation. There have also been efforts to provide special navigation possibilities on the Web, based on the visibility of other users' presence in real time, or "footprints" showing how they have navigated (Munro et al., 1999b). In many cases, there is a possibility to open a direct communication channel among users who are "co-located" in this way.

So-called recommendation systems may be seen as building on social navigation principles. For example, a Website may be constructed by automatically collecting the addresses recommended by other users in online discussions, and providing links to these sites (a system with this capability is described by Hill & Terveen, 1997). Other readers may subsequently contribute by suggesting changes to the structure already built.

Dourish (1999) took the concept of social navigation further, to stand for a general paradigm of collaboration through technology. His discussion emphasizes two aspects of collaborative activity as distinctive for social navigation: awareness of the activitities of others to provide a means for interaction, and the conceptual distinction between "places" and "spaces," where a place-centric view implies that there are other people inhabiting the information space, providing opportunities for mutual interaction and information sharing.

Visions of the Web as a Universal Medium for Knowledge Work

The unique possibilities of exchanging knowledge and drawing on others' work have been the source of many visions about the WWW for knowledge workers, following in the trace of Bush's (1945) "memex." In fact, the original idea of the Web was to support distributed collaboration and exchange of ideas between researchers (Berners-Lee, Cailliau, Luotonen, Nielsen, & Secret, 1994). One vision could be the Web as a "platform" for constructing places of information resources but also of knowledge where experts in a topic can be contacted. Shneiderman (1998) used the term *genex* for describing a development of the concept *memex* applied on the potential of the Web. He proposed: "Appropriate genex design would enable problem solvers to locate and build on previous work easily, explore numerous alternatives rapidly, consult conveniently, and propagate solutions widely" (p. 99).

A similar vision, presented by Holtzblatt (1999), is the "knowledge crystal." By describing skills, knowledge, and procedures within the field of customer centered design, researchers are invited to jointly represent knowledge using the new medium, the Internet.

These examples should be seen as ideal models of shared knowledge among researchers on a global network. There are already numerous examples of knowledge communities on the Web, where researchers voluntarily share information about their field. Web-based environments are also being designed for educational purposes, supporting both document repositories and synchronous text communication within distributed groups of professionals.[2]

Buckingham Shum (1998) discussed methods of enhancing the Web with special mechanisms aiming to support the collective development and use of scientific knowledge. According to Buckingham Shum, "the Net, particularly the Web, provides an unprecedented opportunity in scientific history to locate, interconnect and analyse ideas and documents" (p. 16). But also, "The Web is becoming a more chaotic place every day. As the signal to noise ratio gets worse, research communities need better support for tracking developments and finding relevant documents" (p. 16). The solution proposed by Buckingham Shum is to supply metadata schemes that describe semantic relationships between scientific documents and that enable a researcher to search for general patterns of ideas and arguments within a large space of related contributions.

Dilemmas of Sharing Knowledge

It is clear that the Internet and the Web are potential tools for knowledge sharing and competence development among knowledge workers. Our point of departure in the KnowHow project is a democratic model where all participants can use the medium on the same terms. Communication, and maybe even more, competence development on the Web, build on an implicit assumption that everyone wants to cooperate, contribute, and give and take. However, it can be expected that some users will only take without

---

[2]One example is Tapped In™, a shared teacher professional development workplace, patterned after a real-world conference center. It began developing its community in the summer of 1997 and grew to over 8,500 members and over 15 partner organizations by May, 2000. Studies about the use of Tapped In™ show that teachers benefit from using this workplace as a place for informal discussions and collaboration, to exchange tips and advice, and to share educational resources rather than as a space for importing "traditional classrooms" online (see Cerratto, 2001; Cerratto & Waern, 2000).

giving, because it in many situations is very hard to make people contribute (Kollock & Smith, 1996). This does not always have to be a problem, at least not as long as this group does not grow too large.[3] To contribute with information implies taking responsibility with respect to its quality, so as to avoid misleading or false information. These different aspects of cooperation are relevant for individuals, groups, and organizations.

A particular tension on an individual basis exists in the desire for obtaining Web information in relation to one's own willingness to be visible on the net. If you are visible, people will notice you and perhaps offer information. However, there is a cost in being visible; for example, people will expect you to continue providing information and to keep existing information updated.

A PRESTUDY OF INTERNET COMMUNICATION

In a prestudy to the KnowHow project in 1997 (reported in Lantz & Severinson Eklundh, 1999), we performed in-depth interviews with a group of 10 individuals from research, development, and information areas about their use of electronic networks for communication and knowledge exchange. The study was explorative, and aimed to identify relevant research questions for the project. The following issues were addressed:

- How do the users conceptualize the Internet? How do they distinguish between the Internet and an intranet?
- To what extent are the users willing to fetch and collect material on the global net? How do they manage to find the information for which they look?
- What is their attitude about being visible on the net?
- Do users give hints to each other about relevant information and contacts? To what extent are new contacts established on the network?
- How is the Internet used for communication and for supporting the individual's development of competence?

The participants (4 women and 6 men) were well educated and were researchers, teachers, technical developers, and information professionals. All of them had occupations that involved large amounts of information acquisition for themselves and for others. Typical work tasks were writing doc-

---

[3]The problem of unequal participation is well known and has frequently been discussed with respect to other electronic media. For example in Usenet newsgroups, discussions tend to be dominated by a few active individuals (see Whittaker, Terveen, Hill, & Cherny, 1998), and many others participate only as passive "lurkers."

uments, communicating with other people, searching for information, distributing information, and attending related meetings. Most of the participants had a role that allowed them to organize their own work and plan for future activities.

The respondents had reached such a level of expertise that they had to take responsibility for their own competence development. They visited conferences, read literature, participated in relevant courses and seminar series; they regarded the Internet as a competence supporting tool.

The View of the Internet.   The Internet was described by the respondents as a protocol or a language that is necessary for enabling communication among the connected computers. When asked to use a metaphor for describing the Web, the telephone or a net was used. When asked to compare the Internet with intranets and explain the differences, the respondents first laughed. Then they explained, "Well, one is world-wide and one is local."

Security was felt to be higher on an intranet because it is closed. An intranet can be specifically designed for a group, so cooperation can also be facilitated in a different way than it can be on the Internet. It is only a support to people who have access; everybody else is excluded. Some participants felt isolated behind the "fire-walls," not being able to communicate freely with others outside their own organization. One respondent gave the example: "When I visit a conference, others sometimes give me their home page URL (Uniform Resource Locator) but I can never do the same since I am on an intranet."

Search and Navigation.   When navigating on the Web, users collect bookmarks of sites to which they want to return. After a period of Web use with a growing collection of bookmarks, the bookmarks must be structured in some way, and organizational problems may sometimes emerge. These may be similar to those appearing in E-mail communication (Bälter, 1998; Lantz, 1998; Whittaker & Sidner, 1996) and lead to a need for cleaning and filing of bookmarks, an activity that is not well supported, according to Nielsen (1997).

Bookmarks are used when the user knows where to go; otherwise search engines are used. Some of the respondents reported that they had noticed that search tools have specialized in different topics. When the respondents learned which search tools are reliable and if they also have other sources of information on a certain topic, the result can be more complete. One example given was a librarian who asked to search for information about a very uncommon disease. The results were to be delivered to a doctor who had just received a case. In addition to literature on the subject found at the library, the librarian could also add information found on the Web. This information consisted of an information sheet about the disease, names of contact-persons, and a homepage for children with the disease. The doctor and the sick child's family could then use all of this information.

Home Pages. Most of the respondents had a personal home page, on which they were careful to include only professional information. For certain respondents, there were difficulties in constructing a home page and they needed technical help. Some organizations had home pages with links to all employees, and standards were emerging for the build-up of these.

Visibility on the net was experienced in different ways. Some respondents reported that they were afraid of receiving too much information or too many contacts if appearing on the Internet. Others preferred to use traditional publishing media for increasing their professional visibility in an effective way.

Communication and Cooperation. For the participants in the study, E-mail was the primary communication tool in their daily work. This meant that E-mail was used irrespective of whether the receiver was in the next room or across the world. However, if a response was needed quickly, the telephone was used. Also, home pages can be used for communication, and E-mail can sometimes be sent directly from the home page. Contrary to our expectations, it was not felt to be necessary to meet first face-to-face. In fact, we have seen several examples of contacts started via Internet where the involved subjects first met after several years.

For the users in the study the Internet was not seen primarily as a tool for cooperation. However, an example was given by a respondent about a project group spread over Sweden and working in libraries. They had a coordinator that administrated the home page and a number of persons responsible for different areas. The home page was the uniting node, and communication was managed via E-mail and distribution lists. For such cooperation to work, everyone is responsible and one person acts as coordinator.

Cooperation on the Internet would normally be more indirect, such as users giving each other hints about relevant information. However, some users never did this and did not receive hints from others; giving hints can sometimes be excluded because of the climate at work, or that the fear of overloading information to colleagues is greater than the wish to offer information. Often, a work group knows about the other group members' interests and forwards them relevant addresses and information.

The experiences from the prestudy confirmed that the Web has a potential as a platform for sharing knowledge across geographical boundaries. The study opened the way for more specific studies within the KnowHow theme, investigating how people use Internet and the Web for professional collaboration, and how the technology supports these activities.

KNOWLEDGE COMMUNITIES ON THE WEB:
A STUDY OF THE OESTER '96 PROJECT

People working in knowledge professions often have interests in several projects. This leads to working with different colleagues in different settings, regarding type of group and context. Often, the colleagues are at other work sites and the interaction between these experts are mostly formal meetings. Hence, it is easy to see that an expert's work situation is often very isolated; there is no one to ask for advice or initiate discussion.

The most obvious need is to communicate with other experts in the same area and to develop one's competence, not only by reading a book, giving a course, or attending conferences. Face-to-face meetings (formal or informal) are very important, but there are cases when a mediated way to communicate is a good substitute or even a better solution.

One example of this is the Oester '96[4] project, the subject of a case study in KnowHow. The project started in 1997, involving 11 countries and working with different political aspects of the Baltic region. Here experts working within knowledge professions were offered use of the Web as a place to collect or present information, chat, or use mailing lists. Part of the site is open to the general public; other parts are closed and only available for the members of the project group. These experts work in several projects, sometimes distributed via the Website because the cooperating persons are located in different countries.

Results from the questionnaire sent to the project leaders showed that the site mostly was used as an open library, both internal and external. The respondents of the questionnaire knew that all reports were available at the site. The purpose of this Website is not to develop the participants' competence—in fact, this was never an issue. The overall aim of the Website is to signal democracy, that is, to work very openly, presenting all final reports and plans for the future of the different parts of the project.

In interviews with some of the questionnaire respondents, it turned out that the need of performing work with a democratic model in mind is helpful to aid cooperation among delegates in different countries. The idea of using the Website as a place for competence development within a group can be viewed in terms of common ground (cf. Clark, 1996). As a new delegate enters the project, it is easy to read all previous documents on the Website, to look at the lists of participants, the time schedules and organization, which leads to understanding the overall common ground (i.e., what everybody else in the project learned by participating).

In the questionnaire, there were also questions about an internal part of the Website (i.e., the intranet, including facilities for communicating via

---

[4]The name of the project has been changed for reasons of the integrity of participants.

chat and distribution lists). Only a few of the respondents reported that they had used the internal part, and it turned out that 2 years later, it was closed, probably due to the low interest on the part of the project's participants. One interviewee said that taking advantage of the information at the Website contributes to the development of competence because it enables an attendant to follow the ongoing work and also use part of the reports from different parts of the project. It is one way to take advantage of others' knowledge and put this to good use.

Another subject saw it as direct and indirect competence development, where *direct* is related to the specific work task performed within the project and *indirect* is information about which others can pose questions. The Website can be used for one's own reasons but also as a reference library for others who want to know more about the project.

SHARING KNOWLEDGE IN AN ORGANIZATION

The Web has great potential for sharing knowledge and fostering collaboration within organizations. So-called intranets are established in many organizations as a channel for intraorganizational communication and information. Using the same protocol as the Internet, but with restricted access, the intranets may provide both information archives and platforms for direct communication among the organization's members; the intranets can function as an "organizational memory."

Organizational Memory. To support sharing of knowledge within an organization, a collaborative system can be designed to store the knowledge in a large repository of information. Such systems are often referred to as *organizational memory systems*, or lately also *knowledge management systems*; the information can be retrieved and used in the future.

Examples of organizational memory systems are gIBIS (Conklin & Begeman, 1988), and Answer Garden (Ackerman, 1994; Ackerman & Malone, 1990; Ackerman & McDonald, 1996). The purpose of the gIBIS system was to explore the capture of design history, to support computer mediated teamwork, and to investigate hypertext navigation of very large information spaces. In Answer Garden, commonly asked questions about an application domain were stored, together with the answer, in a common repository. In a newer version of Answer Garden, there is also the possibility of finding and interacting directly with an expert.

The concept organizational memory has been criticized for not accounting for how remembering actually takes place in organizations (Bannon & Kuutti, 1996). Bannon and Kuutti (1996) also pointed out that it is difficult to predict what knowledge or information within an organization, will be of interest in the future and thereby is worth storing. This involves a trade-off between cost of storing and the cost of reinventing, but how is this trade-off decided? Bannon and Kuutti (1996) also argued that if the "activity" during which the "storing" takes place differs from the one in which the "remembering" takes place, the information may be reinterpreted or even misinterpreted. It is a question of what needs to be stored and what can be left as assumed knowledge.

Asking for Information.   Bannon (1986) argued that people would rather ask other persons for advice than search through a manual for information. He found, when interviewing administrative and clerical personnel, that the major source of information about the computer systems used were other users (see also Kraut & Streeter, 1995). One person in his study expressed that sharing an office with a person more experienced within a certain area provides an ideal environment for solving problems related to the area. Bannon (1986) pointed out the importance of a common view of the problem, expecially in the case of a novice–expert conversation (see also Clark, 1996). In face-to-face conversation, interruptions and follow-up questions can provide feedback about the participants' understanding of the current dialogue, and the conversation can gravitate to an appropriate level of understanding.

There is also a difference between formal and informal sources of information. A formal source can be a computer system help desk, whereas an informal source can be a person who does not officially have the task of helping other persons. The reason that formal sources often fail in their mission is because the persons working the source do not know enough about the particular topic and because the persons are often remotely located (Bannon, 1986). Instead, informal sources such as colleagues are chosen because they are physically available, they are personal friends, or they are known to be experts on the topic. Investigations show that people working in software design projects prefer to ask nearby colleagues rather than use formal information sources (Eveland, Blanchard, Brown, & Mattocks, 1994; Waterson, Clegg, & Axtell, 1997). The reason is that the colleagues better relate the question to the problem. Also, people outside the group of local colleagues can be important when searching for information (Kraut & Streeter, 1995).

Knowledge Nets: An Alternative Approach for Intraorganizational Communication.   One way to support the sharing of knowledge within an organization is to give references to persons with the requested knowledge, as opposed to presenting the knowledge itself represented in some computer application. The knowledge net approach (Groth, 1999) is based on this principle.

The idea has similarities to social navigation, in that it builds on the importance of using other people as resources. However, a knowledge net builds on using the computer to store references to other persons who are then contacted directly. A knowledge net can be viewed as a "time-window," that is, the knowledge referred to is what is relevant today—the knowledge people have at the moment.

One characteristic of the knowledge net approach is that the given references should encourage and support ongoing communication between individuals. This means that just providing a list or database of references is not sufficient. Another main characteristic is that the knowledge providers are also those who should benefit from the system. In other words, there should be a focus, not on what management is asking for, but on what the individual is interested in sharing with others. A crucial issue in the knowledge net approach is that the individuals' knowledge is described in an open-ended way; this makes it possible for the knowledge providers to decide how to describe their knowledge and how much of it they want to share with others. Still, technical support for the process of entering information should be available, for example, using templates and forms.

However, the use of a specific system supporting people in finding "who-knows what" might not be the ideal solution. Rather, simple means for showing people's present activities and availability in combination with structured information about projects and other activities within the organization might be even better.

The Web as a Basis for a Knowledge Net. Some knowledge net like applications already exist and can be found on the Web. One such application is the Referral Web (Kautz, Selman, & Shah, 1997), which is an interactive tool that helps people find short referral chains between themselves and experts within a certain area. The Referral Web uses publicly available Web pages to create *a referral chain.* A referral chain is created by searching for names and following links on Web pages. If two or more names occur in close proximity on a Web page, then this is seen as evidence of a direct relationship between these persons. Hence, no information needs to be explicitly entered by the users. Unfortunately, the Referral Web was never used within the organization it was created for, a domain of artificial intelligence (AI) researchers.

The Referral Web was thus intended to be used within a specific domain of users. However, there also exists Web-based tools for knowledge exchange between individuals that are globally available on the Internet. One is Abuzz,[5] which provides online communities with tools to share knowledge through people-to-people interactions. Another is Experts Ex-

---

[5]http://www.abuzz.com/

change,[6] a knowledge sharing community on the Web where different topics are available for discussion. A third example is Six Degrees,[7] which is an online community with the possibility to interact, communicate, and share information and experience with others.

In addition to these specific systems supporting contacts between people, well-structured personal home pages on the Web in combination with search facilities may also serve as a simple knowledge net. This issue was addressed in a longitudinal study in the KnowHow project.

A Study of the Use of Home Pages on the Web. Personal home pages[8] give an individual user of the Internet, or of an intranet, an opportunity to present personal information to other users. These pages on the Web can, therefore, be seen as a source of knowledge about individuals within a network, The network is either global, that is, available to everyone on the Internet, or local, that is, available only to the specific users of a certain intranet.

According to Instone (1996), home pages constitute the most visible Web genre. People visit the "home sites" of other persons with interests that are close to their own topic of interest where they expect to find new information about the topic (either directly or via links).

Erickson (1996) claimed that home pages are the very cornerstone of the social character of the Web; navigating via home pages is like asking someone else who is likely to know the answer to a question. Also, home pages provide a possibility to create an identity on the net by a portrayal of oneself in terms of interests, activities, and so on.

Given that personal home pages already contain information about individuals' knowledge and competence, it is of interest to explore the extent to which they can function as a knowledge net. With this question in mind, we performed a longitudinal interview study about the use of personal home pages among people from knowledge-oriented professions (Groth, 1999, Groth & Lantz, 1997). Although home pages are often available on a global basis, we were especially interested in their use for sharing knowledge within an organization.

In 1996, a group of 22 persons from three different organizations were interviewed about their personal home page. In combination with the interview, the personal home page was demonstrated. Two of the organiza-

---

[6]http://www.experts-exchange.com/

[7]http://www.sixdegrees.com/

[8]A home page on the Web is the intended entry point of a logical information structure (usually called a Website) from which all other pages on the site may be reached, directly or via other pages, by hypertext links. A *home page* can refer to an individual, a group or an organization. If a home page is written (partly or wholly) by and about an individual, it is called a *personal home page*.

tions were research facilities with personal home pages accessible from the Internet. The subjects from the research organizations had been advised by their managers to have a personal home page. The third place was a software development company using an intranet where people could voluntarily present personal home pages. All subjects in each organization belonged to the same department and they were chosen because they had a personal home page. After 1 year, 7 researchers, and 3 software developers were interviewed once again about the changes made to their home page. The home pages of all 14 researchers and of the 3 software developers were also examined. After yet another year, the home pages of the 14 researchers and one of the software developers were once again examined.

At the beginning of the study, most persons interviewed had used the Web for more than a year. As many as 13 subjects had used it from the beginning of the Web, in 1993/1994. Also, most subjects used the Web every day, and the most common activity was to search for specific information, often related to the subject's work tasks. Eleven of the subjects, all from the research groups, searched for articles or research reports. The subjects also reported that they searched for other persons' home pages because they wanted to find, for example, links to other sites about subjects that they knew the author was interested in, or information about the author such as a picture, contact information, or written reports.

The Web was also used to find solutions to specific problems, and to look for conferences, courses, or organizations of interest. Finally, it was used for looking up nonprofessional information such as weather reports, apartments, friends, movies, and so on.

About half of the subjects had had a home page for more than a year. The reasons reported by the subjects for having made a personal home page were because they found other persons' home pages useful, they wanted to distribute their publications, they wanted to try out the new medium, and because they considered it a good way to find information about other persons.

The results of the study showed that contact information and information about projects or work that the author was involved in were information items that the subjects both found interesting on other persons' home pages and had included on their own home page. The reasons given for including project information were because they wanted other persons to know what they do, and to distribute information about projects. Contact information was included to give other persons the possibility to make contact.

In a similar study of personal home pages, Bly, Cook, Bickmore, Churchill, and Sullivan (1998) found that 75% of the examined personal home pages contained project-related information. Bly et al. (1998) mentioned that the authors of the home pages wanted to facilitate the access to project information and thereby provide pointers to their work. For a knowledge net, project-related information may be crucial. However, in order to get an understanding of the author's skills, the work/project related information needs to be more detailed. Contact information is important in a knowledge netlike application because the "expert" needs to be contacted by, for example, E-mail, phone, or in person.

In our study, only a minority of the subjects had not made any changes to their home page in 1996, and when comparing the home pages from 1996, 1997, and 1998 it was found that most people had made some changes to their home page. Reasons given for updating the information were that the information on the page was outdated, new, interesting links had been found, new projects had been started, more information had been added that made a new layout of the page necessary, and so on. The fact that the subjects tend to update the information on their personal home page is of interest for a knowledge netlike application, where the validity of the information is important. Bly et al. (1998) reported that one of the authors in their study thought the work of having a personal home page was worthwhile because it was important that other persons had the possibility to find out about this person and his or her work. This is interesting from a general perspective of the Web as a medium for sharing knowledge, and the dilemmas of equal participation discussed in the beginning of this chapter. It shows a willingness to provide personal information for others, although the author's own benefit from the work of supporting the home pages may be marginal.

Another finding was that some of the subjects said that looking at an unknown person's home page made them feel more familiar with that person. Bly et al. (1998) mentioned that some of their subjects reported using personal home pages as an introduction to someone they were going to meet. They also found that the personalization of a home page was important.

It seems that a main group of readers of people's home pages are colleagues. The respondents in our study thought that information about research projects, publications, and contact information would interest these colleagues. Also, students were mentioned as a possible group that could be interested in a home page. The information on the home pages described, in most cases, what "project" the owner of the page is involved in and what areas she or he was interested in. The subjects presented their knowledge rather than their opinions (although this may also be found on some home pages). They did not seem to be afraid of presenting what they knew, wanted to do, and had been doing in the past.

Also, the subjects found the information included on other persons' home pages of interest, which suggests that what is presented on personal home pages is of relevance for a knowledge netlike application. It was mainly contact information, publications, and project or research information that was found interesting. Bly et al. (1998) found that personal home pages are often used by the author's colleagues to get access to other material. This, together with the findings that some of the subjects had been contacted about their information on their home page, shows the interest for personal information. In this regard, many people may have, consciously or unconsciously, used personal home pages as a knowledge net.

GROUP COLLABORATION THROUGH THE WEB

In addition to its role as a medium for sharing knowledge in global and local networks, the Web is also increasingly used to support actual collaboration in small or moderate-sized groups. This is not a feature that is inherent in standard Web protocol; instead, the demands of collaboration support usually require extensions in terms of either server or client software, or both (Dix, 1997).

The research on computer-supported cooperative work in the last 10 years has so far yielded few widely used collaborative systems. However, there have been a number of important insights through the empirical studies of existing systems. Grudin (1988) showed that it is important that users who have to change their work due to a new system are also the ones that will benefit from changing. Further, there must be a working infrastructure for collaboration, and it should be easy to switch from individual to group collaboration. The last two requirements suggest that the Web is a suitable basis for building cooperative systems.

Collaboration can be defined in different ways, which has consequences for what is included here. A weak definition of collaboration is assumed, for example, in Terveen and Hill (1998): "Links between web sites can be seen as evidence of a type of emergent collaboration among Web site authors" (p. 35). They conducted a quantitative study of such linking behavior by using a special algorithm to detect the connectivity among Websites in various domains.

A definition of collaboration in such terms would imply that almost all use of the Web is a kind of collaboration. Here, we restrict the word *collaboration* in the way suggested by Dix (1997), that it requires a common task and a channel for direct communication between participants of a group. Thus, for a Web-based application to support collaboration, it should (a) provide some representation of the collaborative task and its artifacts, (b) make it possible for users to interact with and manipulate these artifacts, and (c) facilitate users' communication with each other about the task.

A central concept in computer-supported cooperative work is *awareness*. In its original form, it stands for the co-workers' ability to perceive and understand the activities of others as a context for their own work (Dourish, 1999; Dourish & Bellotti, 1992). When people are working in the same building, they normally observe others' activities in subtle and straightforward ways. For example, when leaving one's own office, one may hear voices, or see someone passing at the end of the corridor, which makes it possible to infer the state of others' activities. In contrast, in mediated collaboration, awareness of others' activities must be deliberately designed in a way that is adapted to the users and the tasks at hand.

The Web does not in itself support users' awareness of each other. In the context of searching for information, this has recently been argued as a weakness by proponents of the *social navigation* paradigm, who have attempted to make traces of users' activities more explicit. Certain efforts have also been made to construct Web-based support for local work group awareness; for example, @ Work (Sandor & Tollmar, 1996), which allows a group of users to extend their home pages with information about their current whereabouts on a day-to-day basis.[9] Furthermore, Web-based virtual environments have been developed in which users have an explicit representation as an avatar, and that are thought to encourage synchronous group interaction and support peripheral awareness.

Sharing and Reviewing Documents in Working Groups

A form of collaboration of particular interest for knowledge professionals is the use of the Web for coauthoring documents within working groups. Certain efforts to support collaborative management of documents on the Web have focused on creating a shared repository, including password protection and easy uploading and downloading. A well-known example is the BSCW (Basic support for collaborative work) system (Bentley et al., 1997), which also supports communication between coauthors. However, it is less common that Web-based solutions explicitly support collaborative writing, in the sense of interactive user-document manipulation, support for awareness, and a user–user communication link.

There have been certain efforts in this direction. One example is the Alliance system, which is a structured cooperative authoring application for distributed collaboration (Romero Salcedo & Decouchant, 1997). The system has many interesting properties, but empirical evaluations seem to be missing so far. Sumner and Buckingham Shum (1998) presented a system for sharing and reviewing documents on the Web, as a part of a redesigned

---

[9]@ Work was developed within our own research environment by Sandor and Tollmar (1996). The design was ambitious, for example, including links from people's personal information to the telephone switchboard, in order to be able to update information about work hours and activities. However, the tool never reached a critical threshold of use. A possible explanation is that there were problems of usability in the Web presentation, such as long response times and lack of overview. Also, it is conceivable that people felt it was too much work to update the information, when looking at the benefit they gained from it (cf. Grudin, 1988).

publishing process for scholarly work. In this system, the Digital Document Discourse Environment (D3E), the emphasis is on the encouragement of an ongoing discourse about the documents submitted. Easy-to-use facilities are offered for uploading a document and incorporating it into a reading environment enhanced with communication facilities. The design thus supports an interactive discussion between authors, reviewers, and readers. The system has been evaluated in several case studies, including an online multimedia journal and a mixed-modality conference with a concluding face-to-face discussion.

In the KnowHow project, we developed a series of prototypes for Web-based authoring and communication based on a concept of *four frames*. The idea, first materialized in the Domain Help System (DHS),[10] is that members of a group share and comment on a collection of HTML documents (or document parts), available through selection in a list of hyperlinks. When a comment has been made, it is available immediately together with the previous comments in a special window. The set of comments thus evolve into a dialogue between participants aligned with the document, which serves as communication channel throughout the reviewing process (see Rodriguez, 1999).

There are many obvious advantages of having a collaborative environment fully integrated with the Web, as in this case. The users have direct access to the whole Web and all of its uses—in other words, an existing infrastructure is built upon. Links can be placed within the document and the comments, establishing references to locally or globally available knowledge sources; and the basis for the application is an ordinary Web browser, accessible everywhere.

There are also some disadvantages associated with this solution. For example, it is impossible to control in all aspects how information presented in the system will look to a user, as the users can normally change the appearance of a document through preferences made in their Web browser.

The DHS system has been evaluated in several case studies. At first, it was used in our own laboratory as a tool for updating our Website. The lab members could read others' draft project descriptions and make comments on them. It turned out that comments often referred to the design of the system (described in one of the document sections) instead of the others' documents. Apparently, people with a computer or HCI interest were mostly interested in the novel aspects of the system and less motivated to comment on each others' texts. In fact, some members stated in interviews that they did not favor "public" criticism of draft project descriptions.

---

[10]The Domain Help System (DHS) was developed in a collaboration project between the Interaction and Presentation Laboratory (IPLab) and the Center for User-Oriented IT Design (CID) at KTH.

The DHS system has more recently been used in an educational context for students to give feedback on each other's texts within a course. Through these trials, the system has been gradually improved with respect to usability. In one course, which had an HCI orientation, the same pattern of commenting on the system emerged, whereas this pattern was absent in another course dealing with writing scientific papers. Here, students made many comments on each others' papers, although the focus of their comments was often details of spelling and style rather than the content of the papers.

The problem of awareness was reflected through these studies in the time it took the author of a document to react to a comment. The only way that the system supported awareness was by showing the last comment made in the window (all other comments were available through scrolling). In this way, users could just check if they had read the comment before. In general it took 2 to 3 days on average, occasionally up to as many as 10 days, for the author to reply to a direct question posed to him or her, and in some cases, the author never replied.

Recently, the DHS system has been developed further into a coauthoring system, called *Col•laboració* (Rodriguez, Kim, & Severinson Eklundh, 1999). The system supports not only shared access to HTML documents and comments, but also facilities for awareness, joint editing, and versioning. The focus is on communication among distributed coauthors during the reviewing phase of a shared document.

The work on this project was preceded by a series of interviews with academics about their cowriting practices (Kim & Severinson Eklundh, 2001). The people taking part in this study did not use any specific collaboration software. Instead, they cooperated by exchanging E-mails and commenting on paper versions of their articles. It was clear from this study that users lacked a common infrastructure for collaboration.

Figure 5.1 shows the interface layout of the *Col•laboració* system. The links to the left correspond to sections in the document being written. When a section is selected, its content appears in the upper right frame. The middle right frame is where the comments are displayed, and the bottom right frame contains buttons for available commands. Each section can be edited by the participants who have access to that section, by pressing "Edit Section" and changing the HTML code in a separate window. This function does not allow for flexible authoring, but is aimed at supporting small changes rather than original composition of the document.

The awareness of changes to the document is supported in the following way. As soon as a new comment has been made by one participant, the other participants receive an E-mail message containing the comment. The same thing happens when a new section has been added or deleted. In this way, the user does not have to enter the system to check if something important has happened in the collaborative task.

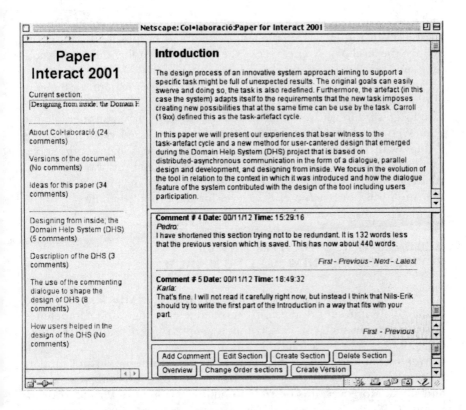

FIG. 5.1. Screen layout of the Col•laboració system.

We evaluated the system in six different writing tasks in which groups of 2 to 9 people participated from an academic background. These case studies showed that coauthors used the system for an ongoing, asynchronous dialogue about the writing task, which served to coordinate their actions and negotiate about changes. In their communication, users often took account of the whole history of comments (including how people had reacted to each other's comments) made between members of the group. Although other writing tools often lack this feature, we found that having access to the comment history is important to promote communication and awareness among coauthors. Also, the notification about new comments via E-mail played an important role to create a sense of other members' current activities and the overall state of the task. Because most users read E-mail on a daily basis, E-mail notification appears to be a good way of supporting awareness with minimal effort and delay.

However, E-mail notifications can easily get overwhelming in periods of intense activity. It emerged early in the case studies that it is not suitable to make every new change in a document section cause a new email message. In fact, even with the present design, it should be possible for users to change the level of awareness set by the system, depending on the task context and their own preferences.

Altogether, the experiences of DHS and *Col•laboració* point to the conclusion that groups with an existing common ground (Clark, 1996), in relation to a task, and who are motivated to collaborate, have considerable use of a Web-based tool for communication about shared documents. For groups with less incentive to collaborate or whose collaboration serves merely to acquire course credits, sharing knowledge in this way may sometimes be perceived as an extra burden or task, which means that their participation will not reach a critical level for the group's benefit.

WEB-BASED COLLABORATIVE VIRTUAL ENVIRONMENTS: A NEW MEETING MEDIUM

In many organizations, experts work mostly alone. Nevertheless, they need to meet colleagues for discussions, knowledge exchange, and competence development. In such contexts, computer support for distributed real-time collaboration may be a relevant work tool.

Web technology enables distributed storing of information and support for synchronous as well as asynchronous communication using text, audio, and video. Moreover, it is possible to build Collaborative Virtual Environments (CVEs) with relevant information for a specific group, for example, experts in a domain (cf. Lea, Honda, & Matsuda, 1997). Apart from synchronous communication—usually by text-based chat—the system offers a graphical representation of a shared environment and participating users. The graphical representation of a user is referred to as his or her *avatar*.[11] Users of CVEs can be seen as "visitors" who need visual embodiments to provide mutual awareness and orientation in the virtual environment (Hedman, 2001).

Not many groups of experts use CVE technology, although it is available relatively easily, and studies in natural settings are rare. Research on CVEs has mainly been performed in experimental settings, focusing on presence, enjoyment and feelings of group accord, and subjective reactions such as shyness and conflict (Slater, Sadagic, Usoh, & Schroder, 1998) and leadership (Tromp et al., 1998).

In a recent case study by Lantz (2001), a work group consisting of four researchers were observed under three conditions: face-to-face, chat, and

---

[11]The term *avatar* originates from Hindu mythology, where it indicated the temporary body that a god inhabits while visiting earth.

CVE, in regular meetings. The CVE was an open world in Active Worlds™ consisting of a building with an exhibition area, surrounded by trees on a lawn, and a blue sky.

Results from the analysis of the data, collected via observations and questionnaires distributed after each meeting, showed that both chat and the CVE were experienced as very slow. This could be explained both by limitations in the technology itself, and by the fact that the participants were not skilled "chatters," that is, they had not developed a language of "shorthand" efficient in a chat environment. Another reason for delays could be that participants were performing other parallel activities during the meeting, such as talking on the phone, seeing a visitor, or reading E-mail. This has also been discussed by Bowers, Pycock, and O'Brien (1996b).

Ratings of efficiency were obtained by asking questions about overall efficiency, task oriented work, and the number of items handled on the agenda. It turned out that the CVE was rated as more efficient and task oriented than face-to-face meetings. This can be explained by the fact that social talk was a substantial part of the face-to-face meetings, whereas meetings in the chat and CVE focused on the tasks to be performed. Regarding communication and the representation of each participant by name, the chat environment was very difficult to use. Extreme discipline was necessary, and a set of rules for communication was developed. It was necessary to follow only one thread of discussion, and rules were needed for organizing the turn-taking among participants. In the CVE, the discipline and rules were not as important. Because participants were represented by avatars, their position in the CVE and their spatial relations in the group made turn-taking more or less transparent. People would usually talk in the order of their spatial positions in the environment, and discussing one topic at a time was facilitated.

Overall, the participants were able to enter, navigate, and communicate in the CVE although they did not have any previous experience of using this particular technology. Using a common meeting spot in the CVE seemed to be preferred compared to just using the built-in chat function. All three ways to perform meetings were rated as being enjoyable, although the level of enjoyment decreased for the chat and CVE after the first meeting.

The results indicate that face-to-face meetings are needed in order to facilitate learning and competence development, for example, for brainstorming. Also, participants are in favor of knowing each other before starting to communicate in the CVE. Bowers, Pycock, and O'Brien (1996a) stated that the overall design of CVEs should be considered with respect to how they afford social interaction and not just in terms of navigability, capability of presenting information, or aesthetic appeal. Our study also indicates that the following design elements of a CVE are important for distributed meetings: improved communication facilities (e.g. speech interface, support for turn-taking); support for common material, (e.g., documents), and support for parallel activities (e.g., writing).

More recently, an experimental study has been performed by Sallnäs and Hedman (2001) investigating to what extent and in what way collaboration in CVE is affected by an audio or video connection in comparison to text chat. This study gives additional evidence of the properties of text chat in comparison with other ways of communicating in a CVE by analyzing dialogues conducted in each medium.

Thirty pairs of subjects performed a decision-making task that was presented to them as a written scenario. A CVE was constructed in the ActiveWorlds™ system, and had the appearance of a simple exhibition with information stations (see Fig. 5.2). The stations included posters with pictures of different model cars and corresponding movie clips with information about the cars. Humanlike avatars represented the subjects. The task was, for each pair of subjects, to go through the exhibition, and together, decide on a car. This involved discussing both the information available in the CVE and the subjects' individual preferences, based on prior knowledge that was relevant to making the decision.

Twenty-seven dialogues out of 30 were transcribed. These dialogues were coded into 12 categories according to Bales' (1976) Interaction Process Analysis (IPA) by two people independently. Results show that the amount of communication and thus the number of code units was significantly

FIG. 5.2. The collaborative virtual environment used in the experimental study.

lower in the text chat condition than in the other conditions. However, no significant difference was found between the voice and video conditions with respect to the amount of communication between subjects; the number of code units was almost the same.

The IPA analysis showed that the subjects' verbal behavior in the text chat condition differed in several respects from the other conditions. Subjects both provided more information and asked for more information in the voice and video conditions than in the text chat condition. This was mainly because they investigated and discussed more of the information displayed in the CVE. Many of the questions and much of the information shared in the audio and video conditions concerned personal issues, such as how large subjects' families were, or personal experiences relevant to the information displayed. Subjects also explored the CVE more completely, and consequently had more to discuss. Furthermore, subjects shared more opinions in the voice and video conditions as they negotiated more extensively in those conditions than in the text chat condition. They often discussed and analyzed the information carefully, while at the same time communicating their personal preferences. In the text chat condition, negotiations were crude and were more based on appearances of cars than on information about functionality and preferences. Subjects did not seem as engaged in the discussion in the text chat condition and the dialogues exhibited numerous misunderstandings.

Subjects showed more agreement in the video and voice conditions than in the text chat condition. This might be because it was easier to give fast feedback in the voice and video conditions than in the text chat condition. Subjects also showed more tension-releasing behavior in the voice and video than in the text condition. They were joking more and often expressed satisfaction regarding individual or cooperative behavior. However, there were also examples of this in the text chat condition. "Smileys" (emotionally expressive symbols created with standard keyboard characters) were used by the subjects in order to communicate a joke or feelings of satisfaction.

When studying the percentages of dialogue acts, it emerged that a substantial part of the communication in all three conditions was focused on problem solving. The reason why more than half of the dialogue is focused on problem solving in the text chat condition might be that, because communicating in this medium is harder, most of the effort is put into actually solving the task.

The communication in the voice and video condition was more socially oriented than in the text chat condition. More feedback was given in the voice and video condition that either intervened or was communicated in parallel to the other person's utterances. This is evidently hard to accomplish in the text chat condition.

Video as an added information channel did not seem to make a great difference in comparison to the voice mode. This result is in agreement with previous research about the use of video communication in problem-solving tasks (see Whittaker, 1995; Whittaker & O'Conaill, 1997). It was noticed, however, that the video channel was used in certain typical situations:

- During long pauses in the conversation—to attract the partners attention, or to see if the partner was busy, or ready to interact;
- when problems were encountered, that is, navigational, or interface-related—to establish mutual awareness of pressing situations;
- during greetings, and during discussions prior to important decision making, to establish eye contact, according to traditional social norms.

Thus the video channel, although not used heavily, did serve important functions. It was used to structure the conversation, to establish and maintain mutual awareness, and to allow certain kinds of social interaction that would otherwise not have been possible.

CONCLUSIONS

Through the work in the KnowHow project, we have begun to look into the complexity and the promises of the Web as a medium for communication and knowledge exchange. The area is vast, and the studies reported here should be seen as just a beginning. However, we do feel that using a combination of empirical studies and explorative design work is a promising approach that may lead to new insights as well as to concrete recommendations for the design of collaborative tools on the Web.

The Web is constantly changing, both in terms of contextual and technical conditions. It is difficult to state general conclusions from the work presented here, and it is clear that longitudinal studies are necessary to increase our understanding with respect to some of the questions studied. Nevertheless, the research reviewed and our own studies support the picture of the Web as a potentially powerful social infrastructure for knowledge work, the actual realization of which depends on contextual conditions well known from previous studies of collaborative work. Web technology can help people accomplish tasks together in new ways, across geographical boundaries, but the extent to which such cooperation actually takes place is dependent on a range of situational factors. These include participants' motivation to share knowledge and be visible to others, the constraints of their tasks and the cooperative climate in their everyday work situation. In addition, Web-based tools must be designed to fulfill usability requirements and be easily integrated with people's existing work tools—

factors that currently meet considerable challenges for developers as well as researchers.

For example, the studies of home pages and the experiences from the *Col•laboració* design work show that the Web affords truly new ways of collaboration, using technology easily available to virtually everyone. At the same time, it seems clear that people will only accept a new Web-based tool if they gain something particular from it. There is not always a balance between individuals' need for updated information and their own willingness to supply such information. More stable patterns of collaboration may emerge slowly, under the influence of certain well-known examples of constructive Web use, and with the emergence of a new generation of network-oriented users.

ACKNOWLEDGMENTS

The research reported here has been supported by the Swedish Transport and Communications Research Board, and the Swedish Foundation for Strategic Research through the Graduate School for Human–Machine Interaction.

We are grateful for the constructive comments given by Olfe Bälter and Teresa Cerratto on an earlier version of the chapter.

REFERENCES

Abrams D., Baecker R., & Chignell M. (1998). Information archiving with bookmarks: Personal Web space construction and organization. In *Proceedings of ACM CHI '98 Conference on Human Factors in Computing Systems* (pp. 41–48). New York: ACM Press.

Ackerman, M. S. (1994). Augmenting the organizational memory: A field study of Answer Garden. In *Proceedings of ACM CSCW '94 Conference on Computer-Supported Cooperative Work* (pp. 243–252). New York: ACM Press.

Ackerman, M. S., & Malone, T. W. (1990). Answer Garden: A tool for growing organizational memory. In *Proceedings of ACM Conference on Office Information Systems* (pp. 31–39). Cambridge, MA, USA: ACM Press.

Ackerman, M. S., & McDonald, D. W. (1996). Answer Garden 2: Merging organizational memory with collaborative help. In *Proceedings of ACM CSCW '96 Conference on Computer-Supported Cooperative Work* (pp. 97–105). New York: ACM Press.

Bales, R. F. (1976). *Interaction process analysis: A method for the study of small groups.* Chicago: University of Chicago Press.

Balsvik, G. (1999). Electronic networks and knowledge creation: A study of new learning perspectives related to the context of a media profession. [Tech. rep. TRITA-NA-P9911, NADA]. Stockholm: Royal Institute of Technology.

Bälter, O. (1998). *Electronic mail in a working context.* Doctoral thesis [IPLab-155, TRITA-NA-9820]. Stockholm: Royal Institute of Technology.

Bannon, L. J. (1986). Helping users help each other. In D. A. Norman & S. W. Draper (Eds.), *User centered system design: New perspectives on human–computer interaction* (pp. 399–410). Hillsdale, NJ: Lawrence Erlbaum Associates.

Bannon, L. J., & Kuutti, K. (1996). Shifting perspectives on organizational memory: From storage to active remembering. In *Proceedings of HICSS-29* (Hawaii International Conference on System Sciences), The Institute of Electrical and Electronics Engineering Inc.

Bellotti, V., & Rogers, Y. (1997). From Web press to Web pressure: Multimedia representations and multimedia publishing. In *Proceedings of ACM CHI '97 Conference on Human Factors in Computing Systems* (pp. 279–286). New York: ACM Press.

Bentley, R., Appelt, W., Busbach, U., Hinrichs, E., Kerr, D., Sikkel, D., Trevor, K., & Woetzel, G. (1997). Basic support for collaborative work on the World Wide Web. *International Journal of Human-Computer Studies, 46*(6), 827–846.

Berners-Lee, T., Cailliau, R., Luotonen, A., Nielsen, H. F., & Secret, A. (1994). The World Wide Web. *Communications of the ACM, 37*(8), 76–82.

Bly, S., Cook, L., Bickmore, T., Churchill, E., & Sullivan, J. W. (1998). The rise of personal Web pages at work. In *Proceedings of ACM CHI '98 Conference on Human Factors in Computing Systems (Summary*; pp. 313–314). New York: ACM Press.

Bowers, J., Pycock, J., & O'Brien, J, (1996a). Talk and embodiment in collaborative virtual environments. In *Proceedings of ACM CHI '96 Conference on Human Factors in Computing Systems* (pp. 58–65). New York: ACM Press.

Bowers, J., Pycock, J., & O'Brien, J, (1996b). Practically accomplishing immersion: Cooperation in and for virtual environments. In *Proceedings of ACM CSCW '96 Conference on Computer-Supported Cooperative Work* (pp. 380–389). New York: ACM Press.

Buckingham Shum, S. (1998, December). Evolving the Web for scientific knowledge: First steps towards an "HCI Knowledge Web." *Interfaces Magazine, 39.*

Buckingham Shum, S., & McKnight, C. (Eds.). (1997). Special issue on World Wide Web usability. *International Journal of Human-Computer Studies, 47*(1), 1–218.

Bush, V. (1945, July). As we may think. *Atlantic Monthly, 176,* 101–108.

Card, S., Robertson, G., & York, W. (1996). The Web-book and Web forager: An Information workspace for the World Wide Web. In *Proceedings from ACM CHI '96 Conference on Human Factors in Computing Systems* (pp. 111–117). New York: ACM Press.

Carleson, F., Lundberg, T., & Nässla, H. (1997). Magazines and electronic Web channels— The reader's point of view. In *Proceedings of ACM CHI '97 Conference on Human Factors in Computing Systems* (pp. 253–254). New York: ACM Press.

Cerratto, T. (2001). Collaborative learning in synchronous text-based environments [Tech. rep. TRITA-NA-178, NADA]. Stockholm: Royal Institute of Technology.

Cerratto, T., & Wærn, Y. (2000). Chatting to learn and learning to chat in collaborative virtual environments. *A Journal of Media and Culture* 3(4). Available at http://www.apinetwork. com/mc/0008/learning.html

Clark, H. H. (1996). *Using language.* Cambridge, UK: Cambridge University Press.

Conklin, J., & Begeman, M. L. (1988). gIBIS: A hypertext tool for exploratory policy discussion. In *Proceedings of ACM CSCW '88 Conference on Computer-Supported Cooperative Work* (pp. 140–152). New York: ACM Press.

Dix, A. (1997). Challenges for cooperative work on the Web: An analytical approach. *Computer Supported Cooperative Work: The Journal of Collaborative Computing, 6*(2/3), 135–156.

Dourish, P. (1999). Where the footprints lead: Tracking down other roles for social navigation. In A. J. Munro, K. Höök, & D. Benyon (Eds.), *Social navigation of information space* (pp. 15–34). London: Springer Verlag.

Dourish, P., & Bellotti, V. (1992). Awareness and coordination in shared workspaces. In *Proceedings of ACM CSCW '92 Conference on Computer-Supported Cooperative Work* (pp. 107–114). New York: ACM Press.

Dourish, P., & Chalmers, M. (1994). Running out of space: models of information navigation. Short paper presented at HCI '94, Glasgow, Scotland.

Erickson, T. (1996). The World-Wide Web as social hypertext. *Communications of the ACM,* 39(1), 15–17.

Eveland, J. D., Blanchard, A., Brown, W., & Mattocks, J. (1994). The role of "help networks" in facilitating use of CSCW tools. In *Proceedings of ACM CSCW '94 Conference on Computer-Supported Cooperative Work* (pp. 265–274). New York: ACM Press.

Finn, K. E., Sellen, A. J., & Wilbur, S. B. (1997). *Video-mediated communication.* Hillsdale, NJ: Lawrence Erlbaum Associates.

Groth, K. (1999). Knowledge Net—A support for sharing knowledge within an organisation. Licentiate thesis [IPLab-156, TRITA-NA-9902]. Stockholm: Royal Institute of Technology.

Groth, K., & Lantz, A. (1997, September). *Personliga hemsidor—funktion eller passion?* [Personal homepages—function or passion?]. In STIMDI '97, Linköping, Sweden.

Grudin, J. (1988). Why CSCW applications fail: Problems in the design and evaluation of organizational interfaces. In *Proceedings of ACM CSCW '88 Conference on Computer-Supported Cooperative Work* (pp. 85–93). New York: ACM Press.

Hedman, A. (2001). Visitor orientation: Human-computer interaction in digital places. Licentiate dissertation [ISBN-91-7283-049-2, TRITA-NA-0103, ISSN-0348-2952]. Stockholm: Royal Institute of Technology.

Hill, W. C., & Terveen, L. (1997). Involving remote users in continuous design of Web content. In *Proceedings of DIS '97: Designing interactive systems: Processes, practices, methods, & techniques* (pp. 137–145). New York: ACM Press.

Holtzblatt, K. (1999). Customer centered design as discipline. In M A. Sasse & C. Johnson (Eds.), *Proceedings of INTERACT '99* (pp. 3–17). Amsterdam: The Netherlands: IOS Press.

Instone, K. (1996). HCI and the Web. *SIGCHI Bulletin, 28*(4), 42–45.

Kautz, H., Selman, B., & Shah, M. (1997). The referral web: Combining social networks and collaborative filtering. *Communications of the ACM, 40*(3), 63–65.

Kim, H.-C., & Severinson Eklundh, K. (2001). Reviewing practices in collaborative writing. *Computer-Supported Cooperative Work: The Journal of Collaborative Computing, 10*(2), 247–259.

Kollock, P., & Smith, M. (1996). Managing the virtual commons: Cooperation and conflict in computer communities. In S. C. Herring (Ed.), *Computer-mediated communication: Linguistic, social and cross-cultural perspectives* (pp. 109–128). Amsterdam: J. Benjamins.

Kraut, R. E., & Streeter, L. A. (1995). Coordination in software development, *Communications of the ACM, 38*(3), 69–81.

Lantz, A. (1998). Heavy users of email. *International Journal of Human-Computer Interaction, 10*(4), 361–379.

Lantz, A. (2001). Meetings in a distributed group of experts: Comparing face-to-face, chat and a collaborative virtual environment. *Behavior and Information Technology, 20*(2), pp. 111–118.

Lantz, A., & Severinson Eklundh, K. (1999). *Kommunikation och kompetensutveckling via elektroniska nätverk: En förstudie* [Communication and competence development via electronic networks: A prestudy]. [Tech. rep. IPLab-159, TRITA-NA-P9903]. Sweden: Royal Institute of Technology.

Lea, R., Honda, Y., & Matsuda, K. (1997). Virtual society: Collaboration in 3D spaces on the Internet. *Computer Supported Cooperative Work, 6*(2/3), 227–250.

Munro, A. J., Höök., K., & Benyon, D. R. (1999a). Footprints in the snow. In A. J. Munro, K. Höök, & D. R. Benyon (Eds.), *Social navigation of information space* (pp. 1–14). London: Springer Verlag.

Munro, A. J., Höök, K. & Benyon, D. R. (Eds.). (1999b). *Social navigation of information space.* London: Springer Verlag.

Nielsen, J. (1997). The telephone is the best metaphor for the Internet. Available at http://www.useit.com/alertbox/9705b.html/

126

Perlman, G. (1998). Web-based user interface evaluation with questionnaires. Available at http:/www.acm.org/~perlman/question.html

Rodriguez, H. (1999). The domain help system [Tech. rep. TRITA-NA-P9912, CID-56]. Stockholm: Royal Institute of Technology.

Rodriguez, H., Kim, H.-C., & Severinson Eklundh, K. (1999). Using the Web as infrastructure for collaborative writing and document design. Poster presented at ECSW '99 (6th European Conference on Computer-Supported Cooperative Work), Copenhagen.

Sallnäs, E.-L., & Hedman, A. (2001). Exploring communicative modes for a virtual environment: A social psychological analysis [Tech. rep. IPLab-181]. Sweden: Department of Numerical Analysis and Computer Science, Royal Institute of Technology.

Sandor, O., & Tollmar, K. (1996). @Work: The design of a new communication tool. *Presentation at the ERCIM W4G workshop on CSCW and the Web*, Sankt Augustin, Germany.

Sellen, A., & Harper, R. (1997). Paper as an analytic resource for the design of new technologies. In *Proceedings of ACM CHI '97 Conference on Human Factors in Computing Systems* (pp. 319–326). New York: ACM Press.

Shneiderman, B. (1998). Codex, memex, genex: The pursuit of transformational technologies. In *Proceedings of ACM CHI '98 Conference on Human Factors in Computing Systems* (pp. 98–99). New York: ACM Press.

Slater, M., Sadagic, A., Usoh, M., & Schroder, R. (2000). Small group behavior in a virtual and real environment: A comparative study. *Presence: Teleoperators and Virtual Environments, 9*(1), 37–51.

Sumner, T., & Buckingham Shum, S. (1998). From documents to discourse: Shifting conceptions of scholarly publishing. In *Proceedings of ACM CHI '98 Conference on Human Factors in Computing Systems* (pp. 95–102). New York: ACM Press.

Tauscher, L., & Greenberg, S. (1997). How people revisit Web pages: Empirical findings and implications for the design of history systems. *International Journal of Human–Computer Studies, 47*(1), 97–137.

Terveen, L., & Hill, W. (1998). Evaluating emergent collaboration on the Web. In *Proceedings of ACM CSCW '98 Conference on Computer-Supported Cooperative Work* (pp. 355–362). New York: ACM Press.

Tromp, J., Bullock, A., Steed, A., Sadagic, A., Slater, M. & Frécon, E. (1998). Small group behavior experiments in the Coven Project. *IEEE Computer Graphics and Applications, 18*(6), 53–63.

Waterson, P. E., Clegg, C. W., & Axtell, C. M. (1997). The dynamics of work organization, knowledge and technology during software development. *International Journal of Human–Computer Studies, 46*(1), 79–101.

Whittaker, S. (1995). Rethinking video as a technology for interpersonal communications: Theory and design implications. *International Journal of Human–Computer Studies, 42*(5), 501–529.

Whittaker, S., & O'Conaill, B. (1997). The role of vision in face-to-face and mediated communication. In K. E. Finn, A. J. Sellen, & S. B. Wilbur (Eds.), *Video-mediated communication* (pp. 23–49). Hillsdale, NJ: Lawrence Erlbaum Associates.

Whittaker, S., & Sidner, C. (1996). Email overload: Exploring personal information management of email. In *Proceedings of ACM CHI '96 Conference on Human Factors in Computing Systems* (pp. 276–283). New York: ACM Press.

Whittaker, S., Terveen, L., Hill, W., & Cherny, L. (1998). The dynamics of mass interaction. *Proceedings of ACM CSCW '98 Conference on Computer-Supported Cooperative Work* (pp. 257–264). New York: ACM Press.

Chapter 6

Social Considerations in Online Communities: Usability, Sociability, and Success Factors*

Jonathan Lazar
Towson University

Jennifer Preece
University of Maryland, Baltimore County

The term "online community" is becoming increasingly popular. With the growth of the Internet, millions of people are taking part in online communities. Businesses are trying to build online communities to sell their products. Support communities are growing for people with similar illnesses or circumstances. Hobbyists are getting online and taking part in communities. Building an online community does not consist of merely placing software on the Internet. In reality, online communities are neither designed nor do they just emerge. How software is designed affects community development. The way people interact in a community contributes strongly to its long-term evolution. People's behavior cannot be controlled but it can be influenced. The community's purpose, people's roles in the community, and policies set-up to guide behavior, influence how people behave. The web can support multiple forms of communication, each with its own criteria, each with its own form of "community."

Communities with good sociability have social policies that support the community's purpose and are understandable, socially acceptable and practicable. Usability is concerned with making interfaces consistent, controllable, and predictable, which in turn makes them easy and satisfying to use. Usability plus sociability can produce thriving online communities. Online community research builds on the research literature in areas as di-

---

*The foundation for the first portion of this chapter is an article that appeared in *Information Impacts Magazine.*

verse as Computer Science, Human–Computer Interaction, Psychology, Sociology, Communication, and Library Science. This chapter discusses online communities, and introduces the concepts of *usability* and *sociability* in online communities. A discussion of success factors for online communities is also presented.

WHAT IS AN ONLINE COMMUNITY?

Is an online community when you install community software? Is a community a group of users? Is it when users feel warm and fuzzy inside? A very basic definition of an *online community* could be a set of users who communicate using computer-mediated communication and have common interests, shared goals, and shared resources. However, the concept of an online community can be pleasant and reassuring, or it can conjure disturbing thoughts, such as hate groups plotting heinous crimes. We all have our own notion of what an online community is; it is not hard to understand, but it is slippery to define and tricky to measure. The situation is further complicated by there being many different definitions of "online community" in use at once. Online community is a buzzword, especially now that e-commerce entrepreneurs are realizing that online communities can help expand their markets and bolster sales. The Internet is to business what 747 jumbo jets are to transportation. It provides fast, inexpensive communication and information transfer throughout the world. But a community is more than just a stream of messages. Suffice it to say—there are many interpretations of the term including its wide usage in e-commerce. There are a number of different characteristics of an online community, including:

- A shared purpose: for example, focus on an interest, need, information, service, or support that provides a reason for belonging to the community;
- people: who interact with each other and who may take roles within the community;
- policies: language and protocols that guide people's interactions;
- folklore and rituals that bring a sense of history and accepted social norms. (Preece, 2000)

Background

Information from a disembodied source has limited value and soon lacks appeal. Think about getting the same information about a serious medical problem from the following three sources: a website with no distinguishing features; the National Institutes of Health (NIH) website, or a doctor with whom you have developed a relationship of trust over the past 8 years. How would you react to each? Some people would be highly skeptical about the unknown website. You would probably accept the information from the NIH because it is such a reputable institution, but what a cold, impersonal way to get this information. It would be much more pleasant to have a trusted doctor with whom to talk. The way that information is conveyed can affect your emotional reactions to it and the way that you subsequently behave.

Now, consider how you would react to the staff of an e-commerce company singing the praises of its products and services. Depending on the firm's marketing skills, you may be influenced more or less positively. However, you are likely to be much more influenced by hearing about the product from a friend or even from another customer. This is why online communities have become such a hot topic for e-commerce. They entice people to e-commerce sites. The favorable comments of other customers are believed by entrepreneurs to be a cheap and effective form of marketing. E-commerce providers want to extend their markets and they see online communities as a way of achieving this goal.

All areas of our lives can potentially benefit from online communities, but they are specially promising for health, education, and e-commerce. Already millions of patients are forming support groups. Those with rare diseases or who are immobilized may particularly benefit. Education is being revolutionized. Distance education is more easily available for those in full-time employment or those who are unable to travel. E-commerce, too, is latching on to the benefits of online communities. Like the 20th-century architects and town planners, software designers and community developers can together profoundly shape the online community landscape.

No two communities are the same. Just as Berkeley, California, is different from Halifax, Canada, online communities are also very different from each other. There are a number of different ways to classify characteristics of an online community. An online community could be classified based on how it is related to a physical community. Some online communities are based on a specific town or region, such as the Blacksburg Electronic Village or the Seattle Community Network (Lazar & Preece, 1998) and are known at community networks. The Blackburg Electronic Village (http://www.bev.net) focuses on the people, events, government, and community resources in Blacksburg, Virginia, USA. Similarly, the Seattle Community Network (http://www.scn.org) focuses on the people, events, organizations, and community resources in Seattle, Washington, USA. In these types of online communities, community members see each other face-to-face on a frequent basis. Other online communities are based on periodic face-to-face contact, where the community members may see each other a few times a year, or once every few years at meetings, conferences, retreats, swap meets, and so on. For instance, in the Computer–Human Interaction online community sponsored by the Association for Computing Machinery http://www.chiplace.org/, members may be geographically distributed and communicate electronically year-round, but may only meet face-to-face at one of the conferences held during the year. Other communities, such as role-playing communities and support communities have no face-to-face contact among community members (Lazar & Preece, 1998). Online communities could also be classified based on the supporting software used by the community. For instance, some online communities are supported using listservers, USENET, bulletin boards, Internet Relay Chat, chat rooms, or combinations or more than one of these tools (Lazar & Preece, 1998). These software tools may differ in the type of interface (text-based, graphical, etc.), as well as the time lag (synchronous vs. asynchronous). For instance, listservers can deliver community messages directly to an individual's e-mail inbox, and provides asynchronous communication. A chat room might require special software, and is synchronous group communication.

Ideally, individuals' needs are compatible with the community's, but sometimes they are not, so policies are needed to ensure harmony and deal with serious misconduct. More minor problems occur when people fail to observe social protocols either because they do not know them or because they deliberately choose to ignore them. We can all draw on personal experiences of when we were unsure how to behave, what to say, or whether or not to laugh. Online communities generally have policies and social protocols. Some are widely known and accepted by most established Internet users, but others may be specific to a particular online community. Putting in place basic policies so that members know what to expect from each other provides a framework for initial social growth. This is known as *sociability* (Preece, 2000). As the community develops and forms its own character, its social policies and structure also evolve. Successful communities are more likely to develop when early social planning constrains the community just enough to discourage inappropriate behavior while facilitating the community's evolution. Getting this balance correct requires skill, sensitivity, and an appreciation that the community's purpose and needs may change over time. Sociability focuses on social planning and social processes, which jointly lead to good social policies. Sociability is concerned with planning social policies that encourage development of congenial and appropriate social interactions. By focusing on usability and sociability, community planners can influence the potential success of online communities. Communities evolve organically, influenced by the interactions of their members. However, carefully planned social policies have a big impact on the future development.

Usability

Although online communities develop and continuously evolve, only the software that supports them is designed. Software with good usability supports rapid learning, high skill retention, low error rates, and high productivity (Preece et al., 1994). It is consistent, controllable, and predictable, making it pleasant and effective to use. Shneiderman (1998) has formulated three general principles for software usability:

- *Consistency*. Consistent software uses the same terms and procedures for achieving the same functionality throughout the program. For example, if *exit* is used to leave part of a community platform, such as a bulletin board, then *exit* should be used consistently throughout the platform. Using *quit* sometimes and *exit* at other times will confuse users. The notion of consistency is far-reaching. For example, sequences of actions should also follow the same format. Color should be used consistently. Layout, too, should be consistent and so should typography. For instance, font type and size, capitalization, justification, and positioning of titles need to be consistent throughout a website. Consistency is an important part of usability inspections (Nielsen, 1994).
- *Control*. Users want to be in control. They want software that supports but does not take away their sense of control so they can do what they want, when they want and not be constrained by the software.
- *Predictability*. Software that is consistent and controllable is predictable, too. Predictable software enables users to continually build on their experience. Users do not want surprises. Users know that if a particular set of commands worked in one situation, it will work in another, similar situation. Their confidence and skills increase with experience.

Usability and sociability are closely related. Consider for example, registering to belong to a community. The decision to enforce a registration policy is a sociability decision. It strongly impacts who comes into the community and potential social interactions. The mechanics of registering are determined by software design and involve usability decisions. The design of the registration form, how it is displayed, the nature of prompts, and help messages associated with completing the form are usability issues.

The study of usability is not new (Nielsen, 1994; Preece, 1990). What *is* new is a greater appreciation of its value in software design, as Internet access has become more ubiquitous. As an increasing number of online communities are integrated into websites, web usability has become important. The following guidelines are grouped into three broad categories: navigation, access, and information design (Preece, 2000).

Navigation. Successful websites are designed with good navigation and provide navigation support. The phrase, "lost in cyberspace," is understood by every web user. The following six guidelines encourage good navigation.

- Avoid frames. Frames prevent book marking and destroy consistency because users have no idea where they will end up after clicking on a link. Frames destroy the users' ability to develop safe and reliable mental models of the site's content and design (Nielsen, 2000). If the user has a mental model of a web page as being one document, a framed document that actually consists of three Hypertext Markup Language (HTML) documents will not match the user's mental model.

- Avoid orphan pages that are not connected to the home page. If users try to access these pages independently, they cannot get to the rest of the site. This is frustrating and is one of the biggest maintenance problems (Nielsen, 2000).

- Avoid long pages with excessive white space that force scrolling. Users do not like to read material on screen. They generally skim and fail to scroll to the bottom of long pages (Lynch & Horton, 1999; Van Oostendorp & Van Nimwegen, 1998). This was more problematic in the early days of the web. Users are now more tolerant and knowledgeable. Too many links to find a known item is also problematic, so a balance is needed (Nielsen, 2000).

- Provide navigational support. Designers need to give users a strong site map, which is present wherever the user is in the site. *Site maps* provide an overview that helps users develop correct mental models of how different parts of the website relate to one another (Nielsen, 2000). A site map is like a directory at a shopping mall; it lets users know where they are and where they can go (Lazar, 2001).

- Avoid narrow, deep, hierarchical menus in which users are forced to burrow deep down into the menu structure. Empirical evidence indicates that broad, shallow menus have better usability (Shneiderman, 1998), because they require fewer clicks for the user to reach their task goal (Rosenfeld & Morville, 1998). Such menus draw on users' ability to recall information rather than remember it. The home page for Yahoo™ (http://www.yahoo.com), which has 100 or so links, is good example. Many items are placed at the highest surface level, while keeping links logically organized in a compact layout. This design supports usability even though it appears to contradict the well-known guideline of allowing plenty of white space in the paper. White space is traded off for compactness in favor of fitting information onto the screen.

- Provide consistent look and feel for navigation and information design (Nielsen, 2000; Preece et al., 1994; Van Nimwegen, Pouw, & Van

Oostendorp, 1999). This is particularly important if the site contains several pieces of software. Moving from one part of the site to another should be straightforward, and the experience should be seamless. Users should not be forced to deal with multiple, different interfaces that do not match or work well together. If it is impossible to achieve this because some software modules are imported, users should be warned about the differences between the different software products, and users should be provided with advice on how best to deal with any problems that may arise.

Access. Another aspect of usability is how the user accesses the webpages—through a web browser. Browsers are sensitive to slight errors in URLs, and many users do not have state-of-the-art equipment and efficient Internet access. The following three guidelines encourage good access support.

• Avoid complex Uniform Resource Locators (URLs), which are long and include unusual characters that lead to typing errors. This, in turn, results in unsuccessful searches and frustration. The longer the URL, the more likely that the user will make a typing error. For example, the following URL invites typing errors: http://www.cmaisonneuve.qc.ca/~lan/sbk/CW98/MALcolmZ/laughrt.2.html (Nielsen, 2000)

• Avoid nonstandard link colors. Links to pages that have not been seen are generally blue (Lynch & Horton, 1999). Those that have been seen are indicated with purple or red links. This has become a strong standard, and although there is no cultural basis for blue text being an unvisited link, the user expects that blue text represents an unvisited link (Lazar, 2001). Changing it causes problems and breaks with generally accepted web design consistency.

• Avoid long download times that annoy users (Nielsen, 2000). Web users' tolerance depends on how much they want the information, but a limit of 15 seconds is a reasonable guideline. Research indicates that users' perception of content value is influenced by download time and their patience can be tested (Ramsay, Barbesi, & Preece, 1998; Sears, Jacko, & Borella, 1997). With a very long download time, users may also think that they have made an error (Lazar & Norcio, 2000). Avoiding gratuitous graphics and animations helps to keep download times to a minimum and ensures that users with less sophisticated equipment can access the material.

Information Design. Information design (i.e., content comprehension and aesthetics) contributes to users impression of the community, its purpose, whether it is professional, reputable, and can be trusted (Lynch & Horton, 1999; Rosenfeld & Morville, 1998). The following five guidelines support good information design:

- Outdated or incomplete information is to be strongly avoided because it creates a poor impression with users (Lazar, 2001; Powell, Jones & Cutts, 1998; Small & Arnone, 2000).

- Good graphical design is important. Some rules translate directly from design to paper but others do not. Reading long sentences, paragraphs and documents is difficult on screen, so break material into discrete, meaningful chunks to give the website structure.

- Avoid excessive use of color. Color is useful for indicating different kinds of information (Preece et al., 1994; Shneiderman, 1998). A change of color should signal a change in information type. Soft background colors are preferred with contrasting color for text. Avoid strong saturated primary colors for both background and text. Remember also that a small percentage of people are color impaired. Green and red together are particularly problematic for some people. The golden rule is "use color conservatively." However, this rule is challenged by design fashion. Wired™ magazine, for example, uses saturated colors and background patterns. Different uses of color not only signal different moods and content, they are also signals to different demographic populations. Wired™ targets "techies," many of whom are young males. Choice of color has become so strongly associated with cult images of youth and technology that guidelines established for readability are frequently flaunted. Selection of colors and design need to be related to the purpose of the site, the population of users and their tasks.

- Avoid gratuitous use of graphics and animation. Apart from increasing download time, graphics and animation soon become boring and annoying. What may be cute and amusing on the first few visits to the page, becomes annoying as exposure to it increases (Zhang, 2000). However, appreciation for different graphical design styles is also related to users' age.

- Consistency both within pages (e.g., use of fonts, numbering, terminology etc.) and within the site (e.g., navigation, menu names, etc.) is important for usability and for aesthetically pleasing designs (Lynch & Horton, 1999). For example, simple rules like starting all menu names with a capital letter rather than mixing upper and lower case makes the site look professional. Using the same menu names throughout the site improves navigation.

Sociability

Sociability focuses on social interaction. Communities with good sociability have social policies that support the community's purpose and are understandable, socially acceptable, and practical (Preece, 2000). Success of an online community is encouraged by a blend of well-designed software (i.e., usability) and carefully crafted social policies (i.e., sociability). Developing these communities is challenging for several reasons: First, online communities are a fairly new phenomenon and the body of research knowledge and practitioner experience on which to build is small. There is no formula for a thriving online community. Second, communities are dynamic, so they continually change and evolve. What may be important early in the life of a community may not be significant later on. Third, success is determined by three key factors: usability, sociability, and their affect on the interactions of community members. Developers have little or no control over community members, except in some e-commerce communities where interaction is strongly managed. However, developers can do much to set the tone of a community by designing or selecting software with good usability and developing suitable sociability (Preece, 2000).

Defining the community's purpose is important so that would-be members know what to expect (Lazar & Preece, 1998). Highly motivated people may be prepared to browse web pages and messages, but most people want to find out immediately if the community is worth joining. Developers of large, commercial websites will be instructed by management and marketing specialists on how to portray the community. Small teams developing not-for-profit communities, such as the Down Syndrome Online Advocacy Group, will be eager to work with the community to define its purpose (Lazar, Hanst, Buchwalter, & Preece, 2000).

Sociability issues to consider include: What is the community's purpose and what is a meaningful name that conveys it clearly? For example, DSOAG is meaningful only to people who already know about this community. Down Syndrome Group could be a support group, which would be misleading. "Down Syndrome Online Advocacy Group" clearly defines the group's purpose (Lazar et al., 2000). It is important to make sure the home page always portrays the purpose of the community. For example, the home page of drkoop.com has a clear title, statement of purpose, a symbol of the American Medical Association, and a picture of the well-known Dr. Koop. Similar to the marketing concept of product identification, an online community might have a graphical symbol that clearly identifies the community (Lazar, Tsao & Preece, 1999). For instance, there exists an online community related to Quiz Bowl, an academic competition in the USA and UK where students compete in teams, with questions similar to the Jeopardy!™ or Who Wants to Be a Millionaire?™ television shows. For this online community, a picture of astronomer Tycho Brahe was an identifying mascot for the Quiz Bowl online community (Lazar et al., 1999) because it was an already well-established symbol in face-to-face meetings.

There should be a clear statement of purpose that is in harmony with the community's name and home page design. For example, The Down Syndrome Online Advocacy Group (DSOAG) states its purpose succinctly: "Our focus is Down Syndrome research and its funding, so please stay on that topic."

The following sociability guidelines are grouped into three broad categories: registration, trust and security, and governance (Preece, 2000).

Registration. In many communities, users are required to register to take part in the community, and registration is therefore an important aspect of sociability. Should people have to register? There are pros and cons. Having to go through a registration procedure may deter people whose interest might be raised if they could drop in to the community informally to see what is happening. However, registering deters casual visitors intent on disrupting the community. Some communities allow visitors for a limited period with limited privileges. Registration also enables managers to track demographic information that is important to some e-commerce communities.

Some communities deliberately try to restrict access in order to achieve their purpose. In many cases, communities want to limit participation to knowledgeable professionals who are qualified to take part in a discussion. In addition, many religious, ethnic and political discussion groups usually suffer from a large amount of inappropriate and off-topic attacks (also called "flaming"), and therefore, might want only people who share similar interests (Preece & Ghozati, 1998). However, many communities want to encourage people of diverse cultures, races, and genders by promoting an explicit policy of universal access. Who should be encouraged to use the system? A clear statement about access is needed, possibly linked with the statement of purpose. Different versions of the interface may be needed. For example, basic information such as "help" and governance policies could be provided in different languages, and so on. There could be different versions for people with disabilities and reduced technical facilities.

In determining whether to require registration, two guidelines can be used:

• Does the community deal with sensitive issues? Is the community focused on a specific topic where expertise in a specific area is needed to take part in discussions? In these cases, it is a good idea to require registration, and have a policy that specifies who may enter the community (Preece, 2000).

• If registration is required, should visitors be encouraged and under what conditions? Could the visitors read the postings and interactions of other community members, but be limited? In some graphical chat environments, visitors are allowed for a limited period in restricted areas (Preece, 2000).

Trust and Security. Trust and security are important issues in any type of online community, because for users to communicate freely, they must feel that their privacy is protected. The issues of trust and security are especially of great importance in health and e-commerce communitiese. For example, if medical information is provided by a doctor, is there proof of professional status, such as a certificate or affiliation with the American Medical Association, as in the home page of drkoop.com? It is important to distinguish between information provided by expert professionals, and those which are the personal opinion of community members (Preece, 2000). The following sociability guidelines relate to trust and security:

- Formal privacy statements should describe how personal information of community members will be used (Preece, 2000). For community members to feel comfortable discussing sensitive issues, they need to know that their conversations and personal data will not be sold to marketing companies. There are opportunities for some sticky situations, for example, an online community for those suffering from foot fungus could sell their membership lists to a company that provides related medicine.
- For e-commerce communities, information should be given to users, describing what protections are taken to ensure that their transactions will remain secure (Preece, 2000).
- Health-related communities, as well as other communities that deal with sensitive information, should have a disclaimer to protect both community members as well as the community itself. Policies that describe the ground rules for community interaction should be encouraged because they help set up an environment of trust (Preece, 2000).

A healthy alternative to setting rules is to encourage people to communicate more effectively, so that misunderstandings are reduced and frustration is avoided. Pictures, thumb nail icons, links to personal web sites, and personal stories are ways to remind users that a real person exists behind the alias or avatar electron trail. Helping people to more accurately convey meaning and their intentions in correspondence, particularly emotional intentions, helps to reduce ambiguity. Sociability issues that need to be considered include: Is support for personal presence needed? Can people show and tell each other about themselves? Consider providing ways of showing personal pictures, descriptions, links to home pages, and personal stories. Is support for encouraging common ground, empathy, cooperation, and so on needed? For example, the software may support making user intentions explicit, with features such as emoticons (representations of facial expressions, also called "smilies"), which may help to clarify the meaning of messages.

Governance. Another important sociability concern is the issue of governance. *Governance* covers many issues from registration to moderation and democracy. The trick is to get just the right level of policies to set the community on a good course as it evolves. Too many rules, stated too forcefully, will deter people; not enough will provide too little structure. Developers wanting to influence governance, and hence social interactions in the community, rather than letting serendipity take its course, need to work with potential community members. Getting the phrasing and tone right is important, too. Guidelines for governance include:

- It is important to decide whether community owners will govern the community, or whether community members will govern the community. What is the process for this governing? Rules should be provided for voting, and any other processes that require the participation of community members (Preece, 2000).
- What level of free speech is acceptable? Is there any type of communication that should be discouraged? Should racist, obscene, blasphemous and aggressive language be controlled? A short clearly worded statement saying what is acceptable may be useful (Preece, 2000). For example, the Down Syndrome Online Advocacy Group (http://www.dsoag.com) simply requests: "Do not communicate to someone else that which you would not want communicated to you." Early on members of the WELL (a San Francisco Bay-area online community) decided that complete freedom to say anything was important. The amount of complete freedom will obviously be limited by some e-commerce communities because a company will not allow posted messages that denigrate the company.
- How is "nettiquette" defined for communication in the community? (Preece, 2000) What policies define appropriate communication? For instance, in some communities, when you ask a question of community members, it is appropriate and expected to post a list of responses to your question. In other communities, it is considered inappropriate to promote personal products. A netiquette policy defines what type of communication is expected, what type of communication is appropriate, and what type of communication is unwanted. Another important consideration is to specify how the nettiquette rules will be enforced by the moderators.
- Community rules are often enforced by the moderator or mediator. If these rules are unenforced, they may be worthless. If the rules are enforced unevenly, community members may feel that there is bias on the part of the moderator. Moderators have to make judgments, but to avoid controversy, they generally make a clear statement of their policies so that everyone knows what to expect in advance.

DEFINING SUCCESS FOR ONLINE COMMUNITIES

It is expected that all community members, developers, and community leaders will want a successful online community; obviously, no one would want a community that they have developed or been involved with to fail.

However, different stakeholders in the online community may have different definitions of what *success* means (Andrews, 2000). Some of the many
stakeholders include the community members, developers, moderators,
managers, and financial sponsors. Each of these stakeholders might define success differently. The next section defines some of the different
points of view.

Community Founders

Online communities are not spontaneously generated. There is usually an
individual, or group of individuals, who are responsible for the creation of
an online community. The founders of the community spent time securing
the technology, making sure that it was easy to use, and populating their
community with people. These people may have been continuously involved with the community from the start, or these people might been involved with the creation of the community, but are no longer actively involved with the community. Regardless of the level of current involvement,
these individuals are usually interested in the continuation of the community. For these community founders, they want to see that their work was
not in vain. The community founders want to see that people continue to
use and get involved with "their" community. So for these community
founders, success could be measured by the continuous use of the community. A community would not be considered as successful if no one develops
or manages resources, no one posts messages, and membership is low or
nonexistent.

Community Leaders

Community leaders are those who provide leadership within the community,
offering a welcome to newcomers, advice to those who ask, and wisdom
based on past experience. Community leaders also tend to post frequently.
Community leaders are the people who take an active role and are well
known among community members. Community leaders are not necessarily a unique and mutually exclusive classification. The leaders of a community might also be the community founders or the moderators, and the
community leaders certainly are community members. For community
leaders, success could be defined as whether their role is appreciated. If
other community members post to the community leaders and say something along the lines of "thanks for your response; you always provide such
helpful information," this might be considered success. Community leaders
might also define success as a large number of posts, because their leadership helps to "stir up" discussion in the community.

Moderators

Moderators are important figures within the community. They are responsible for tasks such as ensuring that the communication flows well, that communication does not escalate into an all-out war, and that all messages posted are appropriate (Salmon, 2000). The moderators hope that community members will post responsibly, posting only appropriate messages, and not trying to incite other members of the community. In the ideal world, moderators would not need to exist, because all community members would post on-topic, conversation would flow well and continuously, and no one would flame. The only ideal role for the moderator might be to welcome new people to the community. However, in reality, the moderator must often reject posts as off-topic or inappropriate, keep discussions on-topic and active, and periodically remove someone from the community.

A moderator obviously would prefer to have few complaints, and little censorship. A moderator might define success as "happy community members acting appropriately." A moderator would prefer not to reject too many posts. If there are many posts that need to be rejected, it might signal that either (a) a community policy on posting needs to be created, or if a policy already exists; that (b) community members need to be made aware and/or reminded of the policy on posting. A moderator would also prefer that the community members are happy with the moderating, and do not "file" too many complaints. To a certain extent, the success of the moderators is based on the opinions of community members. If the community members are happy with the moderating, the moderator may feel that the community is successful. Conversely, if the community members frequently complain about the moderating, the moderator might feel that the community is not successful. In summary, moderators might define success by the number of complaints, and the number of posts rejected.

Community Members

Community members might define success in a number of different ways. In general, for community members, success is when they "get out of the community" what they came to the community for. Success can therefore be defined in an unlimited number of ways. For some community members, success could be when they gain access to useful information. For other community members, success could mean that they have met people and developed personal relationships. Some community members might consider success to be when they feel a sense of community, a sense of belonging (Roberts, 1998). Other community members might define success as when they feel a sense of support from those going through similar experiences (Preece, 1998). It is possible that success, for an individual user, could be the experience of "talking" without being ignored because of the individual's physical characteristics or disabilities. Visual cues of disability, such as a cane or a hearing aid, do not appear in computer-mediated communication. The only thing that appears in most online communities is your words.

With all of these different definitions of success by community members, how can one measure whether a community is successful? A number of techniques, such as interviews, surveys, and ethnography could be used to interact with community members. The challenge is *what* to ask the community members. Asking a community member, "Do you receive useful information as a member of the community?" would not necessarily be the right question; some members might say "yes," some members might say "no," but this does not mean that they would consider their experience in the online community a waste of time. A better question to ask might be, "What do you think you gain by being involved in the community?"

Although responses to this inquiry might be significantly different, this difference in response is not a problem. The purpose of the inquiry should be to learn more about how the users define success within their community. If statistical data is desirable, then an exploratory investigation should take place first. This exploratory investigation could be in the form of a small number of in-depth interviews with community members. The responses could then be analyzed, and the most-cited reasons for belonging to the community could then be included on a survey that is distributed to a larger number of people within the community.

Business Managers

If an online community is related to a for-profit business or an e-commerce company, success might be defined in a very different manner. For e-commerce companies that are providing online communities (such as the recommender communities on Amazon.com) they are not providing an online community infrastructure so that people "feel good about themselves." Rather, the companies are hoping that more users visit their website, and hopefully more users become regular customers, and sales of products increase. In these cases, success is defined quantitatively. Success might be defined as an increased number of page hits, increased advertising revenue, and/or increased sales. Other possibilities include brand loyalty (Do users feel strongly about coming to YOUR site?), and brand awareness (How many people in the targeted market know of your product?) and image (How do users perceive your product and your web site?)

Quantitative Measures

Defining success in an online community is hard. Defining and examining a number of quantitative measurements of the community is much easier. For instance, it is possible to measure the number of community members (based on the number of people who have subscribed, registered, or logged in), the number of posts per week, the number of posts related to the number of community members, the number of discussion threads, the number of posts read, and/or the amount of time spent in the online community.

The ability to measure these different facets of community life relate to the specific technology used to support the online community. For instance, if the community is supported with a listserver (which requires registration), it is possible to determine the percentage of posters within the total population of community members. If the user is required to login/logout to access community resources, it is possible to determine the average amount of time per week that the community member spends logged into the community. Generally, this information is provided by logs from the supporting software. Although all of these measurements are interesting and can provide useful information, none of these measurements are necessarily measurements of success. A community is not necessarily successful because there are 500 posts a week, or because 3000 people are subscribed to the community, or because 100% of community members have posted a message. An online community is not a "certification exam" where 80% is a passing mark and 79% is a failing mark. There is not a single quantitative measurement that can determine success. Not all stakeholders define success in the same manner, so it is impossible to say, "this online community is successful." Rather, it is preferable to learn more about how each stakeholder group defines success, and then ascertain whether the stakeholder group perceives the online community as successful, based on their specific view of success.

The Importance of Lurkers

Users who do not post messages but read messages posted by others have been called *lurkers* (Nonnecke & Preece, 1999). But even though being a *lurker* can have a negative connotation, it should not be considered bad to be a lurker. In many cases, lurkers are simply interested in the topic of conversation, and are just trying to learn from others. In fact, many lurkers feel that they are part of the community (Nonnecke & Preece, 2000). Lurkers might be new to the topic area, and might not have much to add to the conversation, or they might begin to post at a later time when they become more experienced in the area. Instead of wasting the bandwidth by posting messages repeating what others have said, lurkers sit back, learn, and become knowledgeable members of the online community. It is possible that community governance policies should be put in place to actually encourage lurking. After all, it would be unreasonable to require users to post a message a week, when the users might not have anything useful to say. Enforcing such a policy would encourage worthless posting, which in turn might drive community members out of the community. Governance and participation policies should encourage community growth, not encourage people to leave. Lurking is simply a different communication role.

SUCCESS FACTORS FOR ONLINE COMMUNITIES

There are a number of different considerations that must be addressed to have a thriving and successful online community. It is not guaranteed that following these rules will result in success; rather, these are common problems with common methods for addressing the problems. If these rules are not followed, it is highly likely that the online community will not be successful.

Good Usability

First and foremost, an online community must be easy to use. If the user cannot even figure out how to join the community, chances are slim that they will ever become community members. When a user does become a community member, good usability is necessary to keep them in the community. If the community members are continuously frustrated by their attempts to take part in the community, they will leave. Good usability can also encourage more interaction. If the interaction is pleasant, the community member will be more likely to take an active role. And people do not have an unlimited amount of time. For example, assume that the community member has 30 minutes each day for involvement in the online community. If the community member spends 15 minutes just trying to figure out how to post a message to the community, assuming that they still want to post, they have just wasted 15 minutes that could have been used to read more posts or to actually post more messages. Good usability is necessary for an effective community.

Appropriate and Responsible Moderation

A strong online community needs a good moderator. A moderator walks a tightrope. On one hand, the moderator should encourage free discussion and encourage people to actually build a community. On the other hand, the moderator needs to "step in" when a community member acts inappropriately or when the community member turns out to be someone who wants to harm the community. The level of enforcement might be related to the past history of strife in the community. For instance, many online communities related to religion suffer from flaming arguments and threats

(Preece & Ghozati, 1998). Therefore, in a religious online community, the moderator might have to enforce policies in a strong manner.

In some communities, the moderator might serve as a "sentry," controlling entry into the community. In a physical community (such as a school, fraternal group, group living situation, etc.), an interview might be necessary to ensure that the person will "fit in" and will not harm the community. In some online communities related to professions, the moderator might serve this role checking the "qualifications" of the user wanting to join, for instance, in an online community for anesthesiologists, the users must first present their medical credentials in order to join the community (Lazar & Preece, 1999b). This is good; community members would not want some random unqualified person joining the conversation on anesthesiology technique. In another online community, this one related to professional song leaders, the moderator individually approves potential community members. The user must write a paragraph explaining why they want to be a member of the community. In addition, users may not join the community using e-mail addresses that do not identify who they are "in real life." The idea behind these steps is to make sure that those who are either (a) unqualified or (b) disruptive will not be able to join. By placing these "hurdles" in the way of joining, those who plan to join the community to only be disruptive will likely find another online community in which to be disruptive.

A Reason to Communicate

When people meet in a physical setting, it is likely that they have some type of shared interest. If you randomly placed 25 people in a room, it is questionable whether they would chat for a long time. When people interact online, they interact because they have a shared purpose, a shared goal, a shared experience, and/or a shared interest. If you try to create a community, and place 25 random people in that community, it is unlikely that they would form one. This is not worrisome, because, in a physical setting, it is also unlikely that those same people would interact. In online communities based on specific physical locations (such as towns or regions), people interact online because they would also interact face-to-face, based on their shared experiences, interests, or goals. In online communities that are not based on physical towns, but are based on periodic face-to-face meetings, people interact online because they would also interact at the face-to-face meetings, based on their shared experiences, interests, or goals. People in online communities where there is no face-to-face contact interact online because they have shared experiences, interests, or goals. Regardless of whether they would even want to interact face-to-face, there is still a shared purpose that causes people to communicate. In fact, in some online communities with no face-to-face contact, such as support communities or role-playing communities, community members may never be interested in meeting face-to-face. These community members still have a shared interest or goal, and that is what allows the community to exist.

A Relatively Stable Leadership and Membership

Most physical communities have relatively stable populations. The city of Seattle does not have an entirely new population each year. Different cities have different levels of population stability, based on factors such as industry, weather, and geography. Cities such as New York and Washington, DC have a large number of people who move in and out of the city each year. Cities such as Daytona Beach and Boca Raton, Florida have populations that increase greatly at different parts of the year, based on "snowbirds" who move to Florida during the winter, and students who come to visit on spring break. Cities such as St. Louis and Baltimore have more stable populations. Dan Rodericks, a columnist for the *Baltimore Sun*, commented that you can tell someone who is from Baltimore because they give directions based on where buildings used to be located. The idea is that, if you give directions based on where a certain local landmark existed 10 years ago, that is fine, because everyone has lived there for a long time, and everyone would know the building that used to exist.

This same issue of population stability also occurs in online communities. Some online communities have very stable populations. There are a large number of people who have been involved in the online community for a long time. These "old-time" community members know who the community members are, how to post appropriately, and what is considered acceptable behavior in the community. Conversely, some communities have populations that turn over rapidly. For instance, many of the online communities that are based on school-aged populations (such as high schools, colleges, and graduate programs) have 100% turnover every few years. Other online communities that are based on trends (such as Pokemon™ and Britney Spears) also tend to have populations that change frequently. For online communities that are focused on topics of interest to the university student population, there will be a lot of population turnover. The new users might not be familiar with the community norms or appropriate posting guidelines. These community members might therefore act in an inappropriate manner, simply out of ignorance of the posting policies. In online communities that have great population turnover, it might be useful to post the policies for appropriate community norms on a regular basis. For instance, in one online community based on campus religious groups, the posting policy, mission of the community, and rules on appropriate behavior were posted once a week as a reminder to community members, many of whom had not been community members for long. These reminders serve the same purpose as a sign posted at a park, describing the rules of the park (no boating, no swimming, no smoking, no open fires, etc.). Because people might not visit the park frequently, the rules for the park are posted all over in a clear and obvious manner, so that those using the park will be aware that rules exist, and what the rules are.

**Distributed Nature of Resources
(or Backup Hardware/Software)**

Because an online community is based on computer-mediated communication and shared resources, it is hopeful that these resources will always be available for community members to access and use. If the community is supported by only one web server, and that server crashes and is down for a long time, this will, in effect, kill a thriving community. In the physical world, this is equivalent to a party that suddenly runs out of beverages and food, and the sound system crashes. People then start to leave the party. An online community is like a continuously running party. As long as there is good conversation and useful resources, people will want to be a part of the community. However, if there is a lapse in the availability of the community, it is likely that people will leave and not return.

Plans for system failure are very important to ensure a continuously existing community. If the resources of an online community are distributed (with some web pages run out of California, some out of Maine, a listserver run out of Nebraska, etc.), this offers an automatic protection against a specific system failure. If a technological portion of the community fails, community members will not necessarily leave because the community still exists, and there is much to keep the member in the community (Lazar et al., 1999) Another approach is to provide backup sites (also called mirror sites), in case one site fails; then a number of other sites will still exist to support the community. Of paramount importance is to make sure that file backups are made of the community resources. If a web server fails, it would be a pity to lose the resources that were developed through the hard work of leaders and members. Losing the resources can be a very negative experience for members, who might harbor ill feelings toward those whose responsibility it was to make sure that backups of resources were made. Without the community resources, a number of members might choose to leave.

The Right Level of Registration

Many communities require users to join the community through a registration process. This might be as simple as sending a "subscription" message to a listserver, where the user must only provide their e-mail address, or this might be a process where the user must provide their name, home address, phone number, and demographic information. Some of the technical infrastructure of the online community might require that user information be collected. However, there are at least two goals involved in requiring users to register: 1) population control, and 2) evaluation information

Registration can be used to help control the number of people who join the community. For instance, if no registration is required, anyone can join the community and post messages. However, if a small amount of registration information must be provided (such as an e-mail address to join a listserver), an individual who might have joined the community to cause trouble might think twice. Also, providing registration information ensures at least minimal identification of the community member. Registration might be a small hurdle that troublemakers (or those who are really not committed to purpose of the community) might not be willing to jump over. On the other end of the spectrum, requiring large amounts of information (such as home address, phone number, and demographic information) might deter people from joining the community because they are not comfortable with providing such information. Some communities (such as classmates.com) will only allow users to join and take part in the community if they allow cookies (small amounts of data, about the user actions and/or habits on a specific web site, that are stored on the user's hard drive) to be stored on the user's hard drive. Requiring that the user provide large amounts of personal information might deter the user from joining the community out of privacy concerns. There needs to be a "middle-of-the-road" approach to registration; it needs to be substantial enough that troublemakers or those not committed to the purpose of the community will not join, but registration should be minimal enough that it will not scare potential community members away because of privacy concerns.

Participatory Community-Centered Design

It is well known that the input of users is required to ensure a successful information system (Norman & Draper, 1986) After all, if you have not asked the users what they need, how will you know what to design? This same concept is applicable to designing online communities. This process has been named *participatory community-centered design* (Preece, 2000) Participatory Community-centered design is when you get the community members or potential members involved in the design process. Participatory Community-centered design has successfully been used in developing a number of different types of online communities (Lazar & Preece, 1999b; Lazar et al., 1999, 2000).

Community members should be involved in a number of different planning activities. A needs assessment should be performed to determine whether an online community would be feasible, and if so, what the needs of the community are. Community members should also be involved in developing the community policies, selecting software, performing usability testing, and populating the community. A number of different information gathering techniques is used as part of the participatory community centered design process. For instance, a needs assessment can be performed using surveys, either paper, e-mail, or web-based, depending on how the developers have access to community members or potential members (Lazar & Preece, 1999a) Other techniques used in the participatory community centered design process include interviews, focus groups, and ethnography (Preece, 2000). (See, Preece (2000) for details on the community centered design process).

THE IMPACT OF POLITICAL SITUATIONS

As part of community centered design, it is important to understand what issues are facing the community members. It is very possible that community members might not feel comfortable in speaking out, due to fears of retribution. For instance, in gathering requirements in one online community for sport enthusiasts, it was discovered that a bulletin board was available for community use; however, users were not allowed to criticize a specific company, and if they did, their posts would be erased. In another example, new teachers did not feel comfortable posting their experiences to an online community because their supervisors would regularly read the posts on the online community. Because the new teachers (community members) feared retribution if they were honest (saying something such as, "this teaching technique did not go well"), the teachers did not feel comfortable communicating.

When people communicate using computer-mediated communication, as long as the author of a post is identified, the relationships that exist offline in the physical world will also exist on-line in the virtual world. For instance, in an online community for students of religion, many posts were not reflex responses, but instead were long, referenced arguments, "targeted" toward the deans of admission at a prestigious seminary. It was well-known that the deans of admission at the seminary read the listserver posts, even though they posted infrequently to the listserver. In an online community for new teachers, the community members would not criticize principals because the principals read the posts in the online community and the principals could affect the new teachers' job futures. Middle-level managers in a company would not openly criticize executives because they would be afraid of losing their jobs. If there are situations where there could possibly be a political or a power relationship between community members, it might be necessary to provide anonymity for posts. This, like serving as a moderator, is a "tightrope to walk." On one hand, anonymity allows community members to more freely express their feelings because they do not need to worry about retribution based on the power structure. On the other hand, if users are anonymous, they might feel free to post inappropriate messages or act in a manner that is disruptive to the community.

SUMMARY

Millions of people participate in thousands of online communities. Some communities are narrowly defined whereas others have a broad range of members. What makes a community successful? This is a difficult question to answer because it depends on many factors and on whose perspective you define success. Software design has been supported by well-tried and tested guidelines to ensure that systems are easy to use. However, unlike most software that serves a functional purpose, online communities are strongly social. So sociability is important as well as usability. Usability is concerned with making sure that software is consistent, predictable, and easy and satisfying to use, and sociability focuses on processes and styles of interaction that support social interaction. Developers can control usability, but they cannot control sociability, however, they can do much to influence it. For instance, appropriate and responsible moderation, stable leadership, and an appropriate level of registration can positively influence the sociability of the community. This chapter proposes guidelines for usability and sociability that will help online community developers to build more successful communities.

REFERENCES

Andrews, D. (2000). *Workshop report on Online Communities: Supporting sociability, designing usability*. Workshop held at the Human-Computer Interaction Lab 2000 Symposium and Open House. May 2000. Available at: http://triton.towson.edu/~jlazar/hcil2000/details.html

Lazar, J. (2001). *User-centered web development*. Sudbury, MA: Jones and Bartlett Publishers.

Lazar, J., Hanst, E., Buchwalter, J., & Preece, J. (2000). Collecting User Requirements in a Virtual Population: A Case Study. *WebNet Journal: Internet Internet Technologies, Applications, and Issues, 2*(4), 20–27.

Lazar, J. & Norcio, A. (2000). System and training design for end-user error. S. Clarke & B. Lehaney (Eds.), *Human centered methods in information systems: Current research and practice* (pp. 76–90). Hershey, PA: Idea Group Publishing.

Lazar, J., & Preece, J. (1998, August). Classification schema for online communities. In E. Hoadley & I. Benbasat (Eds.), *Proceedings of the 1998 Association for Information Systems Americas Conference*, pp. 84–86. Georgia: Association for Information Systems.

Lazar, J., & Preece, J. (1999a). Designing and implementing web-based surveys. *Journal of Computer Information Systems, 39*(4), 63–67.

Lazar, J., & Preece, J. (1999b, December). Implementing service learning in an online communities course. In C Rogers (Ed.), *Proceedings of the International Academy for Information Management* (pp. 22–27). Charlotte, North Carolina.

Lazar, J., Tsao, R., & Preece, J. (1999). One Foot in cyberspace and the other on the ground: A case study of analysis and design issues in a hybrid virtual and physical community. *WebNet Journal: Internet Internet Technologies, Applications, and Issues, 1*(3), 49–57.

Lynch, P., & Horton, S. (1999). *Web style guide: Basic design principles for creating web sites.* New Haven: Yale University Press.

Nielsen, J. (1994). *Usability engineering.* Boston: Academic Press.

Nielsen, J. (2000). *Designing web usability: The practice of simplicity.* Indianapolis: New Riders Publishing.

Nonnecke, B., & Preece, J. (1999, January). Shedding light on lurkers in online communities. In K. Buckner (Ed.), *Proceedings of the conference on ethnographic studies in real and virtual environments: Inhabited information spaces and connected communities* (pp. 123–128).

Nonnecke, B., & Preece, J. (2000, April). Lurker demographics: Counting the silent. In M. Czerwinski & F. Paterno (Eds.), Proceedings of the CHI 2000: Human Factors in Computing (pp. 73–80), The Hague, Netherlands.

Norman, D., & Draper, S. (1986). *User-centered system design.* Hillsdale, NJ: Lawrence Erlbaum Associates.

Powell, T., Jones, D., & Cutts, D. (1998). *Web site engineering: beyond web page design.* Upper Saddle River, NJ: Prentice Hall.

Preece, J. (Ed.). (1990). *A Guide to Usability.* Milton Keynes, England: The Open University.

Preece, J. (1998). Empathic communities: Reaching out across the web. *Interactions, 5*(2), 32–43.

Preece, J. (2000). *Online communities: Designing usability, supporting sociability.* New York: Wiley.

Preece, J., & Ghozati, K. (1998, August). In search of empathy online. In E. H. Oadley & I. Benbasat (Eds.), *Proceedings of the 1998 Association for Information Systems Americas Conference* (pp. 92–94). Atlanta, Georgia: Association for Information Systems.

Preece, J., Rogers, Y., Sharp, H., Benyon, D., Holland, S., & Carey, T. (1994). *Human-computer Interaction.* Wokingham, England: Addison Wesley Publishing.

Ramsay, J., Barbesi, A., & Preece, J. (1998). A psychological investigation of long retrieval times on the World Wide Web. *Interacting With Computers, 10*, 77–86.

Roberts, T. (1998, April). Are Newsgroups Virtual Communities? In C. M. Karat & A. Lund (Eds.), *Proceedings of the CHI 98: Human Factors in Computers* (pp. 360–367). Los Angeles, CA, New York: ACM Press.

Rosenfeld, L., & Morville, P. (1998). *Information architecture for the world wide web.* Sebastopol, CA: O'Reilly and Associates.

Salmon, G. (2000). *E-moderating: The key to teaching and learning online.* London: Kogan Page.

Sears, A., Jacko, J., & Borella, M. (1997, March). Internet delay effects: How users perceive quality, organization, and ease of use of information. In J. Preece & M. B. Rosson (Eds.), *Proceedings of the CHI 97: Human Factors in Computing* (pp. 353–354). Atlanta, Georgia, New York: ACM Press.

Shneiderman, B. (1998). *Designing the user interface: Strategies for effective human-computer interaction.* (3rd ed.). Reading, Massachusetts: Addison-Wesley.

Small, R., & Arnone, M. (2000). Evaluating the effectiveness of web sites. In S. Clarke & B. Lehaney (Eds.), *Human-centered methods in information systems: Current research and practice* (pp. 91–101). Hershey, PA: Idea Group Publishing.

Van Nimwegen, C., Pouw, M., & Van Oostendorp, H. (1999). The influence of structure and reading manipulation on usability of hypertexts. *Interacting with Computers, 12*(1), 7–21.

Van Oostendorp, H., & Van Nimwegen, C. (1998). Locating Information in an Online Newspaper. *Journal of Computer-Mediated Communication, 4*(1). Available online at: http://www.ascusc.org/jcmc/

Zhang, P. (2000). The effects of animation on information seeking performance on the world wide web: Securing attention or interfering with primary tasks? *Journal of the Association for Information Systems, 1*(1). Available at: http://jais.aisnet.org/.

Part III

ANALYSIS OF COMPUTER-MEDIATED (COLLABORATIVE) COMMUNICATION

Educational Technology and Multimedia From a Cognitive Perspective: Knowledge From Inside the Computer, Onto the Screen, and Into Our Heads?

Erica de Vries
Laboratory for Educational Sciences, University of Grenoble II, France

Computer programs specifically designed for educational settings form a large share of the multiple uses of multimedia technology for human information processing. In an educational setting, multimedia, or more generally, the way information is presented, is the essential passageway from information stored in computer memory to knowledge constructed by the learner.

A computer program for learning embodies a specific view on the knowledge in a domain, and on the way in which learners acquire knowledge. This chapter claims that the way in which multimedia are used in effect is a result of theoretical views on how learning takes place and on what role the computer should fulfill in the ideal learning context. After an organization of existing research into three subfields, the chapter examines the consequences of multiple perspectives on learning and multiple educational approaches for multimedia research.

MEDIA, MULTIMEDIA, AND HYPERMEDIA RESEARCH

Ever since teaching and learning can be mediated, that is, may take place with an intermediary such as a book or a blackboard between teacher and learner, the question can be asked as to which is the optimal way of transferring knowledge. This is a rather delicate question because it needs specifying what is meant by *the optimal way* and by *transfer of knowledge*. For a long time, the question has been treated in terms of establishing the instructional method that is most cost-effective and that produces high outcomes expressed in learning results. With the development of each new technology, the efficiency question can be asked again, giving rise to a new line of research comparing existing methods with an approach involving new technology. This section briefly structures the field into three different subfields corresponding to the three major debates that have been taking place in this area: the fields of media, multimedia, and hypermedia research.

Media

The first debate centers around the question of whether or not using different media for teaching has an effect on learning. In the context of this question, a *medium* denotes the channel for passing on information. Possible media are a human, a book, a radio, a television, or a computer. According to Clark (1983), one of the participants in the debate, a particular medium does not influence learning because it can be considered as a mere vehicle for delivering instruction. Clark describes two confusions that, he argues, are at the origin of studies that report media effects on learning. The first confusion is between a medium and the instructional method selected, for example, when comparing a human and a computer (media) delivering respectively a lecture and large numbers of exercises (instructional methods). The learning effects measured then can be imputed to the instructional method rather than to the medium. The second confusion is between a medium and its media attributes, for example when a learning effect is attributed to video (medium) whereas in fact the effect is caused by the possibility of zooming in on details (media attribute). Because an attribute may not be exclusive to a medium, zooming in on details can be done on video but also on the computer, Clark (1983) argued that it is unjustified to impute the effect to the medium. According to Clark, the two sources of confusion have led to a large number of unjustified claims about the appropriateness of particular media for teaching and learning.

In reaction to Clark's (1983) reasoning, one could argue that it is a rather artificial operation to want to separate a medium from its defining characteristics. This argument can be found in Kozma (1991). In Kozma's interpretation, a medium consists of a technology, a symbol system, and a number of processing characteristics. By *technology*, Kozma means the physical, mechanical, and electronic aspects that determine the function of the medium, and the surface characteristics that make something be an instance of a specific type of medium. For example, a television is something that emits sound and pictures and that has a screen. But more important are the symbol systems (text, pictures) a medium can employ and the processes that can be performed with it. For example, a radio cannot be used to display pictures (symbol system) and a book cannot easily be used to search for all the occurrences of a certain word (processing characteristic). Following Kozma's (1991) reasoning, it is more fruitful to focus on the influence of different symbol systems and processing capabilities on learning. He makes a strong case for this type of research by stating that the choice of a medium in fact does not enforce exploiting all of its possible symbol systems and processing capabilities (a television that becomes radio, a video-disc player that becomes broadcast television). It is only the capabilities actually used that can be expected to have an effect on learning processes and outcomes. Consequently, Kozma's (1991) review of the media question focuses on the specific characteristics of symbol systems that can be used in a particular medium. *Effects on learning* are studied by looking at how learners construct, structure, and modify their representations of the information, and the quality of the information processes that act on these representations. The main measures used involve free or cued recall of the presented information and tests involving comprehension and solving new problems (see Kozma, 1991, for an overview).

Both aspects of a medium, the symbol system and the processing capabilities, are at the heart of the second and third subfields dealt with in this section, respectively the multimedia and hypermedia research fields.

Multimedia

The second debate focuses on the benefits of multimedia for learning. Multimedia in this context designates concurrent or consecutive presentation of information using text, pictures, sound, animations, and so on. Studies in this field involve comparisons of two or more ways of presenting information such as text and pictures, animations and narrations, or printed and spoken text. In addition, some comparisons focus specifically on whether the information is presented concurrently or consecutively and in which order. At the outset, studies in the field aimed at establishing the value of adding illustrations to instructional texts. Numerous overviews to the literature demonstrate the importance of the issue (e.g. Levie, 1987, Mayer, 1993). With the introduction of the computer, the field has exploded due to the possibilities of using animations and narrations. Multimedia research now embodies all research into presenting information and literature overviews on this enlarged field have started to emerge (e.g. Najjar, 1996). In this line of research, the technology for presenting information is not specifically considered as part of the setting. For example, studies focusing on learning with text and pictures may use pieces of paper or a computer screen as a display device. However, studies may focus on the particular characteristics of the symbol system employed. For example, texts and pictures provide stability, whereas sound or animations are transient. Examples of factors studied are visual versus auditory, verbal versus nonverbal, transient versus stable, symbolic versus nonsymbolic, and unimodal versus multimodal presentations of information. Whereas in media research, learning benefits are measured in terms of memory and comprehension of the presented information, multimedia research in addition involves the question of the cognitive factors that can account for learning benefits, that is, information processing advantages of particular symbol systems. In other words, multimedia research deals with why one way of information presentation works better than another rather than only proving that it does. It stresses explanation of the results in terms of cognitive processes rather than only establishing media differences in terms of learning products. Such explanations are sought in a number of directions. For example, augmenting text with pictures, animations, narrations, and so on, could represent advantages through effects related to motivation and repetition (Glenberg & Langston, 1992), and dual coding and mental model construction (Mayer, 1997). Conversely, difficulties might arise due to limitations of working memory and the high cognitive load associated with the integration of multiple sources of information (Chandler & Sweller, 1991; Mayer & Moreno, 1998).

Hypermedia

The third debate, largely instigated by the development of hypermedia technology, concerns the type of access to information. Traditional media involve decisions regarding the order in which information is presented. The development of hypermedia, more specifically, the introduction of electronic linking, has made it possible to leave part of these decisions to the learner. Whereas multimedia techniques are used to present information in different formats, hypermedia techniques allow manipulating access to the information. This feature introduces the idea of interaction of the learner with the information presented. The learner is thought to profit from hypermedia because it enables self-paced, in-depth, and nonlinear access to vast amounts of information structured in a way that is compatible with the workings of the human mind. Detailed overviews of these claims regarding educational hypermedia can be found in Dillon and Gabbard (1998) and in Tergan (1997a, 1997b).

With the development of hypermedia, a number of studies focused on the effects of differences in the structure of presentations on learning. Types of access are keyword, index, linear, hierarchical and network structures of information. Learners typically are asked to study the information at their own pace and are allowed to navigate, crisscross, or browse the information guided by their own curiosity. Learning outcomes in these studies are often measured in terms of comprehension and quality of written essays (Dillon & Gabbard, 1998). Individual choices of learners are considered to be an asset of hypermedia, but at the same time constitute a problem in hypermedia research. If different hypermedia structures lead to different consultation patterns, should effects on learning be attributed to the structure of information or to the fact that the learners have seen a different subset of information? In any case, there are many issues in the field of hypermedia for learning that remain to be investigated.

Summary of the Conditions and Factors Studied

Table 7.1 summarizes conditions and factors studied in media, multimedia, and hypermedia research. Combining these conditions and factors gives rise to an infinite number of possible ways of presenting information. As has become clear by now, this chapter does not give an overview of the research itself. The overviews of the literature and the meta-studies mentioned in the former sections can be consulted for the details. Ideally, this kind of metastudies will eventually lead to recommendations on the presentation technique to be used for a particular type of knowledge and a particular type of audience. Those overviews will also lead to a number of new research questions to be addressed.

Two remarks can be made regarding studies in the three research lines. The first remark pertains to the prevalence of the use of the computer. The

TABLE 7.1
Conditions and Factors in Media, Multimedia,
and Hypermedia Research (Nonexhaustive)

Research Line	Conditions	Levels of Factors
Media research	Human	Presence–Distance
	Book	Passive–Active
	Television	
	Radio	
	Computer	
Multimedia research	Text	Visual–Auditory
	Scrolling Text	Verbal–Nonverbal
	Illustration	Stable–Transient
	Animation	Static–Dynamic
	Graphic	Unimodal–Multimodal
	Animated Graphics	Simultaneous–Consecutive
	Narration	Manipulable–Nonmanipulable
	Sound	
Hypermedia research	Keyword Search	Free Order–Forced Order
	Index	Structural–Semantic Links
	Linear Acces	
	Hierarchy	
	Network	

computer has become the technology with which many of the media and multimedia conditions can be implemented. Developing an educational application becomes a subject of a discipline called *instructional design*, in which decisions about media, multimedia, and hypermedia choices have to be made. These decisions are important in any situation, not just in situations in which comparisons between presentation conditions are at stake.

The second remark pertains to the theoretical view on learning. The bulk of the research has been carried out in a teaching-as-delivery tradition, that is, the expository approach to teaching and learning. A theoretical perspective has an influence both on the way multimedia and hypermedia are used and on the way learning outcomes are assessed. Nowadays, other theoretical views on teaching and learning coexist, influenced in part by the augmented use of the computer. The existence of these alternative perspectives calls for a redefinition of the field of educational technology.

EDUCATIONAL TECHNOLOGY: THEORIES AND FUNCTIONS

A theoretical perspective determines the view on what learning is, how learning takes place, and how instruction should be carried out to accomplish learning. Approaches to educational technology implicitly or explicitly embody such a theoretical view on learning and instruction. The theoretical perspective may remain implicit, in particular in cases in which the development of an educational program has largely been incited by advances in technology (technology driven). On the contrary, the theoretical view may also be explicit, in particular when an educational program is especially designed as an implementation of a theory of learning and instruction (theory driven). The development of educational programs is part of the larger domain of instructional design. As in other design domains, theory plays an important role in the decisions taken while developing new artifacts (Duffy & Jonassen, 1991). Theory is one of the information sources used by designers. In fact, three levels of information can be distinguished: a theoretical level (concepts), a functional level (performance requirements) and an artifact level (materializations; see De Vries & De Jong, 1999). For example, a proponent of the teaching-as-delivery perspective thinks of learning as the intake of information (theoretical level), conceives of achievement of this goal through a well-designed presentation of the information (functional level), and designs a particular multimedia or hypermedia application (artifact level). Although the three levels are closely related to each other, a position at one level does not fully determine positions at the other levels. The process of design involves establishing relations both between and within levels. Decisions at the artifact level about the form that the product ultimately will have are not taken arbitrarily but are influenced by the functional level, which in turn is influenced by the theoretical level.

The previous section showed the dominance of the teaching-as-delivery perspective in studies investigating educational multimedia and hyper-media. The main objective in such a perspective is the transfer of information taking place between some sender (designer, teacher, researcher) and some receiver (user, learner, subject). This has important consequences for the type of situation studied. The material is presented using a particular technology (medium, format, and structure); a subject studies the material and subsequently performs some criterion task in order to establish the amount of learning that has taken place. Learning measures (dependent variables) include memory (recall), comprehension (paraphrases and inferences) and the resolution of new problems (transfer of learned knowledge). Today, different theoretical perspectives on learning and instruction co-exist partly inspired by technological developments. These perspectives have an impact on the way technology is exploited. They might for example preclude a more active role of the learner besides simply studying material. So what is needed at this point is to specify these alternative perspectives at the theoretical and functional level. The theoretical and functional levels will subsequently provide input for how to implement these viewpoints in multimedia for learning, that is, the artifact level. Ultimately, these levels will prescribe how learning should be assessed, and in particular how learning with the designed artifacts should be evaluated.

Theoretical Perspectives on Learning and Instruction

This section presents the four most widespread theoretical viewpoints on learning and instruction. For the sake of argument, they are presented in their more extreme form. On one hand, this may cause differences between viewpoints to appear as largely exaggerated or artificial. On the other hand, such extreme viewpoints are often encountered in the literature describing a specific type of educational computer program. In any case, a clear presentation of the differences between the viewpoints will help understand the differences at the functional level to which they precisely give rise.

The Behaviorist Perspective. The behaviorist perspective on learning involves determining the relationships between instructional manipulations or stimuli on one hand, and outcome performance or responses on the other (Mayer, 1987). For example, in operant conditioning (Skinner, cited in R. L. Atkinson, R. C. Atkinson, & Hilgard, 1983), learning depends on the consequences of behavior. In order to teach some desired behavior, the environmental stimulus, the desired response behavior, and the reward or reinforcement have to be established. By giving the reward upon occurrence of (steps in) the desired behavior, the latter will take place more often. Learning in this view has taken place when the appropriate stimuli–response associations have been established.

The Cognitivist Perspective. The cognitive perspective on learning includes the factors just mentioned (instructional manipulations and outcome performance), but in addition involves factors such as the characteristics of the learner, learning processes, and learning outcomes (Mayer, 1987). According to this approach, instructional manipulations affect learning processes (paying attention, encoding, retrieving) and thus learning outcomes (acquisition of new knowledge). These learning outcomes in turn influence outcome performance. In addition to establishing the relationship between instructional manipulations and outcome performance, the cognitivist approach is concerned with the states and processes that allow an understanding of these relationships. The objectivist tradition is said to underlie cognitivism (Duffy & Jonassen, 1991) because the world is seen as being structured and organized in terms of entities, properties, and relations independent of individual experience. Learning, in this view, simply means acquiring this objective knowledge structure. The cognitivist view largely underlies the teaching-as-delivery tradition already mentioned. A specific branch of the cognitivist view studies expertise; the knowledge and skills possessed by individuals that are proficient in a specific domain, such as, for example, chess, medicine, and electronic troubleshooting. The main objective of this enterprise is to model domain knowledge, that is, to develop knowledge representations that can account for human performance. In the cognitivist view, learning has taken place when the learner has acquired the knowledge structure of the domain.

The Constructivist Perspective. The constructivist perspective stresses the active involvement of learners in building their own knowledge. The starting points of constructivism are several, summarized by Paris and Byrne (cited in Boekaerts and Simons, 1995). The most important is that learners are actively searching for information as a result of intrinsic motivation. Understanding is more than information take-in; learners structure, organize, and generalize raw information. Organization of and reflection on incoming information means that understanding is never finished; learners correct themselves, and learned knowledge is constantly refined. Reflection on one's own learning makes learners build theories on learning goals, tasks, strategies, and possibilities. Constructivism provides an alternative epistemological base to the objectivist tradition (Duffy & Jonassen, 1991). The main argument of constructivism is that, rather than independently existing in the world, meaning is imposed on the world by the individual. The results of knowledge construction are therefore specific to the individual learner. This position makes it difficult to establish learning because it makes no sense to grade the knowledge construction of one individual as being better than that of another. Both constructions are unique, and any assessment is considered to be normative. Extreme cases of constructivism do not preclude assessment of learning.

The Situationist Perspective. The situationist perspective on learning highlights the idea that the learned knowledge has to be used in real life contexts (Brown, Collins, & Duguid, 1989). Traditional classroom teaching is thought to lead to so-called inert knowledge; abstract knowledge is acquired, but is inaccessible in situations where it is needed (Perfetto, Bransford, & Franks, 1983). According to the proponents of the situationist perspective, authentic activities, that is, the ordinary practices of a domain culture rather than traditional classroom activities are needed for knowledge to be constructed in a form that will be exploitable in the future. An important aspect of learning situations involving authentic activities is the social context in which they take place (Lave & Wenger, 1991). Meaning is not bound to the individual but socially constructed through negotiations among past and present members of the community involved in a domain. A group of individuals involved in the same domain has also been called a *community of practice.* Part of the learning process is to become a member of such a community by adopting the range of appropriate behaviors. In this view, learning has taken place when a person is able to participate and to behave as a member of the community.

The Functional Level: Approaches to Educational Technology

The four Theoretical perspectives on learning and instruction described in the previous section co-exist and give rise to the definition of different functions to be fulfilled by educational technology. As stressed before, a particular position on the theoretical level initiates aspirations on the functional level, but does not fully determine it. In other words, there is no one to one relation between positions on the theoretical and on the functional level. This section presents seven essentially different approaches to educational technology that originated from either one of the four theoretical perspectives. The main difference stressed here is the function that the computer is intended to fulfill or the role that it plays in the instructional situation. Each function roughly corresponds to a type of computer program that exists and that can be read about in the literature or that can be bought today. Two more aspects allow clear distinguishing between these functions. First, the function of the computer is closely related to the specific activity that is proposed to the learner. A range of different learner activities are encountered in presenting the seven functions. Second, each position on the functional level has an essentially different way of dealing with domain knowledge. The objective of this characterization of educational technology approaches is to come to a typology of uses of the computer for learning that than will help us to set a new research agenda for exploiting multimedia.

Presenting Information. One of the first imagined uses of the computer consists of simply presenting information. This approach corresponds to traditional computer-assisted instruction (CAI). Alessi and Trollip (1991) argued that programs for presenting information, called *tutorials*, are appropriate as a first stage of teaching. The role played by the computer is therefore an expository one. Just like a textbook, a tutorial may contain texts and pictures, explanations, examples, and some questions to assure that the learner has assimilated the information before continuing on with the next part.

Using the computer for presenting information is the most straightforward example of the cognitivist perspective to learning and instruction. The knowledge to be acquired is first digested by a teacher or a pedagogical expert, and then put in a form that is judged suitable by the experts, that is, the domain knowledge is put into an organized presentation of information. In this sense, the computer program incorporates the decisions of the domain experts on how to present the domain for teaching purposes (Wenger, 1987). Principles on how to analyze and structure domain knowledge for the purpose of designing instruction can be found in Gagné (1985) and Merrill (1983). The activities proposed to learners also reflect the cognitivist perspective: The learners are supposed to turn pages, study information, and answer to questions.

Administering Exercises. The second imagined use of the computer consists of giving large sets of exercises to the learner. Computer programs fulfilling this function were at first called programmed instruction and later on called *drills*. The main role played by the computer is as an exercise storage and administering device. The program presents sequences of exercises or items that aim at training the learner in a particular aspect. In the general case, this stage is preceded by an expository stage. Its purpose is to allow the learner to acquire speed and accuracy in a particular skill (Alessi & Trollip, 1991).

Drills are inspired by a behaviorist or Stimulus-Response associationist view of learning. For each exercise, the desired behavior of the learner consists of giving the correct answer and the reward consists in some combination of three: being able to go to the next exercise, getting some auditory or visual response of the system, or simply knowing that the right answer was chosen. An excellent review of behaviorism and programmed instruction and the systems that incorporated this approach can be found in Burton, Moore, and Magliaro (1996). It is a delicate matter to speak of knowledge in the behaviorist approach. Knowledge has to be defined in terms of performance or observable behavior. Strictly speaking, there is no knowledge in the computer or in the head of the learner. What is to be learned are the associations between an item and its correct response. The learner's main activity is completing sets of exercises as quickly and correctly as possible.

Genuinely Teaching. A challenging possibility lies in the development of programs that would make the computer act like a human teacher or tutor. This ambition lies at the heart of the project of developing Intelligent Tutoring Systems (ITS). Such a system needs knowledge of the domain to be taught (domain model), knowledge of the student, that is, level of schooling and possible misconceptions (student model), pedagogical knowledge for adopting a teaching strategy (pedagogical module), and the capacity of communicating with the student (human–computer interface). The domain knowledge is explicitly represented (according to Wenger, 1987) in a form that is presumably similar to the knowledge representation of a human expert. The pedagogical module is necessary to decide which part of the knowledge to process next and in what way. The role of the computer in an ITS equals that of a domain expert that can individually teach, coach, and guide the student. Depending on the particular program, this includes playing a teacher, a coach, a fellow student, and so on. The activities carried out by the learner vary according to the particular pedagogical strategy at hand, for example, dialoguing with the system, game playing, problem solving, but the theoretical idea behind it is that the learner eventually acquires the expert model contained in the tutoring system. Therefore, intelligent tutoring systems constitute another implementation of the cognitivist viewpoint on learning and instruction. Examples of experimental ITSs are Scholar and West, developed by respectively Carbonell (1970) and Burton and Brown (1975), both cited in Wenger (1987). *Scholar* teaches the geography of South America by dialoguing on the basis of a semantic network representation. *West* guides the learner while playing a game that involves arithmetic and comparing his or her performance with that of an expert on a number of aspects. An overview of these and other systems can be found in Wenger (1987).

Providing an Information Space For Exploration. A relatively new role for the computer instigated by the development of hypermedia and multimedia is to provide large information spaces for the learner to explore. Hypermedia systems contain text, sound, pictures, videos, and so on, accessible through electronic links. They furnish visual and auditory information that can be integrated in a teaching sequence. The difference with classical tutorials is that the information is organized respecting relations between domain concepts but with no particular presentation order or teaching objectives in mind. The role of the computer is therefore to provide a large space of information that can be explored in any direction by the learner.

The knowledge view advocated is one that argues that it is sufficient to provide a kind of semantic network that exemplifies the topic organization of the domain: a free-access presentation. Hypermedia can be seen as implementing a cognitivist perspective to the extent that the match between the organization of knowledge in the computer and in human memory is stressed. However, when stressing the active role of the learner in exploring the information space, hypermedia can be seen as applying principles of the constructivist perspective on learning. The main activity executed by learners is to browse and explore the information space following their momentary interest. The order in which the information is accessed is therefore dependent on learner actions. The learners' motivation is important, and learners are thought to structure and organize their knowledge as they browse through the information.

A specific form of constructivism interested in hypermedia is *cognitive flexibility theory*. Cognitive flexibility theory (Spiro, Feltovich, Jacobson, & Coulson, 1991, Spiro, Vispoel, Schmitz, Samarapungavan, & Boerger, 1987) is based on the observation that transfer of knowledge to other than the instructional situation is hard to be obtained especially in complex domains. Knowledge is in a sense confined to the facts learned at school, leading to inert knowledge. In their view, essential aspects of knowledge in complex domains are contained in cases. These cases should be presented and studied, highlighting the thematic organization of the domain. Knowledge acquisition for transfer is best acquired by studying cases in the context of different themes and studying themes exemplified by different cases. This form of instruction, according to Spiro et al. (1987, 1991), requires easy access to information, and that is what they implement in hypertext systems. In their proposed systems, learners can browse through different cases and different themes of a domain. In the authors' view, the active involvement of the learner in crisscrossing the domain will lead to individual knowledge construction. The knowledge so constructed is thought to be more flexible and more readily available for application in new situations.

Providing an Environment for Discovering Natural Laws. Another approach to educational technology is to use the computer for modeling the laws of a domain, such as the laws of biology, physics, or chemistry. These environments, called *simulations*, imitate part of reality. For example, in a simulation of a falling object, the learner might be able to change the values of relevant input variables, for example, weight, height, and/or gravity, and then observe the changes caused in the relevant output variables, for example, speed and elapsed time. The role of the computer is to provide an environment for testing actions on a system, actions that would be too costly, dangerous, or time-consuming in the real world. This means that the learner has to carry out activities such as formulating hypotheses, designing experiments, and observing and interpreting results in order to gradually discover the laws underlying the simulation. This type of environment can therefore be recognized as another implementation of the constructivist perspective on learning and instruction. The specific branch of constructivism that advocates the use of simulations is a theory of discovery learning. The approach to knowledge is to model the laws of the domain that are then to be discovered by the learner just as a scientist discovers them in the real world. A theory of discovery learning assumes that learners should execute processes similar to the ones in scientific discovery (see De Jong & Van Joolingen, 1998, for a comprehensive overview). Such processes include defining the problem, stating hypotheses, designing experiments, collecting data, interpreting results, and making new predictions. In order for these processes to work smoothly, some regulative or control (planning, verifying, and monitoring) processes are necessary.

Providing an Environment for Discovering the Laws of Abstract Domains. An even more innovating use of the computer is to provide an environment for the discovery of the laws of abstract domains. Whereas simulations imitate some part of the world, so called *microworlds* incorporate the laws of abstract domains, but the difference between the two is a subtle one. The main criterion is that a microworld can give feedback on actions in abstract domains for which the same kind of feedback does not a priori exist in the real world. The laws of the domain are in a weak sense materialized in the computer environment. The objects manipulated in a microworld have properties associated to both the formal objects of the domain and objects in the real world.

Examples of such domains, and the microworlds that materialize them are programming in LOGO™ (Papert, 1980) and first-order logic in Tarski's world (Barwise & Etchemendy, 1990). LOGO provides a programming language that allows giving commands for a turtle to move on the screen thereby producing drawings. Watching the movements of the turtle on the screen gives immediate feedback on the commands issued. In order to draw more complex figures, the learner needs to break them down into components and build procedures with control structures.

Tarski's World allows learners to build three-dimensional worlds and to describe them in first-order logic. They evaluate the sentences in the constructed worlds and if their evaluation is incorrect, the program provides them with a game that leads them to understand where they went wrong.

The role of the computer is to allow the learner to discover the laws of an abstract domain by construction-type activities and by interpreting the reactions of the microworld. This type of environment closely relates to a third variant of the constructivist perspective according to which learning heavily relies on metacognitive processes. In order to construct one's knowledge, the learner needs to analyze his or her learning needs, plan, control, verify, and reflect on his or her own activities. In addition to learning the abstract domain, learners are thought to learn to regulate their own learning activities.

Providing Environments for Interaction Between Learners. A final functional role of the computer is to provide support for interaction between learners. There are several ways in which this might be accomplished. These Computer-Supported Collaborative Learning (CSCL) environments can fulfill a number of roles as different as a collective memory, a display device, or a genuine medium for communication. The main idea is that the computer centers attention of several learners, synchronous or asynchronous, present or at a distance. The activities by the learners include discussion, text writing, information gathering, and critiquing. Encouraging interaction between learners as an instructional approach fits in the situationist perspective on learning and instruction. The knowledge view is mainly based on the idea that learners will construct their own knowledge in interaction. Therefore, there is often not really a (re)presentation of domain knowledge as such in the computer. An example of such an environment is Computer Supported Intentional Learning Environment (CSILE; Scardamalia & Bereiter, 1994). CSILE is a network system that allows learners and teachers to create a communal database. Learners can enter text and graphic notes into the database on any topic their teacher has created. All students on the network can read the notes and students may build on, or comment on, each others' ideas.

The seven instructional approaches to educational technology and their main characteristics are summarized in Table 7.2. The approaches have been deliberately formulated as functions to be fulfilled by the computer. Their degree of specification corresponds to the middle level of design information, that is, the functional level. Presenting information and administering exercises (tutorials and drills) are functions not specific to computer-based instruction. Moreover, they do no really exploit the capacities of the computer. Although genuine teaching definitely is not a new educational approach, intelligent tutors do represent a revolutionary use of capacities of the computer. The remaining functions, environments for exploration, discovery, and social interaction, have been invented hand-in-hand with the technologies that allowed their implementation.

Another main instructional approach not mentioned so far is to favor learning by capturing the learner's attention and motivation. This ap-

TABLE 7.2
Seven Instructional Approaches to Educational Technology

Instructional Approach (Functional Level)	Computer Program	Theoretical Perspective	Learner Activity	Status of Knowledge
Presenting information	Tutorial	Cognitivist	Reading	Ordered presentation
Administering exercises	Drill	Behaviorist	Doing exercises	Stimulus-response associations
Genuinely teaching	Intelligent Tutor	Cognitivist	Dialoguing amongst others	Representation
Providing an information space for exploration	Hypermedia	Cognitivist/Constructivist	Exploring	Free-access presentation
Providing an environment for dis-covering natural laws	Simulation	Constructivist	Manipulating, observing	Model
Providing an environment for dis-covering abstract domains	MicroWorld	Constructivist	Constructing	Materialization
Providing an environment for inter-action between learners	CSCL	Situationist	Discussing, writing	Construction by the learner

proach is the main reason for creating educational computer games that aim at fulfilling educational objectives by exploiting motivational aspects and the challenges associated to games. The main role of the computer is therefore to motivate the student to stay at the activity. Educational games vary in the activities proposed to the learner. They can be a disguised drill or other question-answering game, a kind of microworld, or simulation in which to accomplish something.

MULTIMEDIA FOR LEARNER ACTIVITIES: THE ARTIFACT LEVEL REVISITED

As the previous section showed, different instructional approaches can be implemented using a computer. The computer has the potential of providing many different learning environments; it can be seen as a metamedium (Kay, cited in Bruillard, 1997). However, an instructional approach does not fully define a particular instructional environment at the artifact level. Media attributes, symbol systems, and available information processes, instead of being intrinsic to a particular technology, are subject to the choices of the designer. A particular educational computer program incorporates such decisions at the artifact level; it exploits multimedia in a specific way.

Huge amounts of research effort have been devoted to understanding the effects of these decisions with respect to memory and comprehension of presented information (see the first section of this chapter). An artifact intended for presenting information, by its design, is expected to encourage the activities of reading and studying. In other words, it should present affordances for these activities (Gibson, 1979). The term *affordance* refers to the real and the perceived properties of an object that determine how it potentially can be used (Norman, 1988). A well-designed object invites to its appropriated use: a door calls for opening it, a chair induces sitting. Nowadays, learners are not only expected to read and to study, educational computer programs should also invite them to manipulate, observe, and discuss with peers. This is why the notion of affordance is critical for building a science of educational technology (see also a discussion by Pea, 1993). How should multimedia and hypermedia be exploited in order to create affordances for the whole spectrum of different activities?

The answer to this question essentially means shifting research efforts from a concern for reading and studying information exclusively to other activities such as exploring information and discussing with peers (see Table 7.2). An example of such an effort can be found in Suthers (1999). Suthers' approach focuses on environments for critical inquiry in which learners discuss scientific topics and construct so-called evidence maps of the data, hypotheses, and theories under scrutiny. This approach corresponds to the seventh function of educational technology presented in the previous section. There are several ways of implementing these evidence maps: in the form of a threaded discussion, a representation using containment of several boxes, a graph with ellipses, boxes, and arrows, or a matrix with symbols in the cells. The main issue here is to study these different representations on their merits for supporting certain learner interactions. In other words, the question is which representation presents affordances for what kind of interactions? The main focus in Suthers' (1999) case would be on interactions involved in critical inquiry, that is, the main function for which the environment is designed. Naturally, this question demands that the effects of different formats be expressed in the appropriate measures, that is, variables that reflect essential aspects of learners' discourse.

Suthers' (1999) proposal for studying different (re)presentations of information in technology designed for encouraging learner interactions shows only one possible research line. Studying the role, advantages, and drawbacks of multimedia in educational technology involves covering the whole range of learner activities listed in Table 7.2. Thus, the benefits of multimedia should be studied for reading and studying, but also for associating, exploring, manipulating, observing, discussing, and constructing. Dependent variables for measuring these benefits should be inspired by these same activities.

CONCLUSION

This chapter reviewed three levels of design information in the field of educational technology: theories, functions, and artifacts. Multimedia research in educational settings traditionally focuses on reading and studying as main learner activities and on memory and comprehension of the presented information as the main performance variables. Nowadays, the diversity of theoretical perspectives on learning and instruction and the corresponding spectrum of functions to be fulfilled by the technology imply a redefinition of the field of educational multimedia at the artifact level. Particular applications are now being designed to encourage discussing, manipulating, and constructing in educational settings. Multimedia research should follow these developments in order to be able to provide recommendations that will be useful as input of design decisions. In other words, designing particular multimedia applications for learning at present involves paying attention to the way in which learners will work with it (discuss, construct, manipulate, etc.). In fact, the field of education could well be a domain where the repercussions of the digital world are felt in a strong sense. The cognitive skills necessary for functioning in the digital world range far beyond basic skills like reading and writing. The execution of tasks with computers, especially learning tasks, as has been shown in this chapter, today poses strong cognitive demands on the individual. One needs to become proficient in skills such as defining problems, finding information, and collaborating in order to effectively function in professional settings as well as educational settings. This chapter made a case for the exploitation of multimedia for situations involving particular learning activities; this approach might well be appropriate for designing multimedia for task execution in general. Multimedia have to be seen as tools that need to be designed to fulfill specific functions depending on the task context.

Finally, there are also important theoretical and methodological implications. Cognitively relevant variables have to be established for each one of the tasks. This would involve a classification into generic categories of tasks. Moreover, measuring the outcomes of manipulations no longer only involves memory and comprehension, but new performance measures are needed. Should these be defined opportunistically for each particular computer program or would it be possible to define classes of outcomes for each task? Designing and evaluating multimedia for a variety of educational goals considerably enlarges the scope of factors and variables that need to be studied in multimedia research.

ACKNOWLEDGMENTS

The author wishes to thank her colleagues from the Laboratory of Educational Sciences of the University of Grenoble II, and in particular, Jacques Baillé, Philippe Dessus, and Benoit Lemaire, for providing an excellent environment for reflecting on the issues presented in this chapter and for their helpful comments on previous versions of the chapter.

REFERENCES

Alessi, S. M., & Trollip, S. R. (1991). *Computer-based instruction: Methods and development* (2nd ed.). Englewood Cliffs, NJ: Prentice Hall.

Atkinson, R. L., Atkinson, R. C., & Hilgard, R. E. (1983). *Introduction to psychology*. San Diego: Harcourt, Brace, & Jovanovitch.

Barwise, J., & Etchemendy, J. (1990). *The language of first order logic*. Stanford, CA: Center for the Study of Language and Information.

Boekaerts, M., & Simons, P. R.-J. (1995). *Leren en instructie* [Learning and instruction]. Assen: Van Gorcum.

Brown, J. S., Collins, A., & Duguid, P. (1989). Situated cognition and the culture of learning. *Educational Researcher, 18,* 32–42.

Bruillard, E. (1997). *Les machines à enseigner* [Teaching machines]. Paris: Hermès.

Burton, J. K., Moore, D. M., & Magliaro, S. G. (1996). Behaviorism and instructional technology. In D. H. Jonassen (Ed.), *Handbook of research for educational communications and technology* (pp. 46–73). New York: Macmillan.

Chandler, P., & Sweller, J. (1991). Cognitive load theory and the format of instruction. *Cognition and Instruction, 8,* 293–332.

Clark, R. E. (1983). Reconsidering research on learning from media. *Review of Educational Research, 53,* 445–459.

De Jong, T., & Van Joolingen, W. R. (1998). Scientific discovery learning with computer simulations of conceptual domains. *Review of Educational Research, 68,* 179–202.

De Vries, E., & De Jong, T. (1999). The design and evaluation of hypertext structures for supporting design problem solving. *Instructional Science, 27,* 285–302.

Dillon, A., & Gabbard, R. (1998). Hypermedia as an educational technology: A review of the quantitative research literature on learner comprehension, control and style. *Review of Educational Research, 68,* 322–349.

Duffy, T. M., & Jonassen, D. H. (1991). Constructivism: New implications for instructional technology? *Educational Technology, 31*(5), 7–12.

Gagné, R. M. (1985). *The conditions of learning and theory of instruction* (4th ed.). New York: Holt.

Gibson, J. J. (1979). *The ecological approach to visual perception.* Boston, MA: Houghton Mifflin.

Glenberg, A. M., & Langston, W. E. (1992). Comprehension of illustrated text: Pictures help to build mental models. *Journal of Memory and Language, 31,* 129–151.

Kozma, R. B. (1991). Learning with media. *Review of Educational Research, 61,* 179–211.

Lave, J., & Wenger, E. (1991). *Situated learning: Legitimate peripheral participation.* Cambridge, UK: Cambridge University Press.

Levie, W. H. (1987). Research on pictures: A guide to the literature. In D. M. Willows & H. A. Houghton (Eds.), *The psychology of illustration. Volume 1: Basic research* (pp. 1–50). New York: Springer Verlag.

Mayer, R. E. (1987). *Educational psychology.* Santa Barbara, CA: Harper Collins.

Mayer, R. E. (1993). Comprehension of graphics in text: An overview. *Learning and Instruction, 3,* 239–245.

Mayer, R. E. (1997). Multimedia learning: Are we asking the right questions? *Educational Psychologist, 32,* 1–19.

Mayer, R. E., & Moreno, R. (1998). A split-attention effect in multimedia learning: Evidence for dual processing systems in working memory. *Journal of Educational Psychology, 90,* 312–320.

Merrill, M. D. (1983). Component display theory. In C. M. Reigeluth (Ed.), *Instructional design theories and models* (pp. 279–333). Hillsdale, NJ: Lawrence Erlbaum Associates.

Najjar, L. J. (1996). Multimedia information and learning. *Journal of Educational Multimedia and Hypermedia, 5,* 129–150.

Norman, D. A. (1988). *The psychology of everyday things.* New York: Basic Books.

Papert, S. (1980). *Mindstorms: Children, computers and powerful ideas.* New York: Basic Books.

Pea, R. D. (1993). Practices of distributed intelligence and designs for education. In G. Salomon (Ed.), *Distributed cognitions: Psychological and educational considerations* (pp. 47–87). Cambridge, MA: Cambridge University Press.

Perfetto, G. A., Bransford, J. D., & Franks, J. J. (1983). Constraints on access in a problem solving context. *Memory and Cognition, 11,* 24–31.

Scardamalia, M., & Bereiter, C. (1994). Computer support for knowledge-building communities. *The Journal of the Learning Sciences, 3,* 265–283.

Spiro, R. J., Feltovich, P. J., Jacobson, M. J., & Coulson, R. L. (1991, May). Cognitive flexibility, constructivism and hypertext: Random access instruction for advanced knowledge acquisition in ill-structured domains. *Educational Technology,* 24–33.

Spiro, R. J., Vispoel W. P., Schmitz, J. G., Samarapungavan, A., & Boerger, A. E. (1987). Knowledge acquisition for application. In B. K. Britton & S. M. Glynn (Eds.), *Executive control processes in reading* (pp. 177–199). Hillsdale, NJ: Lawrence Erlbaum Associates.

Suthers, D. D. (1999). Representational bias as a guidance for learning interactions: A research agenda. In S. P. Lajoie & M. Vivet (Eds.), *Artificial Intelligence in Education. Open learning environments: New computational technologies to support learning, exploration and collaboration* (pp. 121–128). Amsterdam: IOS Press.

Tergan, S.-O. (1997a). Misleading theoretical assumptions in hypertext/ hypermedia research. *Journal of Educational Multimedia and Hypermedia, 6,* 257–283.

Tergan, S.-O. (1997b). Multiple views, contexts, and symbol systems in learning with hypertext/hypermedia: a critical review of research. *Educational Technology, 27(4),* 5–18.

Wenger, E. (1987). *Artificial intelligence and tutoring systems.* Los Altos, CA: Morgan Kaufmann.

Chapter 8

Analyzing Communication in Team Tasks

Simone Stroomer
TNO Human Factors, Soesterberg, the Netherlands

Herre van Oostendorp
Institute of Information and Computing Sciences,
Utrecht University, the Netherlands

This chapter is about analyzing communication. Communication is an important factor in group and team performance. In performing a team task, the members of a team need to work together, coordinate their actions and share information. In a real team task, the performance of one team member may even depend on the performance of the other team member and on the information this team member distributes. An important means to work together, coordinate actions, and share information is by communication. By analyzing communication in teams, one can learn about team performance and how to optimize this performance. In learning situations, like cooperative or collaborative learning, communication is also an important factor because communicating involves exchanging information, and by collecting information, people can learn about a particular thing. Analyzing the exchange of information may explain something about the way people solve problems and how they learn to do so. With regard to computer mediated education, communication analysis may be helpful to explore training interventions and to find out what kind of information presentation or elicitation is most effective for learning and for team training. Communication analysis may therefore be helpful designing tools that can support learning in a computer-mediated environment. More generally, knowing how to analyze communication enables us to reveal bottlenecks experienced by group members in achieving a team task. On the basis of this knowledge, tools as part of a computer-supported work environment can be designed—or improved—that effectively support group performance.

COMMUNICATION ANALYSIS

Communication has been analyzed by researchers of many different disciplines and with many different aims. Philosophers, psychologists, linguists, sociologists, ethnomethodologists, and artificial intelligence researchers all contribute to the analysis of communication. Because of this multidisciplinarity, many different terms are used to describe communication analysis, like conversation analysis, dialogue analysis, and discourse analysis. These differently named studies were often performed for different goals, which of course resulted in different approaches to communication analysis. The goals of these studies vary from expanding general knowledge of communication (fundamental research) to exploring team performance by unraveling the communication used within a team (an applied perspective). The different goals of these studies and the use of different approaches to analysis make it difficult to compare the results of the studies.

However, in this chapter, some approaches to communication analysis are compared with regard to the methods that were used for analysis (the studies discussed in this chapter are summarized in tables in Appendix A). We focused on team tasks, that is, tasks for which members have to work together and share information to get the job done. Furthermore, we wanted to select and describe studies that are conducted from different perspectives and approaches (see following text). The comparison concerns the *sensitivity, validity,* and *reliability* of the methods of analysis. The term sensitivity means that the method that is used for the analysis can actually measure differences in communication (or in performance) that are evoked by the manipulation of variables in the experiment. The term reliability means that when the same method of analysis is used again—by the same person or by another person—it will produce the same results. The term validity means that the method actually measures what it is supposed to measure (Cook & Campbell, 1979). An important aspect will be the relationship (e.g., the correlation coefficient) between characteristics of communication and quality of task performance. In team tasks, communication (and its characteristics) are part of the process of task performance that leads to the product of task performance. For example, a characteristic of communication can be that a team member provides relevant information without the other team member having to ask for it. This characteristic enhances the quality of task performance, because it enables the team to perform faster than a team in which the team members have to ask for all relevant information. From a process–product perspective, it is important to know whether the method of analysis is able to distinguish communication categories that are significantly—positively or negatively—related to final task performance.

Therefore the goal of this chapter is to explore what kind of method of communication analysis is sensitive, reliable, and valid in order to establish the relationship between characteristics of communication and the quality of performance. In comparing the methods, attention is also paid to the communication units that are used in the analyses and the categorization of these units. These terms, *communication unit* and *categorization*, will first be explained. Communication units are the parts into which conversation is broken down to enable analysis. The part of communication that can be regarded as a separate unit depends on the goal of the analysis and on the categories in which these units have to be ordered or categorized. The kind of categories that are important for analysis also depends on the goal of the study. Together, the goal of the study and the kind of categories determine the length and the function of the units of the communication. There are different levels at which communication can be broken down (H. H. Clark & E. V. Clark, 1977): (1) the topic level (thematic structure), (2) the communicative or interactional level (the speech act), and (3) the message level (the propositional content). At the topic level relatively long fragments of conversation are analyzed to investigate, for example, the kind of topics or the number of topics discussed in a conversation or the way in which contributions are tuned to the topic of conversation. The part of conversation concerning one topic is called *a conversational game* and consists of a closed sequence of utterances (a more extensive explanation of the term *game* is given in the discussion of the study of Doherty-Sneddon et al., 1997). At the next level of unitization, the topic or the conversational game can be analyzed in "pairs that belong together" or "interactional rounds". At this level of analysis, communication units are ordered according to rules of succession. A pair of two adjacent sentences, like question–answer or action–reaction, forms a unit, that is, a pair of sentences that belong together. At the next level of analysis, these pairs of sentences that belong together can be broken down into separate expressions or message units. The length of the expression is determined by the change of turns in a conversation. A turn or an expression can consist of several message units, which are the smallest units that convey meaning: one sentence or even part of a sentence. Message units must be identified post hoc by cues that give an indication of the context of these units. These cues, called *prosody* and *paralinguistic signs of communication* (Gumperz, 1992) are intonation, pitch, tempo, and pause structure. Siegel, Dubrovsky, Kiesler and McGuire (1986) developed a set of guidelines to divide communication into what they called remarks (level of expressions, message units). The most important of these guidelines are: (a) Each remark comprises a clause (subject, verb, object); (b) Count conditional clauses (like sentences containing "if", "then") as one remark; (c) Do not count unintelligible/incomplete remarks or verbal ticks such as "you know."

To make sense out of the separated units of communication, these units can be ordered or classified into categories. What kind of categories should be used depends on the goal of the analysis. Categories can be based on the content of what is said, on the meaning of what is said (depending on the context, different things can be meant by the same content of an utterance), on the kind of behavior the communication refers to, or on the sequence or structure of the conversation.

To describe and compare several studies,[1] they are grouped into three kinds of research: experimental, ethnographic and descriptive. The next section starts by describing these kinds of research.

COMPARING STUDIES

According to Haft-van Rees (1989), studies concerning communication analysis can be grouped into studies originating from linguistics and studies originating from sociology; respectively, analyses with or without a theoretical framework. Studies originating from sociology focus on social interaction between members of a social community and are called *conversation analyses* (Sacks, Schegloff, & Jefferson, 1974). This analysis is not based on a priori theories and therefore distinctions between utterances are only made when the empirical data show that the speakers themselves use these distinctions. Due to the lack of a theoretical framework, it is not possible to generalize the findings of these studies. One of the studies originating from sociology is *ethnomethodology*, which examines the implicit and shared knowledge that members of a social group use to order and interpret their everyday social interactions.

Studies originating from linguistics mainly focus on the relation between form and function of language. This is a more pragmatic analysis and is called *discourse analysis* (Grice, 1978). Variables like age, sex, and class are considered to influence communication. The framework for these studies is the *speech act theory* (Searle, 1969). Because of this theoretical framework, these studies can be systematically interpreted and generalized. However, the framework does not provide the opportunity to examine the interactionally developing interpretation of utterances, though the work by Clark and colleagues extended this framework considerably (H. H. Clark & Schaefer, 1989; H. H. Clark & Brennan, 1991).

---

[1]The studies discussed in this chapter were selected by entering keywords like "communication," "discourse," "conversation," "analysis," "team," and "group" in search engines and on the Internet. An important consideration in this search activity was to finally have sufficient studies in different categories of research. This selection is not meant to be an exhaustive review, but merely a description of differences in approach.

In H. H. Clark's (1996) model of human communication several levels
of communication are defined in which the fundamental, interactive process of *grounding* is assumed to operate. Grounding is the basic process by
which conversation partners keep track of their "common ground" and its
moment-by-moment changes. To put it in other words, speakers assure (by
trying to find positive and negative evidence) whether conversation partners have understood what the speaker meant. The main levels Clark distin-
guishes are briefly: (1) "execution" (of some behavior by the speaker) and
"attention" (by the listener), (2) "presentation" and "identification," (3)
"signaling" and "recognition," and (4) "proposal" and "consideration."
These acts of speaker(s) and listener(s) have to be carefully coordinated.
This model seems sufficiently extensive to cover the dynamic character of
communication during face-to-face settings but also in computer-mediated
environments. For instance, Hancock and Dunham (2001) recently showed
that in using Clark's framework, the availability of a simple, explicit turn
marker during text-based, computer-mediated communication facilitated
the construal of meaning (Level 3) and reduced the number of verbal coordination remarks required to ground communication.

Similar to the division in conversation analysis and discourse analysis
studies, communication analyses can also be divided into experimental and
ethnographic research (Masoodian, 2001). *Ethnographic research* investigates
the natural occurring interactional aspects of communication in real work
environments. Ethnographic research can be compared with conversation
analysis in the way that it investigates a real life situation without a priori
theories about the communication. Experimental research investigates
communication in a controlled experimental laboratory set-up, using sim-
plified group tasks and manipulating variables. Like discourse analysis, *experimental research* is a systematic study and is based on a theoretical framework. A third kind of research can be added to these two groups—the
descriptive research. This kind of research forms a separate group because it
differs in the way the data are gathered and in the purposes for which the
data are used. Unlike the ethnographic study, participants in a descriptive
study perform a task in a laboratory setting instead of working in real-life
environments. However, the descriptive study is also different from an experimental study because no independent variables are varied or manipulated. Descriptive research merely describes the system of analysis that is
used to describe the communication.

In the next sections, several ethnographic, experimental, and descriptive studies of communication analysis are discussed. In the Appendix (see
Table 8A.1), we present a brief overview of the studies now described. In
this overview the studies are represented by a number of features like task,
variables, categories for the communication analysis, communication units,
approach, validity, reliability, and sensitivity.

Ethnographic Communication Research

Kelly and Crawford (1996, 1997) performed two ethnographic studies (Table 8A.1). The first study investigated conversation between students during a classroom physics experiment using Microcomputer Based Laboratories. The classroom communication was broken down into message units in order to see how the actors put these smallest building blocks together to produce larger structures. These larger units (speech acts) often show an intended act by a group member and Kelly and Crawford therefore called them *action units*. Based on these action units, patterns of interaction were identified. Finally, it was analyzed how thematically tied interaction units form sequence units. These different levels of analysis were brought together in a scheme for an overview of the sequence of utterances in time. According to Kelly and Crawford, this kind of analysis can be extended to compare across groups and across time within a group. However, there is no actual proof of the reliability of this kind of analysis because in ethnographic research, it is difficult to repeat a study the exact same way. The validity of this kind of analysis is not mentioned. The term *sensitivity* is not applicable since ethnographic studies do not manipulate variables to sort out a specific effect.

Experimental Communication Research

Compared to the few ethnographic communication studies there are a lot of experimental communication studies. These experimental studies can be subdivided by the kind of task that the participants perform in the experiment. The goal and the content of the task or the assignment influence the process of performance and therefore communication, as mentioned by Erkens, Andriessen, and Peters (Chap. 10, this volume). McGrath (1984) made a division between group tasks based on four performance processes: *generate, execute, negotiate,* and *choose.* The division of these performance processes led to the definition of eight team tasks: creativity tasks and planning tasks (generate), intellective tasks and decision-making tasks (choose), cognitive conflict tasks and mixed-motive tasks (negotiate) and performance/psycho–motor tasks and contests/battles/competitive tasks (execute). In this section, the division between the experimental studies only concerns three of these group tasks: planning tasks (when performance requires a process of generating plans), intellective tasks (when performance requires solving problems for which there is a standard solution or norm), and decision-making tasks (when performance requires solving problems for which there is no standard solution or norm).

Planning Task Experiments

Kanki, Lozito, and Foushee (1989), Waller (1999), Post, Rasker, and Schraagen (1997), Rasker, Schraagen, and Stroomer (2000) and Doherty-Sneddon et al. (1997) used a planning task in their experiments (see Table 8A.2).

Kanki et al. (1989) tried to find a method to analyze the communication between two team members in a flight simulation task. To test the method, existing data of two groups of flight crews were compared for the structure and direction of the communication. The communication unit they used consists of two turns: *initiating speech* and *response speech*. Initiating speech was classified as commands, questions, observations and dysfluencies. Response speech was divided into acknowledgments, responses larger than acknowledgments, and zero response. This analysis was performed at the communicative or interactive level: pairs that belong together. Although nothing is mentioned about the validity and reliability, it is mentioned that the same results were shown in a different research setting, which suggests some degree of reliability. The method is sensitive in the way that the analysis differentiated communication patterns of low-error teams from those of high-error teams.

Communication within flight crews was also analyzed by Waller (1999). Communication was regarded to be the verbalization of the behavior the flight crew performed (like in the illocutionary approach, in which the speech act is considered to be an intention to do or to achieve something (cf. Searle, 1969; Grice, 1978). Instead of classifying communication units, merely the presence or absence of communication was coded every ten sec. Crew performance could be measured in this way because the flight crew can only perform by talking about their task. Nothing was mentioned about the validity of this study though. The intercoder reliability is .79 (Cohen's kappa), though discrepancies in coding were discussed until they were resolved. Concerning the sensitivity, the analysis differentiated crew performance based on the frequencies in the coding categories.

Post et al. (1997) used a computer based, fire-fighting simulation in their experiment. Based on a task analysis, they developed a coding structure to analyze the communication between two team members, who performed the task of observer and decision maker. The communication unit was not specified in advance, but the units were coded according to their meaning or content into categories concerning *data, task, domain knowledge, metacommunication,* and *remaining.* The hypothesis was that for improved performance, communication needs to be more than data communication. Therefore, the frequencies in the other categories, excluding data communication, were counted. However, nothing was mentioned about the validity of this analysis. Also, nothing can be said about the sensitivity of this kind of analysis because only one condition provided communication for the analysis (in the other conditions communication took place by sending standard e-mail messages). The reliability of the study was not mentioned either.

An additional experiment using the same fire-fighting task was performed by Rasker et al. (2000). Groups had different communication opportunities, which led to differences in task performance and to differences in the results. The communication in those teams that had the opportunity to talk during task performance was analyzed. Each utterance that conveyed meaning was scored as a separate communication unit. Based on a task analysis and on earlier category schemes (Post et al., 1997) a coding scheme of five main categories was developed (*data, evaluate activities, evaluate knowledge, team,* and *remaining*). The coding scheme also divided the utterances in statements, questions, answers, and confirmations across different time periods. The question was whether utterances in certain categories would help the team members to develop a more accurate, shared mental model. The groups of the different conditions differed in performance, which could be explained by the differences in their communication. It can be discussed, however, whether it is valid to assume that communication about each other's roles in task performance leads to the development of a more accurate shared mental model and therefore to better performance. The interrater reliability for this analysis was .9 (Cohen's kappa).

Doherty-Sneddon et al. (1997) used a map task in which participants had to exchange information about the map they both had in front of them. They called their analysis the conversational game analysis (the term *game* represents the fact that conversation has rules that both participants know and follow). A game is a closed sequence of utterances aimed at achieving a (sub-) goal. For this multilevel analysis, different communication units were used at different levels of analysis. The units were coded according to their function or content into six types of game categories: *instruct, check, align, query–yes/no, query–open answer,* and *explain.* To obtain valid measures, task performance as well as the communicative process were measured and looked at in conjunction. Looking at only one of these aspects would have led to different or incomplete conclusions. The interrater reliability reached a *good* level by four coders agreeing on where the games began and on the type of game. Regarding the sensitivity of the analysis, discerned the dialogue structures of different conditions.

Only two of these five planning task studies are reasonably similar in their way of analyzing because they used the exact same task: the fire fighting simulation. There were also two studies using a flight simulation task, but they had very different purposes for analyzing conversation.

Decision-Making Task Experiments

Here, four experiments are discussed that used a decision-making task: Adrianson and Hjelmquist (1999, Experiment 1), Dennis, A. R. Easton, A. C. Easton, George, and Nunamaker (1990), Lea and Spears (1991), Van Hiel and Schittekatte (1998) (see Table 8A.5).

Adrianson and Hjelmquist (1999) used a task called the *social dilemma game* in three communication conditions: face-to-face, computer-mediated with the participant's real name, and anonymously computer-mediated. The communication unit was defined as a message expressing one main idea. The coding scheme consisted of five main content categories: *strategy, norm, game reaction, value reaction,* and *metacommunication*. There were no a priori categories; categories were established during the process of analyzing. Subcategories also distinguished between suggestions, agreements, questions, and answers. The research question was whether face-to-face and computer-mediated communication would differ qualitatively and quantitatively. In addition to the coding of the type and frequency of the utterances, the participants had to fill out questionnaires about their communication. The validity of these measures was not mentioned. The correspondence between the coding of two independent coders was 70%, which is reasonably reliable. The analysis was sensitive in the way that it measured differences between the communication contents of the different conditions.

Dennis et al. (1990) compared the type of communication used by ad hoc groups and established groups, both working with an Electronic Meeting System. In the task, two salesmen compete for a sales territory and the participants have to generate solutions and vote for the best solution. The communication was electronic and tagged with the participant's name. Beside measuring the total amount of communication and the equality of participation of the group members, communication was coded in the categories: *uninhibited comments* (not task related), *process oriented comments, directly conflictive/critical comments,* and *indirectly conflictive/critical comments.* The communication unit was determined based on the guidelines of Siegel et al. (1986). The validity and reliability of this study (as well as those of other studies investigating differences between ad hoc and established groups) are questionable because different studies show very different results. However, the analysis was sensitive in the way that it distinguished between the type of communication of both groups.

Lea and Spears (1991) also compared decision-making performances of different kinds of groups. They manipulated two independent variables: (1) whether group or individual identity is made salient, and (2) whether members of a group are co-present or de-individuated (isolated and anonymous). Attitudes of the participants on four controversial topics were measured before and after a group discussion. The comparative participation and the amount of discussion were measured by recording the number of messages and the number of words. Like in the previous study, communication was divided into units according to the guidelines of Siegel et al. (1986). Remarks were coded in three content categories: *discussion oriented remarks, social oriented remarks,* and *situation and system oriented remarks.* This study claims to be valid in the way that it measures the real differences between computer-mediated communication and face-to-face interaction, by avoiding problems of interpretation in, for example, speaking versus typing, although the validity of the analysis itself is not mentioned. The reliability of this analysis also is not mentioned. As for the sensitivity, the results of the analysis are in accordance with the difference between the conditions: greater polarization of the group members is associated with fewer words, shorter messages, smaller proportion of discussion remarks, and more social remarks.

Another study comparing the effects of group characteristics on information exchange is the study of Van Hiel and Schittekatte (1998). They varied gender composition of the groups, accountability (responsibility in the way that accountable people can be made to explain/justify their conduct, and their behavior can be judged by a forum) and group perspective (the presence of another group promotes social in-group identification and in-group liking, which motivates intergroup distinguishing behavior). Four-person groups had to select one of three candidates for the position of chairman. Nine information items about the candidate were read by all group members (shared information) and two items were read by only one member (unshared information). The analysis measured the number of information items mentioned (shared, unshared and total). The communication unit was not defined. The validity and reliability of the analysis were not mentioned. Concerning the sensitivity, analysis of the communication showed differences between groups in the different conditions regarding the distribution of new/unshared information within a team.

Intellective Task Experiments

Experiments using a task for which there is one correct solution, are described in the studies of Dennis (1996), Erkens (1997) and Adrianson and Hjelmquist (1999, Experiment 2) (see Table 8A.7).

Dennis (1996) compared communication during group decision making with or without a Group Support System. Six-person teams had to select one of three students for admission to the university. Four participants received a subset of information favoring the same suboptimal alternative, and two received a subset of information favoring the optimal alternative. Both the amount of exchange of common information and of unique information were scored (with a subdivision of supporting, neutral, and opposing information compared to the prediscussion preferences). The validity of this kind of analysis was not mentioned. A second rater reviewed the information exchange of four randomly selected groups and the two raters agreed on .96 of the ratings (measured as 1–[number of disagreements divided by information exchanged]). The analysis of the total amount of information exchange did not discern the two groups but the analysis of the amount of information split up in unique and common information did.

Erkens (1997) developed a dialogue analysis system: the Dialogue Structure Analysis. By using the Verbal Observation System (VOS), utterances were coded according to content as well as communicative aspects (see also Erkens, Andriessen, and Peters, chap. 10, this volume, in which this study is described in more detail). To test a theoretic model of how a student should behave in performing a team task, Erkens compared the result and the process of cooperative problem solving between student–student teams and student–monitor (simulated team member) teams. The task performed in the experiment (the *camp puzzle*) comprises finding the personal characteristics of six children by combining informative statements about these children. The available information about the six children is limited and distributed among the team-members, but by exchanging and arranging it in a matrix, it is possible to deduce the characteristics of each child. The definition of the communication unit was that it could be discerned by a pause, a comma, or a dot and had a single communicative function. By using the VOS, the communicative aspects of the utterances were scored on several variables: *line number, point of time, speaker, meant recipient, topic index, specification category, kind of sentence, interpersonal reference, explicit illocution, allocation, monitoring, intonation,* and *references.* The variable, kind of sentence, specifies the function of the utterances, which was divided into six categories: *attention signals, informative utterances, argumentative utterances, elicitation, responsive utterances,* and *actions.* The interrater reliability on the VOS variables varied between 64% and 97%. The interrater reliability on the categories within the kind of sentence variable was 70%. Regarding sensitivity, an extensive comparison between the dialogue functions of the two conditions was not possible, because of the differences in data collection (e.g., speech versus messages in writing). However, within teams, the distribution of utterances over the function categories differs between the student and the monitor. With regard to the validity, looking at the pattern of communication made it possible to link the quality of task performance to the quality of the cooperation dialogue (in terms of the function of utterances).

Adrianson and Hjelmquist (1999, Experiment 2) developed a scheme for qualitative coding, in which it would be possible to look at the pattern of communication (questions, answers, agreements, disagreements, number of ideas, and feedback chains). The mode of communication was varied: face-to-face, anonymously computer mediated, and computer-mediated communication in combination with the participant's real name. The communication unit is defined by the expression of one main idea, regardless of how many words, clauses, or sentences it holds. The main content categories are: *information, ideas, solution, strategy, summary, meta communication, jokes,* and *uncoded messages.* The categories were not fixed a priori. Some of the categories were subdivided into given information, questions, and answers. The validity of this kind of analysis was not mentioned. The interrater reliability was 70%. As for the sensitivity, the analysis only measured differences between the conditions (the different modes of communication) on the category "ideas."

The experimental intellective task studies use different communication units in the analyses. The message unit of Erkens is discerned from the rest by a pause, a comma, or a dot (syntactic separating rule), whereas the communication unit of Adrianson and Hjelmquist (1999) is discerned from the rest based on the content of the unit, regardless of the number of words, clauses, or sentences that could be included. And Dennis (1996) did not define a communication unit at all. All these studies were based on a frequency analysis: the number of communication units in the different categories. Adrianson and Hjelmquist (1999) meant to look at the communication pattern, but the only thing that makes their study transcend beyond frequency counting was the subdivision of the categories in given information, questions and answers. This subdivision offers the opportunity to have a look at an interactive aspect of communication.

Descriptive Communication Research

In the analyses of the experimental studies just mentioned, conditions were compared based on the number of communication units in the different categories. However, descriptive studies, as will be discussed, reason that this kind of frequency analysis leaves out important aspects of communication, like the interaction between participants and the sequence of the utterances. The studies that we discuss here as being descriptive research are those of Kumpulainen and Mutanen (1999) and two studies by Bowers, Jentsch, Salas, and Braun (1998) (see Tables 8A.8 and 8A.9).

According to Kumpulainen and Mutanen (1999) studies based on frequency counts in different categories do not highlight the important aspects of communication like the actual interaction process and the construction of meaning in interaction. Partly inspired by sociocultural perspectives and interactional ethnography, Kumpulainen and Mutanen (1999) developed an analysis framework to study the student's verbal interaction in different learning situations. In this framework, peer interaction is seen as a dynamic process. The communication unit in this kind of analysis is a message unit, a meaningful unit of speech. Communication is analyzed at three dimensions: (1) functional analysis of the verbal interaction; (2) cognitive processing: In what way do students approach and process the learning of tasks in interaction?; and (3) social processing: Focuses on the social relationships developed in the interaction. The functional analysis concentrates on the illocutionary force of utterances, which must therefore be identified in the context. For each interaction situation, categories have to be defined on a post hoc basis according to the particular situation. The language functions, that were divided, are listed in the overview of the study in Appendix A. Though validity and reliability are not explicitly mentioned, Kumpulainen and Mutanen (1999) implied that the method is valid and reliable by suggesting that it can be used for crosscultural studies of peer group interaction. To check the validity of the interpretation of the utterances, one can easily return to the original data that are modeled in a structural map. Regarding the sensitivity, this analysis demonstrates the student's different communicative strategies.

In the experiments of Bowers et al. (1998) participants had to perform a certain task during a simulated flight scenario. In the first experiment, a mapping task had to be performed and in the second experiment a new authority, who did not answer, had to be contacted. In these studies, no independent variables are manipulated because these are descriptive studies. The first study compared frequency counts with pattern analysis of the communication during the mapping task. The communication unit used in the pattern analysis was a two-statement sequence, which was called an *adjacency pair*. The categories focused on the interactional function of the communication units. The validity and reliability of this comparison were not mentioned. Concerning the sensitivity, the pattern analysis resulted in a better discrimination between the communication of different performance groups than the frequency count analysis. The second study also compared the two kinds of analysis, but used a different task: contacting an authority, who did not answer. The experiment was set up in the same way as the first experiment, only this time the participants were actual pilots and they performed a different task. Because of the different task, different categories were used, which were based on the coordination and evaluation of an actual aircrew. The communication unit was a two-statement sequence. The validity and the reliability were not mentioned. This kind of analysis was sensitive because, in addition to the discrimination of groups by frequency counts, the pattern analysis provided further details about these differences.

DISCUSSION

To compare different communication analysis studies, it seems useful to group the different studies according to the purpose of the research and according to the kind of task that is used in the research. In this comparison, studies were divided in ethnographic, experimental, and descriptive research. A division according to task was only applied to the experimental studies. This was partly due to the large amount of experimental studies described in this chapter, whereas only two ethnographic and three descriptive studies were discussed. However, a division based on the kind of task that is used may in principle also be applied to ethnographic and descriptive studies. A task-based division of other kinds of research will probably add other kinds of tasks to the division as it was used in this chapter (planning, decision making, intellective tasks) because the original task division of McGrath (1984) contained as many as eight kinds of tasks.

In discussing the different studies selected for this chapter, it appeared that the communication unit and the way in which the analysis was performed were not always described clearly. Most studies discussed here did define the categories, if used, and some studies even mentioned the theoretical framework behind the categories. However, in general, a theoretical framework was lacking and categories were defined on an ad hoc basis.

Most importantly for the comparison and generalizability of the methods of analysis are the validity, reliability, and sensitivity of these methods. A lot of the studies that were described here did not mention detailed information about the validity and reliability of the method of analysis. Most of the time, the validity of the methods was not mentioned at all. More quantitatively, in this chapter we discuss 18 studies (Appendix A) and almost none of them discussed the validity of the analysis or of the set of categories that is used. The exceptions are the studies by Erkens (1997) and Doherty-Sneddon et al. (1997). Often the sensitivity of a method also is not mentioned, but this can often be inferred by looking at the results of the analysis. This way, the amount of information concerning the sensitivity of the communication analyses is more positive: In approximately all studies, the effects of the independent variables are reported (15 of the 16 studies; the two ethnographic studies do not count here). The negative exception is the study by Post et al. (1997). Thus, at least, there is an effect of, for example, group treatment or restriction in communication possibilities on frequencies of certain communication categories, though it is less clear what these frequencies, really mean in terms of validity. Though the reliability of analysis is sometimes referred to by mentioning the interrater correspondence, the interrater correspondence is determined in different ways (negotiating until establishment of joint agreement, percent of correspondence in the scored data, and Cohen's kappa). As to the reliability, the available information is mixed: Ten out 18 studies report their analyses in terms of reliability. In the studies that report the reliability, the degree of this reliability seems to be satisfactory.

All in all, in the studies presented in this chapter, the methodological aspects of the analyses often were not clear or were not mentioned at all. The possibility that these different kinds of research do not differ with respect to the validity, reliability, and sensitivity is therefore still conceivable. In order to find this out, and to make theoretical and practical progress, in future research, the kind of analysis should be described as clearly as possible and as completely as possible.

Even after this comparison of different studies, it is impossible to conclude with a recommendation for one specific method of analysis. However, it is possible to say something about the distinction between the different kinds of analysis. Although the kind of analysis that should be chosen depends on the goal of the research (ethnographic, experimental, descriptive), and on the kind of task that is used (e.g., planning, decision making, or intellective task), it is possible to further distinguish between analysis focussed on content and analysis focussed on the structure of communication. Depending on the goal of a study, a certain task will be used in the study. And depending on both the goal and the task of the study, one can focus on frequency counts of content categories or on documenting the pattern or structure of communication. For example, Waller (1999) simply counted the frequencies of certain utterances to be able to refer to the amount of times in which certain behavior occurred. Opposed to this, Kanki et al. (1989) tried to find a way to predict the performance of teams based on their sequential pattern of communication. This difference between the focus on content and the focus on pattern in analysis is of a more general importance because the choice for one or the other kind of research may also depend on the experience of the participants in the study (group or team) with the task that has to be performed in this study. Experienced team members, for example, may have developed a more or less standard procedure for their communication and information exchange. By analyzing this kind of communication, one probably wants to know about the content of the information that is exchanged in order to test the process underlying the performance of the team. However, when the goal of the study is to look at the effect of changing the standard procedure for com-

munication or when the participants in a study have to perform new kinds
of tasks or when the study involves new teams performing certain tasks, it
might be desirable to extend the analysis of the process as performed by the
team with the pattern of communication.

Kumpulainen and Mutanen (1999) called studies, like experimental discourse analyses that use frequency counts as a method, *process–product-
studies*. In these studies, communication or interaction is categorized in predefined categories of a coding scheme and the participant's achievement
and performance are statistically linked to these frequencies. These relationships provide insight in the relative importance of process distinctions
to final task performance measures. As such, they contribute to our knowledge of the validity of the method of analysis. For instance, the study by
Erkens (1997) mentioned this kind of data. However, if one wants to explore the possibilities of certain interventions in team functioning, it might
be useful to study the pattern of communication by itself, because pattern
analysis can provide additional information about aspects of communication that help a team to perform well; for instance, the way the team members react to each other, and whether it is efficient to repeat certain things
in exchanging information, and so on.

We agree with Kumpulainen and Mutanen (1999), and Doherty-Sneddon et al. (1997) that to obtain valid measures, communication processes as
well as task performance has to be measured and looked at in conjunction.
We want to add, in line with H. H. Clark (1996), that it is particularly informative to analyze the joint actions of speakers and listeners (e.g. Hancock &
Dunham, 2001). That is, on each level of communication, as distinguished
by H. H. Clark (1996), an action of the speaker requires a compatible action of the addressee (listener). A communicative act like "presenting" a
signal (e.g., a sentence or a gesture) is only successful when the addressee
responds with an action to "identify" the signal (Level 2). Progress in communication depends on the successfulness of these joint actions. This kind
of analysis also has to be related to constraints imposed by the specific task
of participants (e.g., a task performed by a cockpit crew versus a task in a
control room of a nuclear power station).

From this point of view, we can conclude that taking the pattern of communication into account when analyzing the communication of a team or a
group will probably add some extra value to the results of the analysis because this information can make the process of task performance more explicit and may therefore increase the validity of the analysis. However, pattern analysis will only be manageable when the task that has to be
performed by the participants is relatively simple, when standardized teamwork is not a requisite, and when the members of the team are not yet at-
tuned to one another.

Whether focusing on the content or on the pattern of communication, it would be useful when the methods and/or the results of studies concerning communication analysis could be generalized to other research settings. To enable this, studies should at least define the communication level used for analysis or the level at which the communication was broken down and analyzed (cf. H. H. Clark, 1996). Furthermore, the categories used to analyze communication should be defined clearly and the theoretical framework, the empirical data, or the task analysis on which the selection of these categories is based should also be mentioned.

REFERENCES

Adrianson, L., & Hjelmquist, E. (1999). Group processes in solving two problems: Face-to-face and computer-mediated communication. *Behaviour & Information Technology*, *18* (3), 179–198.

Bowers, C. A., Jentsch, F., Salas, E., & Braun, C. C. (1998). Analyzing communication sequences for team training needs assessment. *Human Factors*, *40*(4), 672–679.

Clark, H. H. (1996). *Using language*. Cambridge, England: Cambridge University Press.

Clark, H. H., & Brennan, S. E. (1991). Grounding in communication. In L. B. Resnick, R. M. Levine, & S. D. Teasley (Eds.), *Perspectives on socially shared cognition* (pp. 127–149). Washington, DC: American Psychology Association.

Clark, H. H., & Clark, E. V. (1977). *Psychology and language*. New York: Harcourt Brace Jovanovich.

Clark, H. H., & Schaefer, E. F. (1989). Contributing to discourse. *Cognitive Science*, *13*, 259–294.

Cook, T. D., & Campbell, D. T. (1979). *Quasi-experimentation. Design & analysis issues for field settings*. Chicago: Rand McNally.

Dennis, A. R. (1996). Information exchange and use in small group decision making. *Small Group Research*, *27*(4), 532–550.

Dennis, A. R., Easton, A. C., Easton, G. K., George, J. F., & Nunamaker, J. F. (1990). Ad hoc versus established groups in an electronic meeting system environment. In J. F. Nunamaker & R. H. Sprague (Eds.), *Proceedings of the Twenty-Third Annual Hawaii International Conference on System Science* (Vol. 3, pp. 23–29). Los Alamitos, CA: IEEE Computer Society Press.

Doherty-Sneddon, G., O'Malley, C., Garrod, S., Anderson, A., Langton, S., & Bruce, V. (1997). Face-to-face and video-mediated communication: A comparison of dialogue structure and task performance. *Journal of Experimental Psychology: Applied*, *3*(2), 105–125.

Erkens, G. (1997). *Coöperatief probleemoplossen met computers in het onderwijs: het modelleren van coöperatieve dialogen voor de ontwikkeling van intelligente onderwijssystemen*. [Cooperative problem solving with computers in education: Modelling of cooperative dialogues for the design of intelligent educational systems]. Unpublished doctoral dissertation, Utrecht University, the Netherlands.

Grice, H. P. (1978). Some further notes on logic and conversation. In P. Cole (Ed.), *Syntax and semantics, Volume 9: Pragmatics* (pp. 113–128). New York: Academic Press.

Gumperz, J. J. (1992). Contextualization and understanding. In A. Duranti & C. Goodwin (Eds.), *Rethinking context: Language as an interactive phenomenon* (pp. 229–252). Cambridge, England: Cambridge University Press.

Haft-van Rees, M. A. (1989). *Taalgebruik in gesprekken, inleiding tot gespreksanalytisch onderzoek*. [Use of language in Conversation: Introduction to discourse analytical research]. Leiden: Martinus Nijhoff.

Hancock, J. T., & Dunham, P. J. (2001) Language use in computer-mediated communication: The role of coordination devices. *Discourse Processes, 31*(1), 91–110.

Kanki, B. G., Lozito, S., & Foushee, H. C. (1989). Communication indices of crew coordination. *Aviation, Space, and Environmental Medicine, 60*(1), 56–60.

Kelly, G. J., & Crawford, T. (1996). Students' interaction with computer representations: Analysis of discourse in laboratory groups. *Journal of Research in Science Teaching, 33*(7), 693–707.

Kelly, G. J., & Crawford, T. (1997). An ethnographic investigation of the discourse processes of school science. *Science Education, 81*(5), 533–559.

Kumpulainen, K., & Mutanen, M. (1999). The situated dynamics of peer group interaction: an introduction to an analytic framework. *Learning and Instruction, 9,* 449–473.

Lea, M., & Spears, R. (1991). Computer-mediated communication, de-individuation and group decision-making. *International Journal of Man–Machine Studies, 34,* 283–301.

Masoodian, M. (2001). *A review of the empirical studies of computer supported human-to-human communication* [Internal rep.]. Manuscript in preparation, Odense University, Denmark.

McGrath, J. E (1984). *Groups: Interaction and performance.* Englewood Cliffs, NJ: Prentice-Hall.

Post, W. M., Rasker, P. C., & Schraagen, J. M. C. (1997). *The role of communication and coordination in team decision making in a command & control task* (Rep. TM 97 B004). Soesterberg: TNO Human Factors.

Rasker, P. C., Schraagen, J. M. C., Stroomer, S. M. (2000). *The effect of intra-team feedback on team performance after developing a shared mental model* (Rep. TM 00 B010). Soesterberg: TNO Human Factors.

Sacks, H., Schegloff, E. A., & Jefferson, G. (1974). A simplest systematics for the organization of turn-taking in conversation. *Language, 50,* 696–735.

Searle, J. R. (1969). *Speech acts.* Cambridge, England: Cambridge University Press.

Siegel, J., Dubrovsky, V., Kiesler, S., & McGuire, T. W. (1986). Group processes in computer-mediated communication. *Organizational Behavior and Human Decision Processes, 37,* 157–187.

Taylor, J. T., & Cameron, D. (1987). *Analysing conversation: Rules and units in the structure of talk.* Oxford: Pergamon Press.

Van Hiel, A., & Schittekatte, M. (1998). Information exchange in context: Effects of gender composition of group, accountability, and intergroup perception on group decision making. *Journal of Applied Social Psychology, 28*(22), 2049–2067.

Waller, M. J. (1999). The timing of adaptive group responses to nonroutine events. *Academy of Management Journal, 42*(2), 127–137.

APPENDIX

An overview of the different communication analysis studies, ordered in ethnographic, experimental, and descriptive research. The studies are presented along a list of categories: the *author* of the study, the *year* the study was published, the *task* the participants in the study had to perform, the *variables* in the study, the *categories* along which communication was analyzed, the *communication unit* into which communication was broken down, the *approach* of the study to communication analysis, the *validity* of the method of analysis, the *reliability* of the method of analysis, and the *sensitivity* of the method of analysis.

TABLE 8A.1
Ethnographic Research

Author Year	*Kelly and Crawford* *1996*	*Kelly and Crawford* *1997*
Task	Grade 12 students worked in groups on microcomputer-based laboratories (MBL) to link oscillatory motion to graphical representations (physics).	Experimentation in a physics classroom.
Variables	None. ethnographic research.	None. Ethnographic research.
Categories	None. Analysis focused on the structure of the conversation.	None. Analysis of the structure of conversation by topical and sequential analysis.
Communication Unit	*Units at the level of the expression:* *Message unit:* smallest unit of linguistic meaning. *Action unit:* one or more message units representing intended act. *Units at the communicative/ interactional level:* *Interaction unit:* one or more action units when (potential) response is induced or suggested. *Units at the topic level:* *Sequence unit:* thematically tied interaction units.	*Message unit:* smallest unit of linguistic meaning
Approach	Ethnographic approach to analysis. Multiple level analysis: at the message unit level, at the communicative or interactional level, and at the topic level.	Ethnographic research in combination with discourse analysis performed at the level of the message unit.
Validity	Not mentioned.	Not mentioned.
Reliability	Not mentioned. Though, according to Kelly and Crawford this analysis system can be extended to compare across groups and across time within a group.	Not mentioned; see previous study.
Sensitivity	Not applicable because there is no comparison between conditions.	Not applicable because there is no comparison between conditions.

TABLE 8A.2
Experimental Research: Planning Tasks

Author Year	Kanki et al. 1989	Waller 1999
Task	Two-person flight simulator.	Professional airline flight crews (3 persons) performed five flights in a full-motion flight simulator.
Variables	*Independent variable:* performance on flight-simulator task (low or high error). *Dependent variable:* frequency ratio of initiating speech, response speech, and of the interaction (I*R).	*Independent variable:* nonroutine events in the simulation. *Dependent variables:* Performance (frequency of errors). Occurrence of three types of behavior (collecting and transferring information, distributing tasks, and task prioritization). Average time.
Categories	*Initiating speech:* Commands Questions Observations Dysfluencies *Response speech:* Larger than acknowledgement Acknowledgment Zero response	Information collection and transfer. Task prioritization. Task distribution. Nonroutine event verbalization.
Communicaiton Unit	Two-part sequences representing initiating and response speech.	For every 10-sec interval, the presence or absence of verbalizations of the three types of behavior was coded.
Approach	Analysis at the level of the communicative act; pairs that belong together.	Analysis at the level of the expression/message unit by coding presence/absence of communication.
Validity	Not mentioned.	Not mentioned.
Reliability	Not explicitly mentioned, though the same results in a different setting also imply some kind of reliability	Interrater reliability of .79, Cohen's kappa.
Sensitivity	By means of this analysis, the communication patterns of low-error teams were differentiated from those of high-error teams.	Based on the frequency scores, the analysis discriminated between the crews with different performance results.

TABLE 8A.3
Experimental Research: Planning Tasks

Author Year	Post et al. 1997	Rasker et al. 2000
Task	Fire fighting task: a computer simulation in which an observer and a decision maker have to rescue as many people as possible by using restricted resources.	Fire fighting task: a computer simulation in which an observer and a decision maker have to rescue as many people as possible by using restricted resources.
Variables	*Independent variable:* The kind of communication: Individuals. Unrestricted communication. Restricted communication without shared knowledge. Restricted communication with shared knowledge. *Dependent variable:* Team performance and (in the unrestricted communication condition), the kind of communication.	*Independent variable:* communication opportunity: free talk, standard e-mail messages or free talk during the first half and e-mail messages during the second half of the experiment. *Dependent variables:* team performance and the kind of communication.
Categories	Data communication Task communication Domain knowledge communication Metacommunication Remaining communication In the categories *data, task,* and *domain knowledge,* communication control (whether a message was received and understood) was also rated.	Main content categories: Data Evaluate activities Evaluate knowledge Team Remaining
Communication Unit	Not specified	Utterance that conveyed meaning (expression/message unit).
Approach	Frequency counts in content categories probably at the level of the expression/message unit.	Analysis at the level of the expression/message unit.
Validity	Not mentioned.	Not mentioned. It can be questioned, though, whether communication about each other's tasks leads to more accurate shared mental models and therefore to better team performance.
Reliability	Not mentioned.	Interrater correspondence of .9 Cohen's kappa.
Sensitivity	Not mentioned.	On some categories, the analysis discriminated between the communication of teams with different performance results.

TABLE 8A.4
Experimental Research: Planning Tasks

Author Year	*Doherty-Sneddon et al.* *1997, Experiment 1*	*Doherty-Sneddon et al.* *1997, Experiment 2*
Task	Map task: Participants have different maps and the instruction giver has to tell the instruction follower about the route so that he can reproduce it.	Map task: Participants have different maps and the instruction giver has to tell the instruction follower about the route so that he can reproduce it.
Variables	*Independent variable:* The kind of communication: face-to-face versus co-present audio only. *Dependent variable:* dialogue structure and the map-deviation score for each dialogue.	*Independent variable:* Video-mediated communication with eye contact and video-mediated without eye contact versus remote audio only. *Dependent variable:* The number of games of each type that were initiated per dialogue.
Categories	*Games (categories according to the function of communication):* Instruct Check Align Query yes/no Query open answer Explain	The first dialogues of each pair of participants were game coded (see categories of first experiment).
Communication Unit	Two levels of analysis: *Conversational game* (at the topic level): closed sequence of utterances aimed at achieving goal. *Moves* (at the communicative level): the different turns within the conversational game.	No unit mentioned. However, filled pauses ("ehm" or "uhm") were also coded and an analysis on the number of words was performed so the communication level that was scored was probably at word level.
Approach	Multilevel analysis: at the topic level (games), and at the communicative level (moves).	Full transcriptions of the dialogues, including filled pauses, false starts, repetitions, and interruptions. Analysis performed at the level of the interactional act in which moves are combined to games.

(Continued)

196

TABLE 8A.4
(Continued)

Author Year	Doherty-Sneddon et al. 1997, Experiment 1	Doherty-Sneddon et al. 1997, Experiment 2
Validity	To adequately compare and evaluate, different kinds of communication task performance as well as the communicative process were measured and looked at in conjunction because looking at only one of these aspects would have led to different (incomplete) conclusions.	Not mentioned.
Reliability	Coding reliability: Four coders reached a "good level" of agreement regarding where the games began and regarding the game type.	Three expert coders reached a good level of agreement regarding the coding of the games in the different game categories.
Sensitivity	The analysis discerned the dialogue structures of the different conditions.	The analysis discerned between the number of words and turns in the different conditions.

TABLE 8A.5
Experimental Research: Decision Making Tasks

Author Year	Adrianson and Hjelmquist 1999, Experiment 1	Dennis et al. 1990
Task	Social dilemma game	Electronic Meeting System: "Parkway Drug Case": ranking answers from best to worst.
Variables	*Independent variable:* The kind of communication: face-to-face versus computer mediated communication. *Dependent variable:* the communication pattern (salient features).	*Independent variable:* type of group: established or ad hoc. *Dependent variable:* Amount of communication Equality of participation Type of communication
Categories	Strategy Norm Game reaction Value reaction Metacommunication	Uninhibited comments (nontask communication) Process oriented comments Direct conflict Indirect conflict

(Continued)

TABLE 8A.5
(Continued)

Author Year	*Adrianson and Hjelmquist* *1999, Experiment 1*	*Dennis et al.* *1990*
Communication Unit	Unit expressing one main idea, distinguishable from the rest of the discourse with regard to content, regardless of how many words, clauses or sentences.	To determine the separate units, they used the method of Siegel et al. (1986).
Approach	Analysis at the level of the expression/message unit.	Frequency counts of units in the different categories at the level of the expression/message unit.
Validity	Not mentioned. (Besides measuring communication by coding the type and frequencies, it was also measured by a questionnaire that participant filled out).	A significantly negative correlation of the quality of decision with the number of conflictive or critical comments in ad hoc groups. The interpretation of the results may not be unambiguous because there was significantly more variation between established groups than between ad hoc groups.
Reliability	Interrater correspondence of 70%.	Different studies comparing ad hoc and established groups have shown different results: in some, ad hoc groups perform better; in some, established groups perform better, and in some, as in this study, there is no difference between the two. So the reliability of this study can also be questioned.
Sensitivity	The analysis discriminated the communication of the different conditions.	The study significantly distinguishes between the type of communication that occurred in established and in ad hoc groups.

TABLE 8A.6
Experimental Research: Decision-Making Tasks

Author Year	Lea and Spears 1991	Van Hiel and Schittekatte 1998
Task	Discussion on four controversial issues (nuclear power, privatization of industry, government subsidy of arts, positive discrimination for minority groups) using an electronic mail system. Performed by first-year psychology students in groups of three.	Hidden profile task: Four-person groups of first year psychology students had to select one of three candidates running for chairman.
Variables	*Independent variables:* Salient group versus individual identity. Participants co-present versus deindividuated (= physically isolated). *Dependent variables:* Opinion before and after the discussion. Estimation of attitudinal position of coparticipants. The number of messages, words, comparative participation rates, and so on.	*Independent variables:* Homogeneous / heterogeneous gender composition of the group. Context perspective (control, intergroup, accountability). *Dependent variables:* Alternative chosen (before and after the discussion). Consensus. Discussion time. Number of items mentioned. Proportion of shared vs. unshared information.
Categories	Number of messages (e-mail). Number of words. Message length. Number of remarks. Number of discussion-oriented remarks. Number of social-oriented remarks. Situation and system-oriented remarks. Paralanguage use.	Number of items mentioned. Shared information. Unshared information.
Communication Unit	Unitization according to the method of Siegel et al. (1986) (at the expression/message level).	Not specified.
Approach	Frequency counts in the three content categories at the level of the expression/message unit, based on an underlying theoretical framework.	Analysis probably at the topic level.

(Continued)

TABLE 8A.6
(Continued)

Author Year	Lea and Spears 1991	Van Hiel and Schittekatte 1998
Validity	Not mentioned.	Not mentioned.
Reliability	Not mentioned, though other studies in this field may show different results.	Not mentioned.
Sensitivity	The results support the difference in the amount of polarization between the conditions in the way that greater polarization was associated with fewer words, shorter messages, smaller proportion of discussion remarks, and more social remarks.	The only difference between the groups, as demonstrated by this analysis, was the total number of items mentioned.

TABLE 8A.7
Experimental Research: Intellective Tasks

Author Year	Dennis 1996	Erkens 1997
Task	Hidden profile task: Six-person business student groups had to select one student from a set of three for admission to the university.	Logigram/logikwis: Puzzle in which the personal characteristics of 6 people have to be found by combining the aspects of the given information and putting it in a matrix.
Variables	*Independent variable:* Interacting with or without a Group Support System (computer). *Dependent variables:* The amount of exchanged information. New information learned by each group member. Whether the group decision matched the decision indicated by the information discussed. Decision quality (the proportion of groups making the optimal decision) for groups with and without GSS.	*Independent variable:* The communication partner: communication between two students or communication between a student and the monitor of the program (simulated team-member). Because of this manipulation, the kind of communication also differed: verbal versus in writing via menu structures respectively. *Dependent variables:* task performance of the groups and the process of performing measured by the communication of the team.

(Continued)

TABLE 8A.7

(Continued)

Author	Dennis	Erkens
Year	1996	1997

Categories	*Exchanged information:* common or unique task-information. The unique information was subdivided in supporting, neutral and opposing information as compared to the prediscussion preferences of the participants.	Communication functions: Attention signals Informative utterances Argumentative utterances Elicitation Responsive utterances Actions
Communication Unit	No unit specified.	Discerned by a pause, comma, or a dot and has a single communicative function (expression/ message unit).
Approach	Probably analysis at the level of the expression/message unit.	Analysis at the level of expression/message units. Concerning the pattern of the communication the effectiveness of transitions between two utterances was also analyzed.
Validity	Not mentioned.	The communication pattern linked the quality of the task performance and the quality of the cooperation dialogue.
Reliability	Two raters agreed on 96% of the ratings.	The interrater reliability for the VOS system varies from 64 to 96%. Within the function categories, the interrater reliability was 70%.
Sensitivity	The analysis of the amount of information exchange did not distinguish between the Group Support System (GSS) and the non-GSS groups. However, the distinction between unique and common information did: GSS groups exchanged a lower proportion of unique information.	Within teams, the distribution of utterances over the function categories differs for the student and the monitor.

TABLE 8A.8
Experimental Research

	Intellective tasks	*Descriptive Research*
Author	*Adrianson and Hjelmquist*	*Kumpulainen and Mutanen*
Year	*1999 Experiment 2*	*1999*
Task	Criminal puzzle	Design task in geometry (constructing three dimensional objects pictorially represented on a plane).
Variables	*Independent variable:* The kind of communication: face-to-face versus computer-mediated communication. *Dependent variable:* The communication pattern (questions, answers, agreements, disagreements, number of ideas given, and feedback chains).	No independent variables, because descriptive research. Analysis at three dimensions: Functional analysis Cognitive processing Social processing
Categories	Information: background from the written material. Ideas: information giving, elaboration or inference about suggestions. Solution: discussion about solution and consensus decision. Strategy: statements referring to strategy. Summary: summarizing what has been said. Meta-communication: statement referring to communication itself. Jokes: statement without the purpose of being a serious suggestion. Uncoded messages: comment to an earlier text (without question).	*Language functions:* Informative Reasoning Evaluative Interrogative Responsive Organizational Judgmental (agree/disagree) Argumentational Compositional Revision Dictation Reading aloud Repetition Experiential Affectional
Communication Unit	Unit expressing one main idea, distinguishable from the rest of the discourse with regard to content, regardless of how many words, clauses or sentences.	Message unit: a meaningful unit of speech.
Approach	Analysis at the topic level; counting frequencies in content categories.	The functional analysis is at the level of the expression/message unit.

(Continued)

202

TABLE 8A.8
(Continued)

	Intellective tasks	Descriptive Research
Validity	Not mentioned.	Because the conversation is modeled in the structural map, it is easy to return to the original data and check the validity of the interpretation. However, Kumpulainen and Mutanen (1999) mentioned that a more sophisticated analytical framework is required.
Reliability	Interrater correspondence of 70%.	Two researchers analyzed the data, negotiating disagreements until joint agreement was established. According to Kumpulainen and Mutanen (1999) the method can be applied to crosscultural studies of peer-group interaction.
Sensitivity	The analysis only discriminated the communication of the different conditions in the category, *ideas.*	The analysis demonstrated differences in the student's communicative strategies.

TABLE 8A.9
Descriptive Research

Author	Bowers et al.	
Year	*1998, Study 1*	*1998, Study 2*
Task	Simulated flight scenarios in which high coordination demands were imposed while performing a mapping task.	Simulated flight scenarios in which pilots were ordered to contact a new authority, who did, however, not answer.
Variables	No independent variables, because descriptive research. This study compares two kinds of communication analysis, frequency counts (single statement data) and pattern analysis (two statement sequences), on the distinction they make between highly effective and lowly effective flight crews (effectiveness is based on performance on a mapping task)	No independent variables, because descriptive research. This study compares two kinds of communication analysis, frequency counts (single statement data), and pattern analysis (two statement sequences), on the distinction they make between highly effective and lowly effective flight crews. (Effectiveness is based on the time needed to identify the communication problem.)

(Continued)

Author	Bowers et al.	
Year	1998, Study 1	1998, Study 2
Categories	Uncertainty statements Action statements Acknowledgements Responses Planning statements Factual statements Nontask related statements	Leadership Situation awareness Adaptability Mission analysis Standard Assertiveness
Communication Unit	Two-statement sequences (adjacency pairs).	Two-statement sequences (adjacency pairs).
Approach	Analysis of pattern (instead of content) at the communicative or interactional level.	Analysis of pattern (instead of content) at the communicative or interactional level.
Validity	Not mentioned. Still no real pattern/sequential analysis, for the sequence is only as long as two statements and the results are still based on counting the frequencies.	Not mentioned. Still no real pattern/sequential analysis, for the sequence is only as long as two statements and the results are still based on counting the frequencies.
Reliability	Not mentioned.	Not mentioned.
Sensitivity	The pattern analysis did a better job of discriminating between different performance groups than did the analysis based on frequency counts.	In addition to some significant differences in communication between the performance groups demonstrated by the frequency counts analysis, the pattern analysis provided further details about differences between good and poor performers.

Chapter 9

Being There or Being Where? Videoconferencing and Cooperative Learning

Frank Fischer
University of Tuebingen

Heinz Mandl
University of Munich, Germany

Worldwide, virtual universities and other virtual educational institutions have been developing during the last years as an extension to traditional settings. New technologies enable new forms of communication between learners and between teacher and learner. For example, imagine this: As part of a seminar, two learners collaboratively work on a case problem while being spaciously apart but connected via desktop video conferencing on their home computers. Supposing that the Internet will increase in bandwidth and speed, this could be one of the standard virtual learning scenarios. Recently, many studies have been conducted focusing on technological feasibility and aspects of course delivery as well as the implementation of video conferencing technology in organizations. Their results mostly indicate rather encouraging subjective experiences of the learners. For example, subjective evaluations of participating students are often very similar to those in traditional settings. Participants felt that video conferencing was as effective as face-to-face instruction and they appreciated not losing work time (e.g., Langille, Sargeant & Allen, 1998). Video conferencing enables interaction between learners and teachers for whom it would be difficult if not impossible to meet face-to-face (e.g., Sembor, 1997). However, very little is known on how learners really learn collaboratively in video conferences and how the conditions of interaction in video conferencing influence the processes of collaborative knowledge construction. The same is true for the issue of how to facilitate collaborative knowledge construction in a setting like this. Nevertheless, there are some presumptions stemming from discussions and theoretical reflections expressing some severe concerns about learning with such audiovisually supported computer networks. These concerns may not be reflected in the more macroscopic and more subjective results of the research on delivery and implementation. Those presumptions can be reduced to the following statements:

1. In video conferencing, learners are forced to spend more effort on explicitly coordinating their learning activities.
2. Due to the fact that the learning discourse is impaired in video conferencing, less of the more important contents can be discussed.
3. Due to the reduced process quality of collaborative knowledge construction in video conferencing, learning outcomes are lower.
4. Negotiating a common meaning or perspective is more difficult in video conferencing. Therefore, knowledge convergence may be reduced.
5. To foster learning outcomes and knowledge convergence in video conferencing, interactive graphics are adequate means.

We conducted a series of studies to investigate the potential learning opportunities as well as possible negative effects of dyadic desktop video conferencing for cooperative learning. In what follows, we map theoretical aspects as well as results of some empirical studies to these five presumptions.

IN VIDEO CONFERENCING, LEARNERS ARE FORCED TO SPEND MORE EFFORT ON EXPLICITLY COORDINATING LEARNING ACTIVITIES

A main focus in the research on video conferencing-based interaction is on the more formal aspects of communication and on off-task talk. Results of empirical studies show that the time delay between a speaker's utterance and a hearer's perception of it can cause substantial differences in the formal discourse structure. Asynchrony between picture and sound transmission even promotes these differences (O'Connaill & Whittaker, 1997). Moreover, time delay and the asynchronicity between picture and sound are regarded as causes for the higher frequency of unintended overlaps (i.e., two or more persons talking at the same time) and unintended interruptions (Fussell & Benimoff, 1995). To avoid these disturbances, communicants frequently produce longer turns in comparison to face-to-face situations (Anderson et al., 1997).

The reduced range of possibilities in nonverbal interaction might also have a negative effect on communication in video conferencing environments (Heath & Luff, 1993; O'Connaill & Whittaker, 1997). Participants in video conferencing may not have direct eye contact, so it is far more diffi-cult to trace the gaze of the other (gaze tracking or gaze awareness) than in a face-to-face condition. Moreover, deictic gestures directed to specific screen contents may be less well perceived by the video conferencing part-ner. Together, these problems can hinder the development of a shared per-spective on the discussed topic (J. S. Olson, G. M. Olson, & Meader, 1997).

As a consequence of these factors, learners in video conferencing may have to make more explicit verbal efforts to coordinate their activities. This additional coordination effort is regarded as a side effect of the technology. In evaluating the role of explicit coordination for learning outcomes, con-troversial positions can be found. Some researchers assume that when more explicit effort for coordination become necessary, less capacity and time re-main for discussing the more relevant task contents. Therefore, coordina-tion is supposed to have a negative influence on collaborative knowledge construction. From this perspective, the ideal collaboration would be a col-laboration without words (see Cannon-Bowers & Salas, 1998).

Researchers from the sociogenetic research tradition take the opposite position. In this point of view, explicit coordination is of high importance for the learning outcomes. The collaborative verbal coordination during problem solving or decision making is regarded as the precursor of the later individual cognitive and metacognitive approaches to complex tasks. Thus, coordination is regarded as prerequisite for individual self-direction or self-guidance (Rogoff, 1991; see Vygotsky, 1978; Wertsch, 1991).

Recent empirical studies concerning video conferencing, learning, and coordination have reflected those different perspectives. A pilot study con-ducted by Gräsel, Fischer, Bruhn, and Mandl (2001) compared dyads learn-ing in a videoconference with dyads learning face-to-face. Learners in both settings had to negotiate common solutions for a case problem and repre-sent it graphically by using computer-based interactive graphics and text tools. Learners in the video conferencing setting as well as learners in the face-to-face condition used the same software tools. Each of the learners had one keyboard and one mouse. All learners had been made familiar with the learning environment. Subjects were eight university students of educational psychology. The learning discourse was transcribed and ana-lyzed both quantitatively and qualitatively (Fischer, Bruhn, Gräsel, & Mandl, 1999) with respect to different aspects of coordination and collaborative knowledge construction. They especially differentiate task-related coordi-nation from technology-related coordination. The latter apply to the han-dling of the learning environment, e.g., how to use the mouse or which font in which size should be used for representing something on the screen (e.g., "OK I suppose it is the right button there, try it"). The authors sup-posed that an increased proportion of utterances with such content might be the cause of reduced learning outcomes when learning time is kept constant. *Task-related coordination* is revealed by utterances that serve to *coordinate the joint proceeding*, for example the planning of the next step in solving the case problem (e.g., "Let's start with one or two hypotheses"). Results of this pilot study indicate that dyads in video conferencing produce more utterances concerning technology-related coordination than dyads collaborating face-to-face. With respect to task-related coordination, no differences could be found.

A study by Fischer, Bruhn, Gräsel, and Mandl (2000) used a comparable setting but comprised more subjects (48 learners) than the aforementioned study and extended the collaboration time from about 1 hour and one case problem to about 3 hours and three case problems. Moreover, it included measures of individual and collaborative learning outcomes. Results show that learners in the video conferencing environment did not differ from face-to-face learners in terms of the explicit coordination of their learning activities. Moreover, explicit coordination effort does not mean reduced learning outcomes. Even the contrary is true: Differentiating between technical coordination and task-related coordination, the researchers found that cooperative learning in a video conferencing environment does not differ from face-to-face cooperative learning concerning task-related coordination. Furthermore, task-related coordination is not negatively but positively correlated with individual learning outcomes. Even more surprisingly, learners in the video conferencing environment did not produce more utterances related to *technology-related* coordination. This coordination aspect showed a negative correlation with *collaborative* outcomes, indicating that dyads might not perform as well when they have to spend more time talking about technical aspects of their collaboration. Interestingly though, technology-related coordination does not show any relation to *individual* learning outcomes. These effects might indicate that compensatory individual activities, as often reported in literature on technology-based learning environments, play a major role in explaining this result (see Gräsel et al., 2001). A plausible explanation of the seemingly contradictory findings of the Gräsel et al. (2001) study and the Fischer et al. (2000) study concerning technology-related coordination is the learners' *experience* in using the technology. In the Gräsel et al. study, collaboration time was limited to 1 hour. This limited time frame might have demanded too much of the learners and may have caused them to concentrate on the basics, for instance, how to handle the learning environment and how to come to common ground concerning the resources given to them in the learning environment. However, video conferencing with short periods of collaboration time and with inexperienced learners makes up a big part of the realized and the potential uses of video conferencing technology. We know from studies on collaborative learning that insufficient instructional support can result in superficial discourse with minimal collaborative efforts (Webb, Troper, & Fall, 1995). Research is needed to develop instructional means that support inexperienced learners in video conferencing environments. Findings from another empirical study support this explanation: Law, Ertl, and Mandl (1999) reported a pilot study on computer programming in a video conferencing environment. Their subjects were university students of computer science who were highly experienced in using computers and network technologies. No specific problems in collaboratively using the technology could be observed for these dyads.

Taken together, these first empirical results on coordination in educational video conferencing suggest: (a) The validity of two different coordination aspects: a task-related aspect, which is positively related to *individual* learning outcomes, and a technology-related aspect, which is negatively related to *collaborative* outcomes, and (b) The concerns about the high coordination effort in net-based learning environments seem to be supported only by investigations of very short periods of cooperative learning with video conferencing. With longer periods of cooperative learning, or more technology-experienced learners, increased verbal effort on technology-related coordination could not be observed.

DUE TO THE FACT THAT LEARNING DISCOURSE IS IMPAIRED IN VIDEO CONFERENCING, LESS OF THE MORE IMPORTANT CONTENTS CAN BE DISCUSSED

In studies on video conferencing, collaborative knowledge construction has rarely been analyzed systematically. Therefore, approaches from face-to-face cooperative learning are taken as frame of description. In theoretical and empirical papers, the description or analysis of collaborative knowledge construction is often approached by differentiating *content-related* and *process-related* aspects of discourse. Regarding the content-related aspects, a central question is: To what extent, how frequently, or how adequately do learners talk about the specific content of the learning task? Other studies expand their analyses to the process-related aspects of collaborative knowledge construction in discourse. (a) *Content-related aspects.* In literature on cooperative learning, most studies analyze at least the bare quantity of content-related contributions to the discourse. Interestingly, in explaining outcomes, this rather simple approach also seems to be very successful. Cohen and colleagues were able to show in a series of studies that learners contributing more to the learning discourse learn more (e.g., Cohen, 1994; Cohen & Lotan, 1995); (b) *Processes of collaborative knowledge construction.* Other approaches include the analysis of *how* a specific content is contributed to the learning discourse. *Co-construction of knowledge, collaborative knowledge construction,* and *reciprocal sense-making* are examples of terms commonly used in research to describe the cognitive processes relevant to cooperative learning (Dillenbourg, Baker, Blaye, & O' Malley, 1995; Nastasi & Clements, 1992; Roschelle & Teasley, 1995). For example, Renkl (1997) analyzed questions and follow-up questions in discourse, whereas Nastasi and Clements (1992) concluded in their research that rejection of suggestions could be regarded as indicators of cognitive conflicts (Nastasi & Clements, 1992). Bruhn, Gräsel, Fischer, and Mandl (1997; Fischer, Bruhn, Gräsel, & Mandl, 1999; in press) distinguish four processes of collaborative knowledge construction on the basis of the existing literature: Externalization, elicitation, conflict-oriented negotiation, and integration-oriented consensus building. We now describe these processes. After that, findings of recent empirical studies on cooperative learning with dyadic video conferencing will be presented.

Externalization

A necessary precondition for collaborative knowledge construction is that learners bring individual prior knowledge into the situation; only then differing views and opinions become evident in discourse. In recent years, approaches on situated learning have emphasized the important role of externalization. They consider the exchange of different individual concepts to be the essential starting point for the negotiation of common meaning (J. S. Brown, Collins, & Duguid, 1989). Research on misconceptions highlights the fact that externalization is an important requirement for the detection and modification of inadequate cognitive representations (Schnotz, 1998).

The study of Gräsel et al. (2001) showed that video conferencing might lead to decreased externalization of unshared resources from prior knowledge. Compared to a face-to-face setting, learners talked substantially more about information given in a case problem and tried to solve the problem using information given to them in the learning environment. They neglected to use their prior knowledge in their collaborative work on the case. The authors provide different hypotheses to explain this effect, among which the "lack of strategy" hypothesis seems to be the most plausible, learners simply might not have adequate strategies to deal with the complex technology-mediated collaboration in grounding their communication well. However, recent, more large-scale studies were not able to replicate this effect (Bruhn, 2000). Learners in a video conferencing condition externalized unshared knowledge to an amount comparable to that of learners in the face-to-face condition. Again, differences in collaboration time might be an explanation. Whereas in the Gräsel et al. (2001) study, learners collaborated on one case problem for about 60 min, the Fischer et al. (2000) study included three case problems with 180 min of collaboration. Reviews have shown for other kinds of computer-mediated communication that many effects of the medium vanish with increasing collaboration time (Walther, 1996). For example, it has been observed in text-based, asynchronous communication that with increasing exposure to the technology and increased experience with the other group members, structure and content resembles the face-to-face communication more and more (Walther, 1996). But again, remember, that many of the potential applications of video conferencing include short time frames or learners without much experience in using this kind of telecommunication technology.

Elicitation

Another important aspect of collaborative knowledge construction is causing the learning partners to externalize knowledge related to the task. This is sometimes referred to as "using the learning partner as a resource" (Dillenbourg, Baker, Blaye, & O'Malley, 1995). It is plausible to assume that elicitations, frequently in the form of questions, lead to externalizations, which often take the form of explanations. Therefore, elicitations could be responsible for the success of learning (e.g., King, 1994). Empirical studies on learning with video conferencing showed that more questions were asked in the technology-mediated as in the face-to-face environment (Gräsel et al., 2001). However, further analysis of the content of these questions indicate that the increased elicitation effort in video conferencing can be attributed to task-irrelevant technical aspects of using the hardware and software interface (Gräsel et al., 2001). Focusing on task-relevant knowledge, no differences between the two settings could be found. This finding was replicated in follow-up studies (Bruhn, 2000; Fischer et al., 2000).

Conflict-Oriented Negotiation

Cooperative learning with case problems induces learners to come to a common solution or assessment of the given facts. This necessary consensus can be reached in differing ways. Most of the literature on cooperative learning deals with the sociocognitive conflict (see Dillenbourg, 1999; Doise & Mugny, 1984; Nastasi & Clements, 1992): It is assumed that the different interpretations of the learning partners stimulates processes that can result in modifications of knowledge representations. However, from face-to-face collaborative learning, it is known that learners often seem to avoid engaging in sociocognitive conflict. A plausible hypothesis concerning learning in computer networks postulates that more anonymous communication fosters a less inhibited interaction. The example of "flaming" is well-known, collaborators in text-based environments show tendencies to a more aggressive, sometimes insulting communication. According to one of the most prominent explanations, reduced social context cues have the consequence of a more anonymous situation, which in turn fosters the tendency to a less inhibited, sometimes more aggressive communication (Siegel, Dubrovsky, Kiesler, & McGuire, 1986). Yet, the effect of this tendency on learning has not been investigated empirically. Especially, it is unclear whether this tendency would also come up in a video conferencing environment: Here, far more social context information is transmitted compared to text-based, computer-mediated communication (Straus & McGrath, 1994). But would it be enough to be equivalent with the face-to-face condition as is implicated in the "being there" hypothesis (Edelson, Pea, & Gomez, 1996)? Concerning conflict-oriented negotiation, empirical studies support this equivalence assumption for video conferencing; no differences could be found between video conferencing and face-to-face cooperative learning. In the Gräsel et al. (2001) study the dyads in both conditions hardly ever rejected proposals by their partners. Conflict did not play a relevant quantitative or qualitative role. In contrast, in the study conducted by Bruhn (2000), conflict played a more important quantitative role. Differences in learning time could again be regarded as responsible for this difference. Although the studies showed different absolute levels of conflict in discourse, the two *conditions* investigated (face-to-face and video conferencing) did not differ in fostering conflict-oriented negotiation. Clearly, these findings can not refute the reduced social context cues hypothesis for video conferencing. But at least for conflict-oriented negotiation in cooperative learning with case problems, they do support a "medium doesn't matter" hypothesis; no tendency towards a more conflict-related learning discourse could be observed in the video conferencing environment.

Integration-Oriented Consensus Building

The integration of the varying individual perspectives in a common interpretation or solution of the given task is another way of coming to a consensus. It is an attempt to incorporate all individual views in a common perspective. This form of consensus building can be important under some conditions. However, it involves the risk of being only a form of superficial conflict-avoiding cooperation style. The phenomenon has been found that learners, despite views that differ drastically when observed objectively, claim that they are basically in agreement (Larson & Christensen, 1993; Miyake, 1986). One could speak of a tendency on the part of the learners to reach an illusion of consensus. In the Gräsel et al. (2001) study acceptance and agreement dominated in the process of co-constructing knowledge in both cooperation modes. Similarly, in the study of Fischer and Mandl (2001), integration-oriented processes made up a large part of the discourse both in video conferencing as well as in the face-to-face condition. However, both studies could not find any differences between video conferencing and face-to-face cooperative learning concerning integration-oriented consensus building.

DUE TO THE REDUCED PROCESS QUALITY
OF COLLABORATIVE KNOWLEDGE CONSTRUCTION
IN VIDEO CONFERENCING, LEARNING OUTCOMES
ARE LOWER

Until now, investigations on video conferencing were not much concerned with individual learning outcomes. Instead, the quality of the *collaborative* problem solution was in the focus of attention. Findings show that the problem solutions of video conferencing groups hardly differ from the problem solutions of groups interacting face-to-face (Finn, Sellen, & Wilbur, 1997). Apparently, cooperation partners are ready and able for extensive compensatory efforts (see Clark & Brennan, 1991). The question arises, to what extent these findings can be transferred to learning and learning outcomes. As we explain in the following section, a complex structure of dependencies and influences exists between cooperative performance and individual knowledge acquisition.

In the research on cooperative learning, there are different conceptions of what is actually to be understood by *learning outcomes* (see Salomon & Perkins, 1998). Often the individual learner and thus individual outcomes of cooperative learning are in the center of research interest; the goal of any cooperative learning effort is seen in the individual's cognitive or affective development (e.g., Slavin, 1996). Other approaches, however, emphasize collaborative outcomes (e.g., Scardamalia & Bereiter, 1994). We believe that in order to achieve a comprehensive analysis of a cooperative learning setting, both aspects of outcomes should be regarded.

Furthermore, clarification is necessary concerning the *aspects of knowledge* that are intended to be fostered by cooperative learning. Frequently, a positive modification of a knowledge representation is regarded as success in learning. However, fostering adequate knowledge representations does not seem to be enough; in a series of theoretical as well as empirical studies, the phenomenon of *inert knowledge* has been documented sufficiently (see Renkl, Mandl, & Gruber, 1996). Particularly, the problem has been shown that learners frequently are not able to adequately use knowledge on facts and relations in potential application situations. Therefore, simple inferences from an individual's knowledge representation to the application of that knowledge seem to be impossible.

In recent empirical studies on cooperative, problem-oriented learning with video conferencing, a series of different measures for learning outcomes were taken. In the Bruhn (2000) study and the Fischer et al. (2000)

study, individual as well as collaborative outcomes were measured. In order to measure individual outcome, Bruhn as well as Fischer et al. used individual pre- and posttests. These tests included declarative knowledge tests, an individual baseline case, and an individual transfer case as data sources. In addition, they measured collaborative outcomes by means of a collaborative baseline case and a collaborative transfer case. Moreover, they differentiated between knowledge representation (as measured by the declarative knowledge test) and knowledge transfer, which was determined by analyzing the use of concepts and relations in the solutions of the individual case problems.

In short, virtually no differences could be shown. The dyads in the video conferencing environment attained similar *collaborative outcomes*. They did neither produce solutions of lower quality for the case problems, nor did they show less improvement with respect to their collaborative solutions (Bruhn, 2000; Fischer et al., 2000). The learners of the two conditions did not differ concerning *individual outcomes*. Neither concerning the modification of knowledge representation, nor concerning the individual solution to the transfer case problem, substantial mean differences could be found. Taken together, the reported findings can be regarded as evidence against the presumption that learning outcomes in video conferencing are lower.

NEGOTIATING A COMMON MEANING OR PERSPECTIVE IS MORE DIFFICULT IN VIDEO CONFERENCING. THEREFORE, KNOWLEDGE CONVERGENCE MAY BE REDUCED

An important question is, to what extent learning partners come to comparable individual knowledge in a certain knowledge domain (see Roschelle, 1996). The term *knowledge convergence* (Fischer & Mandl, 2001) reflects this aspect. An important aspect of knowledge convergence is the degree in which individual learning outcomes of the former learning partners are comparable in quality and quantity. If one partner of a dyad knows, for example, much more than the other partner at the end of the cooperation, then a low degree of knowledge convergence exists. Fischer (2001) termed this aspect of knowledge convergence as *outcome convergence* (in contrast to resource homogeneity and process convergence). In theoretical work and empirical studies, this aspect is rarely considered. It has been frequently analyzed how learners negotiate a common solution or how they master sociocognitive conflicts. But, do they all acquire the same knowledge quantitatively as well as qualitatively? Or do learning partners acquire the same quantity of knowledge, but within different areas, as is intended by the idea of *distributed expertise in the classroom* (A. L. Brown et al., 1993)? Can it occur under certain circumstances that one partner profits from the knowledge and the skills of the other without facilitating the learning partner's progress? This aspect is particularly interesting in connection with *video conferencing*. It is conceivable that the knowledge convergence of dyads is lower in video conferencing than in face-to-face settings because developing common conceptions about a topic may be strongly mediated by nonverbal signals. The perceptibility of nonverbal signals like gestures makes up one of the clear differences remaining between video conferencing and face-to-face communication (e.g., Fussell & Benimoff, 1995; O'Connaill & Whittaker, 1997).

However, one can also expect unchanged knowledge convergence in video conferencing as compared to the face-to-face condition if the frequently occurring compensatory efforts of participants in computer-mediated communication are taken into account. Possibly, learners compensate for disturbances of communication through explicit-verbal coordination or other linguistic means.

Empirical findings indicate that knowledge convergence is neither lower nor higher in video conferencing than in the face-to-face setting. Fischer et al. (2000) showed that comparing video conferencing to the face-to-face setting, learners' degree of convergence with respect to knowledge representation do not differ. Moreover, learning partners in both conditions applied the new knowledge in a transfer case task to a similar degree of convergence. Interestingly though, the absolute knowledge convergence (representation and transfer) was very low in both conditions. Although learners had the task to reach a common solution, individual transfer from collaboration was often very different (Bruhn, 2000). Especially, there were many dyads with only one learning partner profiting from the collaboration in the sense of individual knowledge transfer, whereas the other partner learned nearly nothing. This effect has recently been reported from empirical research in other settings as well (Jeong & Chi, 1999). To summarize, it would be misleading to say that learners in video conferencing constructed a convergent perspective equally well when compared to learners in the face-to-face setting. Rather learners in both conditions had similarly severe problems to construct shared knowledge and to attain knowledge convergence. However, the characteristics of cooperation via video conference neither facilitate nor hinder knowledge convergence.

TO FOSTER OUTCOMES AND KNOWLEDGE CONVERGENCE IN VIDEO CONFERENCING, INTERACTIVE GRAPHICS ARE ADEQUATE MEANS

So far, the question of how to foster cooperation in video conferencing environments has rarely been considered. The implicit assumption seems to be that the so-called *shared whiteboards* (simple, interactive graphic tools, which can be accessed by all participants simultaneously) contained in standard desktop video conferencing packages provides adequate multipurpose support for collaborative tasks. Whiteboards therefore have to be *domain-unspecific*, i.e., they do not include any constraints or affordances specific to a domain or a task in that domain. From research on cooperative learning face-to-face we know that domain-unspecific support may be related to nonoptimal learning outcomes.

Domain-specific interactive graphic tools, on the other hand, support the learning partners in the qualitative processing of the task. To provide domain-specific structural affordances, domain-specific interactive graphics based, for example, on concept mapping tools, are potentially helpful support for the collaborative construction of knowledge.

The basic principle of concept mapping tools is to visualize concepts on (for example) index cards and to connect these concepts with appropriate relations. Working with such a tool results in a map of interrelated concepts. A main advantage of concept mapping for use in cooperative learning is its adaptability to specific content: By providing certain types (or categories) of index cards and certain types of relations, important abstract concepts can serve as a schema, which focuses the learners' discourse on relevant aspects without undue constraint.

Domain-specific graphic tools have already proven to be effective in supporting processes of individual knowledge construction (e.g., Mandl, Gräsel, & Fischer, 2000). Initial investigations with those tools in cooperative learning environments indicate that they can be used to foster collaborative knowledge construction as well (Bruhn, Fischer, Gräsel, & Mandl, 2000; see also Mandl & Fischer, 2000; Roth & Roychoudhury, 1993). For example, Fischer et al. (in press) reported that dyads with domain-specific graphic tools based on concept mapping were more frequently engaged in conflict-oriented negotiation, presumably because the visual language offered by the tool facilitated more precise statements, thus reducing the tendency for illusion of consensus. Concerning outcomes, domain-specific interactive graphics on the basis of concept mapping fostered the development of a more comprehensive collaborative conceptual model, especially with respect to the integration of prior knowledge and new knowledge in the collaborative solution (Fischer et al., in press). Interestingly though, there were no effects of the domain-specific graphics on the individual outcomes. The knowledge representation as well as the knowledge transfer were facilitated by both kinds of interactive graphics in a similar way. Again, this could be seen as an indicator that collaborative and individual outcomes follow quite different principles.

The Law et al. (1999) study compared a domain-unspecific interactive graphic tool and a simple text-processing tool concerning their potential support for cooperative learning of Java programming in a video conferencing environment. Their qualitative discourse analyses revealed different patterns of use of the graphic tool for learners with different prior knowledge. For example, one dyad with only little prior knowledge on relevant concepts refrained from using the tool, whereas a dyad with more prior knowledge used it frequently and in an effective way. In those dyads using the tool, the graphics seem to provide specific support for explanatory activities. In contrast, planning and evaluation activities were not facilitated by the graphics tool.

Empirical studies by Bruhn (2000) and Fischer et al. (2000) compared dyads supported with a domain-specific interactive graphics tool based on concept mapping with dyads supported by domain-unspecific interactive graphics tool (shared whiteboard) while collaborating via video conference or in a face-to-face setting. Learning partners had the task to represent case problems and their solutions with different interactive graphics tools. Results show that a domain-specific tool fosters collaboration processes in video conferencing effectively, but to a smaller degree as it does in the face-to-face setting (Fischer et al., 2000). Concerning collaborative outcomes, domain-specific interactive graphics were not able to foster the development of more comprehensive collaborative conceptual models, as was the case in the face-to-face condition. Moreover, no differences could be found with respect to individual outcomes: Whether dyads in the video conferencing environment were supported by domain-specific or domain-unspecific interactive graphics tools was irrelevant for the individual improvement concerning knowledge representation and knowledge transfer.

The study obtained similar findings concerning interactive graphics and *knowledge convergence.* One of the central assumptions of the study had been, that domain-specific graphics would foster knowledge convergence more effectively than a domain-unspecific graphic tool. No such effect could be demonstrated. Dyads with both tools had comparable difficulties to reach knowledge convergence. Instead high convergence was only observed in dyads relying heavily on text production instead of including graphic elements in their external representation. These findings suggest that domain-specific interactive graphic tools in collaborative learning per se may not foster knowledge convergence. Possibly, simple text representation tools might lead to higher convergence. The potentially detrimental effects of interactive graphing on important aspects of cooperation have not been investigated systematically yet. It is open to further investigation whether domain-unspecific tools are more adequate to facilitate knowledge convergence than domain-specific tools because they provide learners with more degrees of freedom to use whatever code they like and do not force them to use a new visual language.

CONCLUSIONS: BEING THERE OR BEING WHERE?

In this chapter we focused on the aspects of interaction and collaborative knowledge construction in video conferencing. Presumptions on possible negative effects of that cooperation mode were used as anchor points for theoretical reflection and empirical findings. To sum up, whatever differences were supposed at a theoretical level, findings of the reported empirical studies rarely show any differences between the cooperation modes: In video conferencing, collaborative learning processes were similar and resulted in learning outcomes that were comparable to a face-to-face setting. Except for one of the reported studies, no differences were found concerning task-related as well as technology-related coordination, externalization, elicitation, or conflict-oriented as well as integration-oriented negotiation. The two cooperation modes were comparable both with respect to knowledge representation as well as to knowledge transfer. There are however empirical indicators that video conferencing may have some detrimental effects on cooperative learning when very short periods of time (e.g., 1 hour) were considered (see Walther, 1996, for a detailed discussion of time effects in computer-mediated communication). Because video conferencing sessions of that duration can be seen as being a part of prototypical learning scenarios, more large-scale empirical studies using different learning tasks are required to investigate specific instructional support for short video conferences and for learners with low technology experience. Another difference between cooperation modes showed up with respect to the interactive graphics tool; there were some interaction effects concerning cooperation mode and instructional support. These effects can be regarded as indicating that tools like domain-specific interactive graphics tools, which have proven to be an effective support for cooperative learning face-to-face (see, e.g., Mandl & Fischer, 2000), may possibly not provide the same advantages in video conferencing.

Moreover, analyses of knowledge convergence shed light on a dark spot in the field of cooperative learning in face-to-face as well as in video conferencing settings. In both settings, dramatic dyadic differences both in quantity and quality of the constructed knowledge imply important questions and goals for further research in the field.

Taken together, the findings concerning the outcomes could be seen as support for the "being there" hypothesis. In that respect they are in line with findings from research on video-mediated communication. Empirical studies in that field frequently come to the conclusion that whatever differences regarding processes may be detected, differences between cooperation outcomes do hardly appear (Finn et al., 1997). Moreover, the being there hypothesis might also be valid for the findings on the *process* of collaborative knowledge construction.

However, it is clear that for implementation issues, other questions concerning video conferencing and learning have to be considered as well. For example, *technological aspects* of course delivery by using video conferences have to be regarded. Desktop video conferencing technologies for computer networks outside the laboratory setting are developing quickly but are still far from being a reliable learning technology. The dependence of process and outcome on the features of the specific video conferencing system is perhaps the most clear consensus in research on video-mediated communication (see Bruhn, 2000; Finn et al., 1997).

Other important aspects are learners' as well as teachers' *use of video-mediated communication.* Empirical studies in real-life educational settings showed that video conferencing technology is often not used by students and teachers, who favor instead other facilities like E-mail. Unreliable connections and complicated software use as well as more complex social demands (e.g., making video conferencing appointments) might be reasons for these user preferences (see, e.g., Fishman, 1997). Learners' and teachers' *acceptance of video-mediated communication* has to be studied with respect to longer time frames like semesters for example (e.g., Gomez, Fishman, & Pea, 1998). Furthermore, *social effects* of implementation of video conferencing technologies within a curriculum have to be investigated using different time frames.

Like with other learning technologies, one important reason of low acceptance and rare use might be that the basic problems of any cooperative learning environment have not been considered sufficiently. Research in the area of cooperative learning may provide knowledge and strategies required for composing effective learning teams or designing adequate cooperative learning tasks (e.g., Cohen, 1994; Johnson & Johnson, 1990), for motivating students to collaborate (e.g., Slavin, 1996), and to adequately structure processes of collaborative knowledge construction (e.g., King, 1999; O'Donnell, 1999).

A predominant trend in research on computer-mediated learning is to develop complex learning environments employing different tasks as well as media mixes with multimedia, synchronous and asynchronous text-based communication, as well as video conferencing (e.g., Slotta & Linn, 2000). With "testbed designs" (Gomez et al., 1998) or "design experiments" (A. L. Brown, 1992), researchers try to design and evaluate those prototypical scenarios based on instructional theories and tools as well as on constraints of the content to be learned and learners needs. In the United States and Canada, large-scale research programs are aimed specifically to those issues (e.g., Pea et al., 1999). We believe that this important evaluative and design-related research should be accompanied by more controlled experimental studies analyzing specific interactive and cognitive effects resulting from specific types of cooperative learning tasks supported by specific technologies. In Germany, the core research program, *Network-Based Knowledge Communication in Groups* (Hesse, Mandl, & Hoppe, 1999) is directed towards these issues. It is funded by the Deutsche Forschungsgemeinschaft (DFG) and includes 13 single projects from social and educational psychology as well as from cognitive science and computer science. In combining the goal of understanding and the goal of use more appropriately in future research, we can expect to improve both, the validity of our findings (Stokes, 1997), and the advice for the designers of online learning environments.

REFERENCES

Anderson, A. H., O'Malley, C., Doherty-Sneddon, G., Lanton, S., Newlands, A., Mullin, J., Fleming, A. M., & Van der Felden, J. (1997). The impact of VMC on collaborative problem solving: An analysis of task performance, communicative process, and user satisfaction. In K. E. Finn, A. J. Sellen, & S. B. Wilbur (Eds.), *Video-mediated communication* (pp. 133–156). Mahwah, NJ: Lawrence Erlbaum Associates.

Brown, A. L. (1992). Design experiments: Theoretical and methodological challenges in creating complex interventions in classroom settings. *The Journal of the Learning Sciences, 2*(2), 141–178.

Brown, A. L., Ash, D., Rutherford, M., Nakagawa, K., Gordon, A., & Campione, J. C. (1993). Distributed expertise in the classroom. In G. Salomon (Ed.), *Distributed cognitions* (pp. 188–228). Cambridge, MA: Cambridge University Press.

Brown, J. S., Collins, A., & Duguid, P. (1989). Situated cognition and the culture of learning. *Educational Researcher, 18*(1), 32–42.

Bruhn, J. (2000). *Foerderung des kooperativen Lernens ueber Computernetze. [Fostering cooperative learning in computer networks].* Frankfurt a. M., Germany: Lang.

Bruhn, J., Fischer, F., Gräsel, C., & Mandl, H. (2000). Kooperatives Lernen mit Mapping-Techniken. [Cooperative learning with mapping techniques]. In H. Mandl & F. Fischer (Eds.), *Wissen sichtbar machen. Wissensmanagement mit Mapping-Techniken* (pp. 119–133). Göttingen: Hogrefe.

Bruhn, J., Gräsel, C., Fischer, F., & Mandl, H. (1997). *Kategoriensystem zur Erfassung der gemeinsamen Wissenskonstruktion im Diskurs. [Coding scheme to measure collaborative knowledge construction in the learning discourse].* Unpublished manuscript, Institute of Educational Psychology, Ludwig-Maximilians-Universitaet, Munich.

Cannon-Bowers, J. A., & Salas, E. (1998). Team performance and training in complex environments: Recent findings from applied research. *Current Directions in Psychological Science, 7* (3), 83–87.

Clark, H. H., & Brennan, S. E. (1991). Grounding in communication. In L. B. Resnick, J. M. Levine, & S. D. Teasley (Eds.), *Perspectives on socially shared cognition* (pp. 127–149). Washington, DC: American Psychological Association.

Cohen, E. G. (1994). Restructuring the classroom: Conditions for productive small groups. *Review of Educational Research, 64,* 1–35.

Cohen, E. G., & Lotan, R. A. (1995). Producing equal-status interaction in the heterogeneous classroom. *American Educational Research Journal, 32,* 99–120.

Dillenbourg, P. (1999). What do you mean by "collaborative learning"? In P. Dillenbourg (Ed.), *Collaborative learning: Cognitive and computational approaches* (pp. 1–19). Oxford: Pergamon.

Dillenbourg, P., Baker, M., Blaye, A., & O'Malley, C. (1995). The evolution of research on collaborative learning. In P. Reimann & H. Spada (Eds.), *Learning in humans and machines: Towards an interdiciplinary learning science* (pp. 189–211). Oxford, England: Elsevier.

Doise, W., & Mugny, W. (1984). *The social development of the intellect.* Oxford, England: Pergamon.

Edelson, D., Pea, R., & Gomez, L. (1996). Constructivism in the collaboratory. In B. G. Wilson (Ed.), *Constructivist learning environments: Case studies in instructional design* (pp. 151–164). Englewood Cliffs, NJ: Educational Technology Publications.

Finn, K. E., Sellen, A. J., & Wilbur, S. B. (Eds.). (1997). *Video-mediated communication.* Mahwah, NJ: Lawrence Erlbaum Associates.

Fischer, F. (2001). *Gemeinsame Wissenskonstruktion in computerunterstützten Kooperationsszenarien [Collaborative knowledge construction in computer-supported collaboration scenarios].* Unpublished Habilitationsschrift [professional dissertation]. Munich: Ludwig-Maximilians-Universitaet, Institute of Educational Psychology.

Fischer, F., Bruhn, J., Gräsel, C., & Mandl, H. (in press). Fostering collaborative knowledge construction with visualization tools. *Learning and Instruction.*

Fischer, F., Bruhn, J., Gräsel, C., & Mandl, H. (1999, September). *Combining quantitative and qualitative approaches in analyzing collaborative learning discourse.* Paper presented at the European Assocation of Research on Learning and Instruction (EARLI) Conference, Goteborg, Sweden.

Fischer, F., Bruhn, J., Gräsel, C., & Mandl, H. (2000). Kooperatives Lernen mit Videokonferenzen: Gemeinsame Wissenskonstruktion und individueller Lernerfolg. [Cooperative learning with video conferencing systems: Collaborative knowledge construction and individual learning outcomes]. *Kognitionswissenschaft, 9*(1), 5–16.

Fischer, F., & Mandl, H. (2001). Facilitating the construction of shared knowledge with graphical representation tools in face-to-face and computer-mediated scenarios. In P. Dillenbourg, A. Eurelings, & K. Hakkarainen (Eds.), *European perspectives on computer-supported collaborative learning* (pp. 230–236). Maastricht, Netherlands: University of Maastricht.

Fishman, B. (1997, April). *Classroom use of computer mediated communication: What matters and why?* Paper presented at the annual meeting of the American Educational Research Association, Chicago.

Fussell, S. R., & Benimoff, N. I. (1995). Social and cognitive processes in interpersonal communication: Implications for advanced telecommunications technologies. *Human Faktors, 37,* 228–250.

Gibbons, M., Limoges, C., Nowotny, H., Schwartzman, S., Scott, P., & Trow, M. (1994). *The new production of knowledge: The dynamics of science and research in contemporary societies.* London: Sage.

Gomez, L. M., Fishman, B. J., & Pea, R. D. (1998). The Covis project: building a large-scale science education testbed. *Interactive Learning Environments, 6,* 59–92.

Gräsel, C. (1997). *Problemorientiertes Lernen.* [Problem-oriented learning]. Göttingen: Hogrefe.

Gräsel, C., Fischer, F., Bruhn, J., & Mandl, H. (2001). Let me tell you something you do know. A pilot study on discourse in cooperative learning with computer networks. In H. Jonassen, S. Dijkstra, & D. Sembill (Eds.), *Learning with multimedia—Results and perspectives* (pp. 112–137). Frankfurt: Lang.

Heath, C., & Luff, P. (1993). Disembodied conduct. Interactional asymmetries in video-mediated communication. In G. Button (Ed.), *Technology in working order: Studies of work, interaction and technology* (pp. 35–54). London: Routledge.

Hesse, F. W., Mandl, H., & Hoppe, U. (1999). *Schwerpunkt-Antrag "Netzbasierte Wissenskommunikation in Gruppen". [Proposal for a core research program on "Net-based knowledge communication in groups].* Bonn: Deutsche Forschungsgemeinschaft.

Jeong, H., & Chi, M. T. H. (1999). *Constructing Shared Knowledge During Collaboration and Learning.* Paper presented at the AERA Annual Meeting, Montreal.

Johnson, D., & Johnson, R. (1990). Cooperative learning and achievment. In S. Sharan (Ed.), *Cooperative learning: theory and research* (pp. 23–37). New York: Praeger.

King, A. (1999). Discourse patterns for mediating peer learning. In A. M. O'Donnell & A. King (Eds.), *Cognitive perspectives on peer learning* (pp. 87–115). Mahwah, NJ: Lawrence Erlbaum Associates.

Langille, D. B., Sargeant, J. M., & Allen, M. J. (1998). Assessment of the acceptability and costs of interactive video conferencing for continuing medical education in Nova Scotia. *Journal of Continuing Education in the Health Professions, 18*(1), 11–19.

222   FISCHER AND MANDL

Larson, J. R., & Christensen, C. (1993). Groups as problem-solving units: Toward a new meaning of social cognition. *British Journal of Social Psychology, 32,* 5–30.

Law, L.-C., Ertl, B., & Mandl, H. (1999). *Collaborative learning of Java programming in the graphics-enhanced video conferencing environment: A pilot study* (Research Report No. 113). Munich: Ludwig-Maximilians-Universitaet, Institute of Educational Psychology.

Mandl, H., Gräsel, C., & Fischer, F. (2000). Problem-oriented learning: Fostering domain-specifc and control strategies through modeling by an expert. In W. Perrig & A. Grob (Ed.), *Control of human behaviour, mental processes and awareness* (pp. 165–182). Mahwah, NJ: Lawrence Erlbaum Associates.

Mandl, H., & Fischer, F. (2000). Mapping-Techniken und Begriffsnetze in Lern- und Kooperationsprozessen [Applying mapping techniques and concept mapping in learning and cooperation]. In H. Mandl & F. Fischer (Eds.), *Wissen sichtbar machen. Wissensmanagement mit Mapping-Techniken* (pp. 3–12). Göttingen: Hogrefe.

Miyake, N. (1986). Constructive interaction and the iterative process of understanding. *Cognitive Science, 10,* 151–177.

Nastasi, B. K., & Clements, D. H. (1992). Social-cognitive behaviors and higher-order thinking in educational computer environments. *Learning and Instruction, 2,* 215–238.

O'Connaill, B., & Whittaker, S. (1997). Characterizing, predicting, and measuring video-mediated communication: A conversational approach. In K. E. Finn, A. J. Sellen, & S. B. Wilbur (Eds.). *Video-mediated communication* (pp. 107–132). Mahwah, NJ: Lawrence Erlbaum Associates.

O'Donnell, A. N. (1999). Structuring dyadic interaction through scripted cooperation. In A. N. O'Donnell & A. King (Eds.), *Cognitive perspectives on peer learning* (pp. 179–196). Mahwah, NJ: Lawrence Erlbaum Associates.

Olson, J. S., Olson, G. M., & Meader, D. K. (1997). Face-to-face group work compared to remote group work with and without video. In K. E. Finn, A. J. Sellen, & S. B. Wilbur (Eds.), *Video-mediated communication* (pp. 157–172). Mahwah, NJ: Lawrence Erlbaum Associates.

Pea, R., Tinker, R., Linn, M., Means, B., Bransford, J., Roschelle, J., Hsi, S., Brophy, S., & Songer, N. (1999). Toward a learning technologies knowledge network. *Educational Technology, Research, and Development, 47*(2), 19–38.

Renkl, A. (1997). Lernen durch Erklaeren: Was, wenn Rueckfragen gestellt werden? [Learning by explaining: What if they answer with questions?] *Zeitschrift fuer Paedagogische Psychologie, 11,* 41–51.

Renkl, A., Mandl, H., & Gruber, H. (1996). Inert knowledge: Analyses and remedies. *Educational Psychologist, 31,* 115–122.

Rogoff, B. (1991). Social interaction as apprenticeship in thinking: guided participation in spatial planning. In L. B. Resnick, J. Levine, & S. Teasley (Eds.) *Perspectives on socially shared cognition* (pp. 349–364). Washington, DC: American Psychological Association.

Roschelle, J. (1996). Learning by collaborating: Convergent conceptual change. In T. Koschmann (Ed.), *CSCL: Theory and practice of an emerging paradigm* (pp. 209–248). Mahwah, NJ: Lawrence Erlbaum Associates.

Roschelle, J., & Teasley, S. D. (1995). The construction of shared knowledge in collaborative problem solving. In C. O'Malley (Ed.), *Computer supported collaborative learning* (pp. 69–97). Berlin: Springer.

Roth, W.-M., & Roychoudhury, A. (1993). The concept map as a tool for the collaborative construction of knowledge: a microanalysis of high school physics students. *Journal of Research in Science Teaching, 30*(5), 503–534.

Salomon, G., & Perkins, D. N. (1998). Individual and social aspects of learning. *Review of Research in Education, 23,* 1–24.

Scardamalia, M., & Bereiter, C. (1994). Computer support for knowledge-building communities. *Journal of the Learning Sciences, 3,* 265–283.

Schnotz, W. (1998). Conceptual change. In D. Rost (Ed.), *Handwoerterbuch Paedagogische Psychologie [Handbook of educational psychology]* (pp. 55–59). Weinheim: Beltz PVU.

Sembor, E. L. (1997). Citizenship, diversity and distance learning: Video conferencing in Connecticut. *Social Education, 61*(3), 154–159.

Siegel, J., Dubrovsky, V., Kiesler, S., & McGuire, T. W. (1986). Group processes in computer-mediated communication. *Organisational Behavior and Human Decision Processes, 37*, 157–187.

Slavin, R. E. (1996). Research for the future. Research on cooperative learning and achievement: what we know, what we need to know. *Contemporary Educational Psychology, 21*, 43–69.

Slotta, J., & Linn, M. C. (2000). The Knowledge Integration Environment: Helping students use the Internet effectively. In M. Jacobson & R. Kozma (Eds.), *Innovations in science and mathematics education: Advanced designs for technologies of learning* (pp. 193–226). Mahwah, NJ: Lawrence Erlbaum Associates.

Stokes, D. E. (1997). *Pasteur's quadrant. Basic science and technological innovation.* Washington, DC: Brookings Institute Press.

Straus, S. G., & McGrath, J. E. (1994). Does the medium matter? The interaction of task-type and technology on group performance and member reactions. *Journal of Applied Psychology, 79*, 87–97.

Vygotsky, L. S. (1978). *Mind in society. The development of higher psychological processes.* Cambridge, MA: Harvard University Press.

Walther, J. B. (1996). Computer-mediated communication: Impersonal, interpersonal, and hyperpersonal interaction. *Communication Research, 19*, 50–88.

Webb, N. M., Troper, J. D., & Fall, R. (1995). Constructive activity and learning in collaborative small groups. *Journal of Educational Psychology, 87*(3), 406–423.

Wertsch, J. V. (1991). *Voices of the mind: A sociocultural approach to mediated action.* Cambridge, MA: Harvard University Press.

Chapter 10

Interaction and Performance in Computer-Supported Collaborative Tasks

Gijsbert Erkens
Jerry Andriessen
Nanno Peters
Utrecht University, The Netherlands

Despite a large number of studies on computer-mediated collaborative communication (Dillenbourg, 1999), not much is known about the specific (mutual) relationships between the nature of interaction and communication on one hand and performance (learning, problem solving, and decision making) on the other. In particular, more insight is needed about the crucial characteristics of the interaction and produced discourse, and the relationships with task performance. In this chapter, we focus on interactional processes in computer-supported collaborative learning (CSCL). Our main question is about the relationship between interaction, learning, and problem solving in complex tasks requiring communication with or mediated by computers. First, we discuss our view on collaborative learning and possible applications of computers in this process. Then we present two of our research projects about collaboration in computer-supported tasks and discuss our method for analyzing collaboration in such tasks. In the first project, we found three processes of coordination between the students to be related to the quality of their performance on the problem solving task that they were given. The second study concerns an analysis of the relationship between the coordinated use of conceptual information during interaction and the product of a collaborative writing assignment. We present a model of "collective landscape" for collaborative learning; a collective space of concepts and ideas that serves as a common ground to be maintained and used during negotiation and task execution.

COLLABORATIVE LEARNING

Research on cooperative learning in education has a long-standing tradition. The main interest in this field was triggered by the observation that, in some circumstances, students seem to learn more from their peers than from their teachers. Besides advantages in cognitive learning, cooperation seems to foster social development and interpersonal (or interethnic) attitudes in the class (D. W. Johnson & R. T. Johnson, 1975; S. Sharan & Y. Sharan, 1976; Slavin, 1983). The main research questions concerned the organization and effectiveness of cooperative learning in the classroom as a teaching method. Most of this research on the effectiveness of cooperative learning was directed toward the prerequisites (e.g., heterogeneous vs. homogeneous groups), the comparison with individual learning or whole-class instruction, and the final products of cooperation (C. R. Cooper & R. G. Cooper, 1984; Webb, 1982). Few researchers focused on the questions of why and how cooperative learning could facilitate learning (Doise & Mugny, 1984), or on what actually happens in the process of collaboration between students.

In recent educational research, cooperative learning or collaborative learning is reemphasized (Brown & Palincsar, 1989; Cohen, 1994). This emphasis follows a reformulation of learning as a social process of enculturation in recent constructivistic or situated learning views on cognition and instruction (Cognition and Technology Group at Vanderbilt, 1990; Duffy & Jonassen, 1991). Aspects of collaboration play a central role in the constructivistic approach of learning. "The idea that authentic learning only occurs in collaboration with others has become the central pillar of constructivist orthodoxy and is the one on which practically every other principle is dependent to some extent" (Petraglia, 1998, p.77). Peer collaboration is seen, in a Vygotskian way, as an intermediate stage in the developmental process of internalization of social activities. The (social) learning environment should help and support the learner to construct his or her own knowledge and skills. Brown, Collins, & Duguid (1989) saw learning—both inside and outside school—advancing through collaborative social interaction and through the social construction of knowledge. They mentioned the following salient features for group learning:

1. *Collective problem solving.* Groups may give rise to insights and solutions that would not come about in individual situations.
2. *Displaying multiple roles.* Groups permit different roles needed to carry out an authentic cognitive task to be displayed by and distributed among different members in the group.

3. *Confronting ineffective strategies and misconceptions.* Groups may be effective in confronting and discussing faulty or nonoptimal ideas of individual members.
4. *Providing collaborative working skills.* Group work may give the opportunity to situate experiences for future cooperative working situations.

At this time we would like to add a fifth feature, and that is *co-construction of meaning.* Sometimes, the goal of collaboration is not only the solution of a problem, but this may serve a higher goal: increased understanding of the concepts and beliefs of the domain knowledge involved. Under certain circumstances, collaboration can even be a vehicle of conceptual change (Teasley & Rochelle, 1993).

Collaboration on a cooperative task concerns a complex interaction between task strategies and communication processes. Cooperation requires that the collaborating subjects acquire a common frame of reference to negotiate and communicate about their individual viewpoints and inferences. Obtaining a common ground is crucial in every communicative situation (Clark & Brennan, 1991). The problem with collaboration is that the processes of representation formation and communication often take place implicitly. Natural language communication is implicit by nature; this implies that viewpoints are not always advanced, task strategies are not always open to discussion, and so forth. Although implicitness may be ineffective because it masks differences in knowledge, viewpoints, and attitudes, it also results in efficient and nonredundant transfer of information. To acquire more knowledge about the coordination between communicative and problem-solving processes, it is necessary to investigate, step by step, the interaction between these processes with collaborating students. However, such an approach has been followed only scarcely within the field of cooperative learning, although the necessity of process-directed research has been expressed quite frequently (C. R. Cooper & R. G. Cooper, 1984; Webb, 1982).

In normal educational settings, we can define a *cooperative learning situation* as one in which two or more students work together to fulfil an assigned task within a particular domain of learning to achieve a joint product. In ideal cooperation, the collaborating partners must have a common interest in solving the problem at hand. Furthermore, they should be mutually dependent on the information and cooperation of the other to reach their (shared) goals. Only when the participants have abilities or information that are complementary, cooperation can be fruitful and anticipated. Some authors distinguish cooperation and collaboration, the first referring to situations in which there is role and task division, while the second is reserved for partners working together on the task at the same time. We propose not to make this distinction, as it confounds task characteristics with task strategy.

TYPES OF COMPUTER SUPPORTED COLLABORATIVE LEARNING

The computer can support collaborative learning in several ways. Erkens (1997) distinguished four different types of use:

1. *Computer-based collaborative tasks (CBCT)*. The computer presents a task environment to foster student collaboration. The extra advantages of the medium (compared to collaborating without it) may be the shared problem representation that can function as a joint problem space, the ease of data access, and, in some cases, intelligent coaching. Example systems are Sherlock (Katz & Lesgold, 1993) and the Envisioning Machine (Teasley & Rochelle, 1993).

2. *Cooperative tools (CT)*. The computer is used as a cooperative tool, a partner who may take over some of the burden of lower order tasks, while functioning as a (nonintelligent) tool during higher order activities. Examples are Writing Partner (Salomon, 1993), Computer Supported Intentional Learning Environment (Scardamalia, Bereiter & Lamon, 1994), and Case-Based Reasoning tool (Kolodner, 1993).

3. *Computer mediated communication (CMC)* supports collaborating over electronic networks. The computer serves as the communication interface, which allows interaction and collaboration between several students at the same time or spread out asynchronously over a specific period. E-mail conferencing, virtual classrooms, and discussion forums fall into this category (Henri, 1995). Groupware systems mostly offer both functions; cooperative tools and computer-mediated communication facilities. Educational groupware systems provide tools, representations, and interfaces that support problem solving and communication, such as in Chene (Baker & Bielaczyc, 1995), Belvedere (Suthers, Weiner, Connelly, & Paolucci, 1995), or the Collaborative Text Production Tool (Andriessen, Erkens, Overeem & Jaspers, 1996).

4. *Intelligent Cooperative Systems (ICS)*. To set it off from CT, in ICS, the computer functions as an intelligent cooperative partner (Dialogue Monitor; Erkens, 1997), a co-learner (People Power; Dillenbourg & Self, 1992), or learning companion (Integration Kid; Chan & Baskin, 1990).

The analysis of cognitive processing and dialogue is not equally important in each of these types of use. Especially researchers involved in the construction of CT do not often engage in detailed analysis of discourse. In contrast, CBCT and ICS have been developed by researchers interested in gaining understanding about collaborative learning. CMC presents a mixed case, although it has been acknowledged that discourse analysis is an important tool for understanding electronic collaboration (e.g. Henri, 1995; Baker, 1996), there are problems in finding the right grain size of analysis and in interpreting data for understanding what seems to be a new communication medium, requiring different means of analysis, and a consistent theoretical framework. In the next sections, we discuss our own attempts in analysing the relationship between interaction and performance in the context of two research projects, each involving detailed analysis of communication and collaboration. The first project, the DSA project, was aimed in developing an ICS, an intelligent cooperative system (fourth type). In the CTP project, a groupware program, supporting tools and mediated communication (second and third type) for collaborative writing, was developed.

DSA: THE COMPUTER AS A COLLABORATIVE PARTNER

The objective of the research project 'Dialogue Structure Analysis of interactive problem solving' (the DSA project) is to study the relation between the process of information exchange and the processes of knowledge construction and the use of information during collaborative problem solving. The central question is how students working together coordinate these processes (Erkens, 1997). On the basis of analyses of dialogues of students collaborating on a problem solving task, a prototype of an "intelligent" computer-based collaborative partner has been implemented. This program, the Dialogue Monitor, is the central part of a computer-assisted educational program, which acts as a simulated "peer-student" and collaborates with a human student in solving a problem task jointly.

Analysis of Collaborative Dialogues

The main question of the research in the DSA project is how processes of problem solving on task-related and communicational levels relate to each other when students collaborate. In order to study this relation, a special collaboration task for students 10 to 12 years old has been developed. In this task (The Camp Puzzle), the students have to derive personal characteristics of six children by combining informative statements. However, the crucial information needed to fulfill the task has been split and distributed among the two collaborating partners. By this mutual dependency, the exchange of information and collaboration between the students becomes necessary. The collaborating partners have to exchange the relevant information, explain their reasoning, discuss their task strategies, and negotiate their inferences. The dialogues of 30 couples were studied on the level of content as well as the level of discourse acts with the help of a comprehensive and fine-grained system for the transcription and analysis of dialogue protocols.

The Verbal Observation System (VOS) is meant to transcribe propositional content, as well as pragmatic and communicative characteristics of utterances in the dialogues (Erkens, 1997). The system is based on the extension of the Transactional Exchange Theory by Burton (1981), the study of classrooms discussions by Barnes and Todd (1977), the theory of discourse markers of Schiffrin (1987), and the analysis of question answering by Lehnert (1978). The VOS is a semiautomatic transcription system on the basis of video recordings, containing some 300 communicative and semantic coding categories. Despite the complexity of the system, a sufficient degree of reliability in coding between raters could be achieved. The VOS uses as much as possible literal clue-words in the utterances to encode the communicative function and content. The system is semiautomatic in the way that the encoding of an utterance is being asked for by a computer program step by step for different variables and that the codes entered are being checked on consistency with the sets of categories defined for those variables.

In the VOS, utterances are transcribed along three main characteristics: propositional-content, dialogue act and illocution:

1. The *propositional-content* is encoded in a predicate logic form in which the arguments can be embedded. For example "The friend of Jan comes from Harlem." is represented in a form like (city, (friend, Jan, X), Harlem). The following types of propositions are distinguished: direct assignments, indirect references, equalities, set-distributions, and axioms.

2. The *dialogue act* represents the communicative action of an utterance. Utterances like "Does the friend of Jan come from Harlem?", "But from Harlem comes Jan's friend." or "No, the friend of Jan comes from Harlem!" All have the same propositional content but differ in dialogue act (response, question, counter, and denial). In the VOS, 65 dialogue acts are distinguished, in 19 main categories representing 5 communicative functions: attention signaler, informative, eliciting, responsive, and argumentative. In Table 10.1, the 19 main categories are given, together with their communicative function.

3. The *illocution* category represents explicitly stated illocutionary force as described by Searle (1969). The illocutionary part of an utterance provides the listener with extra information on how to interpret the information transferred. The category system only considers explicitly stated illocu-

TABLE 10.1
Main Dialogue Acts in the Verbal Observation System and Examples

Example	Dialogue Act	Function
"Eh, eh . . ."	implicit attention	attention
"Wait!"	command attention	signaler
"Here it says . . ."	read information	
"Ann lives in Amsterdam."	statement	informative
"Let's write Amsterdam."	proposal	
"Where does Ann live?"	open question	
"Ann from Amsterdam?"	check question (yes/no)	eliciting
"Amsterdam."	reply	
"Ann lives in Amsterdam"	repeat	
"Oh, I didn't know that"	acceptance	
"Yes, all right!"	confirmation	
"No . . . not Ann."	denial	responsive
"Because Ann does"	reason	
"But Jill does not"	counter	
"Then she comes from . . ."	consequent argument	
"If Ann is Jill's friend."	conditional argument	
"And Ann does"	continuation	
"So Ann has to live there"	conclusion	argumentative
<writes in solution-matrix>	writing	action

tion. In the Camp Puzzle, the illocution refers in most cases to the certainty of the information (e.g. "I am sure that . . .", "I think that . . .") or to the source of information (e.g. "that's in my letter," "you said so"). Five levels of certainty and three sources of information (letter, partner, and self) are distinguished in the category system.

Results

In our analyses of collaborative task dialogues, we found that most dialogue acts have a informative, responsive, or argumentative function (Kanselaar & Erkens, 1994). Contrary to what one would expect, the dialogues contain very few open questions (e.g., "In which city does Jan live?") to elicit exchange of information from the partner. The students seem to hold on to another Cooperative Principle (compare Grice, 1975): "If my partner has found something interesting, he will tell me, I don't have to ask for it!" Check questions, that is, Yes or No questions, are found more frequently (e.g., "Does Jan live in Harlem?"). These questions function, mostly, to check information exchanged by the partner.

By lag sequential analysis of the transitions of dialogue acts between the collaborating students, the dialogue structure could be specified by frequently occurring patterns of dialogue acts. Furthermore the most occurring sequences of content related topics of discussion could be specified.

The topic structure could be related to the structure of subproblems on the task-content level (see Grosz, 1978, for similar findings). The sequence of subproblems to be solved in the task is not rigid and a solution path has to be found. For this purpose, topics have to be initiated, tried, agreed on, and evaluated in the ongoing dialogue. This process is called *focusing*. Remarkably, topics are seldom explicitly proposed ("Let's search for the friend of Jan."), but are initiated implicitly by exchanging relevant information concerning a topic. Important phases in the discussion of topics are: (a) attention signaling, (b) topic initiation by exchange of information or eliciting of information, (c) confirming, accepting, or checking of the information transferred, (d) after checking of information: confirming, accepting, or (counter)argumentation and elaborated discussion, and (e) topic closure by concluding, writing a solution, or by initiating a new topic.

In contrast to earlier expectations, no systematic relationship between these dialogue patterns and the task result was found. The dialogues of low-achieving dyads were not structurally different from the dialogues of dyads who achieved a higher task result. On the whole, the same dialogue patterns and the same variation in dialogue acts were found between the two groups of dyads. Differences between dialogues were found in the coordination between the level of content (task strategies and knowledge construction) and the level of communication (exchange and negotiation). Three coordination processes of interaction and performance could be distinguished that were crucial:

1. *Focusing.* Focusing refers to the way the participants maintain the same topic in their dialogue. Coordination of focus occurs by means of signaling of topic shifts, asking for attention before new information is transferred, and by means of explicitly accepting and re-concluding closure of a topic, in this case, before writing down the solution. By these means, both partners make sure that they share the same understanding of the problem and of the steps to be taken to solve it. In low achieving dyads, focus regularly diverged between the participants by misunderstanding the intention of the other's utterance.

2. *Checking.* One of the main findings is that students spend a great deal of time on controlling activities such as checking plausibility and giving information about the status of information transferred. Checking procedures were found to play an important role in the coordination of actions in the analyzed task-dialogues. The plausibility of the information transferred is compared with their own knowledge base before the information is accepted and further used for inference. In low-achieving dyads, the participants were either not critical enough or too critical with respect to each other's contribution.

3. *Argumentation.* Collaboration on a task also means negotiation of knowledge and task strategies. This implies argumentation about the steps

to be taken in order to convince the partner. In contraargumentation, disagreeing with the line of reasoning of the partner, one of the cooperation partners should be convinced in the end. We observed that in most low-achieving dyads, some students accepted inferences from the partner too quickly, while some other low achievers were hardly convinced.

Collaborating with a Simulated Partner

On the basis of these analyses and conclusions, a prototype of the Dialogue Monitor program could be implemented. The Dialogue Monitor is the core of an "intelligent" collaborative partner system (the DSA program) that is capable of engaging in a dialogue with a student and solving a problem task together by simulating a peer student (Kanselaar & Erkens, 1994). The collaborating student is able to communicate with the DSA program by means of a menu-based, Natural Language interface. By several linked menus, natural verbal utterances can be composed.

The Dialogue Monitor program has been experimentally used with 40 students in the highest grade of two elementary schools. In Table 10.2, a dialogue fragment between a 12-year-old student and the DSA program is shown. The fragment is literally translated from Dutch. As can be seen in the fragment, the dialogue has a rather natural flavor with a lot of implicit proposals, interjections ("Yes," "Oh"), nonspecific replies (line 13), plausibility checking (line 2) and unexpected topic shifts (lines 17,19). In fact, most dialogues look, at first sight, rather similar to student–student dialogues, which is promising for the aims of this research.

Students collaborating with the DSA program solved less subproblems of the Camp Puzzle in 45 min sessions compared to students working together. However, they also produced less faulty solutions; probably the written communication leads to more control and accuracy. The number of utterances in the dialogues between student and monitor is only $\frac{1}{5}$ less than the number of utterances in dialogues between two students. However the number of utterances made by the student is notably less than those made by the monitor. In addition, the contributions of the students were mainly informing, supporting, or reacting, whereas the contribution of the Dialogue Monitor were more frequently argumentative and eliciting.

The simulation program was equipped with an adjustment option for "collaborative attitude," that is either a more compliant or a more critical attitude toward the student. This option was experimentally varied in two randomly selected groups of students. The option was shown to have a significant effect on the collaborative activity of the student, which supported the assumption that critical checking of the plausibility of information is of paramount importance for the coordination of collaboration. However, an effect of the adjustment option on the task score could not be demon-

TABLE 10.2
Fragment of a Dialogue Protocol
of a Student and the Dialogue Monitor

Dialogue Fragment Between a 12-Year-Old Male Student and the Dialogue Monitor		
1	student:	"Chris does gymnastics; that is in my letter." . . .*
2	monitor:	"Does Chris do gymnastics?" . . .
3	student:	"Yes . . ."
4	monitor:	"So Chris does gymnastics."
5	student:	"Yes . . ."
6	monitor:	"Oh . . ."
7	monitor:	"We can write that: Chris on gymnastics."
8	monitor:	"Well, I have written it." (i.e., filled in the solution-matrix)
9	monitor:	"All right!" . . .
10	student:	"Let's search: the partner of Jan." . . .
11	monitor:	"Yes . . ."
12	monitor:	"With whom does Jan work?"
13	student:	"And the partner of Jan is a girl; that is in my letter." . . .
14	monitor:	"Oh . . . , the partner of Jan is a girl . . ."
15	student:	"Yes; that is correct." . . .
16	monitor:	"Oh . . ."
17	student:	"From which city does Jan come from?" . . .
18	monitor:	"The city of Jan I don't know; it is not in my letter." . . .
19	student:	"Jan does the same sports as Jill; I am sure of that." . . .
20	monitor:	"So, Jan does the same sports as Jill." . . .
21	monitor:	"Jan does the same sports as Jill; you said that."
22	monitor:	"Jill does swimming; that is in my letter."
23	monitor:	"Then Jan does swimming."
24	monitor:	"We can write that: Jan on swimming."
25	monitor:	"It is written!" (i.e., filled in the solution-matrix)
26	monitor:	"What else do you know?" . . .
27	student:	"Wait a minute" . . .

Note. *. . . = pause > 2 sec

strated. Although the task domain of the DSA program is limited and several weak points have to be solved, it may be concluded that on the whole, the model of coordination of collaborative problem solving, interactive knowledge construction, and dialogue processing that was employed proved to be functional and may be used for the further development of computer-based intelligent collaborative partners (Erkens, 1997).

CONTENT AND PERFORMANCE IN COLLABORATIVE INTERACTION

From process-oriented studies of collaborative learning, it can be concluded that the collaborative learning situation may lead to higher task orientation, more verbalization and elaboration, more mutual criticizing, and better adaptation to one another's level of processing (Cohen, 1994). These factors are supposed to explain the learning effects of collaboration. *Learning* may thus be seen as an interactive process of knowledge construction in which the learner as well as other actors contribute and negotiate. Computer supported collaborative learning (CSCL) environments, tools, and communication media may strengthen the effects of collaborative learning. This strengthening is brought about by the potential of computer programs with regard to visualizing argumentation, cognitive supportive tools, and the possibility of storage of discussion and argumentation during collaboration. In computer-supported collaborative partner systems in which the program is the actor with whom to negotiate, the interactive process of knowledge construction may be influenced directly.

In our analysis of dialogues of students in the DSA project, we found coordination to be a crucial aspect of collaboration. In our view, it is very important to realize that focusing, checking, and argumentation are coordination processes in discourse essentially dealing with content matters. The incidence and the nature of these coordination mechanisms are contingent on characteristics of the knowledge being constructed and the problem to be solved. *Focusing* refers to specific task strategies, that is, subproblems to be solved, and to the concepts necessary to discuss. *Checking* refers to the integration and acceptance of knowledge transferred, and *argumentation* is about specific inferences that may be made. All these processes operate in a virtual collective space that serves as the common ground for further negotiation and task execution. It is our opinion that in order to obtain more insight in the processes of collaborative problem solving, analysis of discourse in relation to content is required. In the collaboration task of the DSA project (The Camp Puzzle), however, the content domain is limited and all the information the participants use is known beforehand and can be specified easily. In a semantically rich and open task, the analysis of content and performance in interaction is much more difficult and laborious. Such tasks cannot be analyzed as if all correct solutions and tasks goals can be fixed and unambiguously assessed. In the next section, we give an example for collaborative writing.

CTP: THE COMPUTER AS TOOL AND COMMUNICATIVE MEDIUM FOR WRITING

Writing clearly is an open task. Writing texts of any length has been shown to be a complex process in which several interrelated processes can be distinguished, each with its own dynamics and constraints (for a review, see Alamargot & Chanquoy, 2001). The main advantage of collaborative writing, compared to individual writing, is to offer a workspace where the writers can receive immediate feedback from each other on their writing actions. Furthermore, the discussions generated by the activity make the collaborators verbalize and negotiate many things: representations, purpose, plans, doubts, and so on. Collaborating writers have to test their hypotheses, justify their propositions, and make their goals explicit. This may lead to progressively more conscious control and increased awareness of the processes (Gere & Stevens, 1989; Giroud, 1999; Roussey & Gombert, 1992).

At our laboratory in Utrecht, we study electronic collaborative text production with respect to the relationship between characteristics of interaction on one hand and learning and problem solving on the other. In the CTP project (Collaborative Text Production), a network-based groupware program has been developed that combines a shared word processor, chat boxes, and private information sources to foster the collaborative writing of texts. The working screen of the program displays several private and shared windows (see Fig. 10.1). The two private information windows at the top (Task Window and Arguments window) both contain task information. The Task Window displays the task assignment and the Arguments window

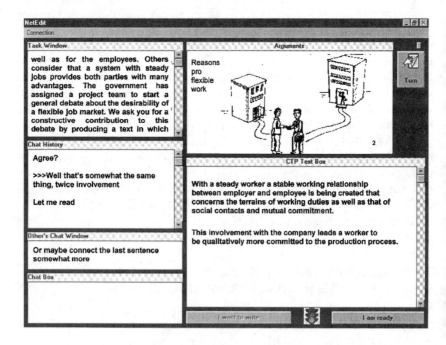

FIG. 10.1.   The collaborative text production tool (CTP; Text box, Chat and Task window translated from Dutch).

displays additional information with which an individual participant is provided. A "turn pages" button may be used to turn the pages when the information is in pictorial format. The Chat Box can be used to communicate information that simultaneously can be seen by the writing partner in the Other's Chat Window. This arrangement allows partners to send messages simultaneously. When a message is ready, pressing the return button will enter it into the shared Chat History, where the previous dialogue is available for review by both participants.

The CTP Text Box is the shared space in which the participants may enter, edit, and revise the text they are currently writing. They both can write in the same text but not simultaneously. Two buttons and a traffic light under the CTP Text Box are used to signal turn-taking intentions and turn giving. The program allows logging of all keystrokes during task execution. The CTP tool is currently replaced by a new groupware program, which is similar in design (Erkens, Tabachneck-Schijf, Jaspers, & Van Berlo, 2000).

The data we report here are from an earlier study (Andriessen et al., 1996); the analysis is new. That study showed that, in the written product, students explored multiple viewpoints and elaborated on their arguments. The program was used to gather data on the effects of external information representations on argumentative text. The discussion by the participants, the chat messages, the button actions, and all changes in the text were logged in a time-based protocol to be used for further analysis. In this experiment, 74 university students in social sciences, working in pairs, were instructed to write two texts considering the problem of the overpopulation of rabbits and considering labor policy on employability. Pairs were randomly assigned to two different conditions. Students were provided with some predefined arguments in textual format or in graphical representations. The graphical representations gave rise to a greater number and variety of self-generated arguments and elaborations of predefined arguments in the written products than did the textual information. This, however, did not relate to more coherent texts or advanced text production strategies. Content elaboration and coherent collaborative writing seemed to rely on different processes.

For the purpose of the current contribution, we present an analysis of content elaboration on a subset of protocols of this collaborative writing task. Our goal is to present data showing the relationship between interaction and task performance in collaborative electronic text production in terms of the concepts used. The main question involves the relation between concepts discussed during interaction at the chat interface and concepts included in the text produced during three phases of collaborative text production. We assume the concepts that the students activate and focus on to be dependent on the activities they employ in fulfilling the writing assignment.

The Collaborative Writing Process

Three major activities are usually distinguished in individual writing: planning, translating, and revising. These activities are supposed to operate in a sequence, with possible recursion. Most models include (at least) the following components (see Alamargot & Chanquoy, 2001, for a critical review):

- *Conceptual or referential planning* comprises the three subprocesses of (1) idea generation, that is, retrieval of ideas from memory and/or from external sources; (2) selection and evaluation of the retrieved ideas; and (3) organization of ideas, relating these ideas to each other, in accordance with goals, instructions, addressee, type of text, and so on. There is much discussion about the nature of the output of the planning process; proposals involve, for example, (pre-) textual structures (such as an outline), or mental networks of relationships (such as a diagram). Such proposals also touch the nature of the next writing process, translating (Hayes & Nash, 1996; Kellogg, 1993).
- *Translating* comprises sequential ordering of the information (linearizing) and linguistic coding of the resulting sequence; the plan is being translated into a grammatically correct and pragmatically adequate linear text.
- *Revising*, during which the writer may modify his or her text, evaluate its adequacy to the assignments (addressee, goal, etc.), and possibly reorganize the initial mental structure. This process probably does not only intervene at the end of the writing phase, but during the whole composing process (Rijlaarsdam & Van den Bergh, 1996).

Process analysis of individual writing has shown a number of activities with different activation over time. This has been the topic of a series of papers by Van den Bergh and Rijlaarsdam, in which thinking-aloud protocol segments were coded according to the type of writing activity, such as structuring (Van den Bergh & Rijlaarsdam, 1996), rereading, and generating (Breetvelt, Van den Bergh, & Rijlaarsdam, 1996), or idea generation (Van den Bergh & Rijlaarsdam, 1999). The frequency of each activity over time was plotted and (by multilevel analysis) correlated with the quality of the resulting text. By these techniques the authors showed that the pattern of writing activities changes over time, and that the same goes for the relation with text quality. Moreover, substantial differences between writers were observed in these respects. Collaborative writing may constitute an additional source of evidence for certain types of activities because it offers an explicit source of data about negotiation. To be able to interpret changes in frequencies of (inferred) activities over time and their relationships with text quality, we need a theory of collaborative writing. As a first step, we propose a framework of content co-construction in collaborative writing: the Collective Landscape Model, by combining the work on individual writing of Galbraith (1999) and the text comprehension model proposed by Van den Broek (Van den Broek, Risden, Fletcher, & Thurlow, 1996; Van den Broek, Young, Tzeng, & Linderholm, 1999).

Collective Landscape Model

Generating and Formulating Content. The generation and formulation by an individual of content that is new for this individual is an important source of learning. Galbraith (1996, 1999) claims that the construction of knowledge is the result of a dialectic between the writer's disposition and the written text. The "knowledge-constituting" model's (Galbraith, 1999) basic claim is that the knowledge encoded in sentences is represented, implicitly, within a distributed network of conceptual relationships, and ideas are synthesized by constraint satisfaction within this network rather than being directly retrieved. The main condition for this dialectic to come into play is a writer trying to express his ideas as propositionally correct sentences that follow each other in one way or another. In this way, a first rough draft of a (part of a) text is developing, not necessarily very coherent, but also different from a list of notes or an organized outline. Only during rewriting of the first draft in a second phase the writer tries to take into account the rhetorical goals of a text. This last process has been described as *problem solving*, possibly leading to knowledge transformation (Bereiter & Scardamalia, 1987). It seems that according to this position, the very fact that during rough drafting, there are no constraints present for organization, planning, or dealing with an audience, allows the activation of the greatest number of (new) ideas. In addition, ideas that are activated and written down give rise to new ideas; in other words, old ideas change because they have been formulated and written down without rhetorical constraints (Galbraith, 1999). Only by writing ideas down, new ideas can come up. In collaborative writing, there is additional input in the form of new ideas and feedback generated by the partner or coming from other external sources. We represent this as a "collective landscape of activated ideas and concepts."

Representing Content. The landscape model (Van den Broek et al., 1999) is based on the activation of concepts during the reading process, leading to the formation of a content representation. During reading, concepts and relations between concepts are activated. The number of concepts than can be active at the same time is limited. Four sources of activation can be described: (1) the text that is currently being processed, (2) the immediately preceding reading cycle, (3) earlier processed information, and (4) other relevant background knowledge of the reader. Together, the limited attentional capacity and access to these sources of activation cause text elements to constantly fluctuate in activation as the reader proceeds through a text. When a concept is activated, other concepts that are connected to it will be somewhat activated as well. This fluctuating of activation of concepts can be described as a landscape of peaks and valleys for each concept across reading cycles (Van den Broek et al., 1996).

We propose to discuss the collaborative writing process as one of collective knowledge construction, in which the individual dispositions combine to a (virtual) landscape of concepts that are activated at a specific moment by making them explicit. Under ideal circumstances, cycles of individual knowledge constitution may be confronted in a collective landscape of concepts activated and discussed. This process is visualized in Fig. 10.2. We use the collective landscape metaphor to represent interactive knowledge building rather than individual learning. The landscape is located outside the individuals participating in the dialogue but it is supposed to represent the concepts that individuals are conscious about to differing degrees. The *collective landscape* can be seen as the result at the content level of the focusing and other coordinating activities of the students collaborating. In fact, the collective landscape represents the change of focus in this process. Checking and argumentation may function to control and to reactivate concepts. In addition, our application output can be explicitly observed on

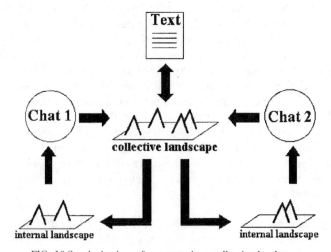

FIG. 10.2.   Activation of concepts in a collective landscape.

two platforms, the chat and the text. The text is the product of collaboration, and is formed during collaboration.

We conceive collaborative writing as a process of collective knowledge co-construction, in which individual knowledge dispositions combine through linguistic externalization in chat and text into a landscape of concepts with fluctuating levels of activation. These concepts are part of the *common ground* of the participants, that is their shared information during interaction (Clark & Brennan, 1991). The purpose of the grounding process, the process of creating common ground, for the subjects is to agree on content (arguments) to include in the text. Of course the concepts activated will also depend on the information and knowledge that the students already have of the subject matter and of the positions pro or con that can be taken.

Research Questions

Collaborative writing is analyzed here with respect to the conceptual dimension of interaction (Baker, 1999). We consider concepts as being active in the collective landscape if mentioned in either chat or text during a specific cycle of collaborative writing. The comparison between chat and text in terms of concepts shows the relationship between content discussed and content actually used in the text. The comparison allows to specify to what extent discussion contributes to the content of text production, for different moments during writing and for different (opposing) positions to defend: pro steady or pro flexible work. In the analysis that follows, we try to address two questions: (1) What is the relationship between the concepts produced in the chat and those in the resulting texts measured during three phases of collaborative interaction? and (2) Is this relationship affected by the content of the position to be defended?

We expect the results to be different according to the phase of the writing task in which participants are involved. For practical reasons, we distinguish three periods of writing. The first period is ended when the participants have written their first draft, the third period is ended by the final text and the second period is determined by the middle text between the first and final text. So every phase contains a chat period followed by a text. Figure 10.3 pictures the writing process in three phases. We focus on the co-construction of knowledge during this process, by comparing the concepts that are produced during three phases of writing, at the level of interaction in the chats, and those in the text.

During a phase predominantly characterized by content generation, we expect many new concepts to appear in the chat discussion, some of which may later be selected for and included in the text. During a phase predominantly characterized by selection and formulation of content, we do not ex-

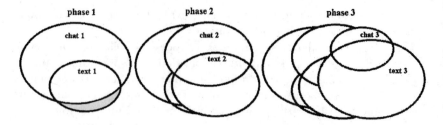

FIG. 10.3. The writing process in three phases.

pect much new information to appear and a high overlap between the concepts included in the text and those introduced in the chat. During a phase characterized by revision and reflection, we expect rewriting, editing and reordering of information, which may eventually lead to new concepts directly being introduced in the text itself. Such expectations are general, and obviously not precise, but not much is known about strategies for collaborative writing. With respect to argumentative text production, each of these phases presents its specific problems to writers (Coirier, Andriessen, & Chanquoy, 1999), which we address in another chapter (Andriessen, Erkens, Van der Laak & Peters, 2001).

Method

Fourteen dyads of university students collaborated 75 min with the CTP program to write an argumentative text on labor policy. A total of nine dyads defending the position pro steady work and five dyads the position pro flexible work. The program offered each student three arguments in advance. One of the students received three arguments supporting the advantages of flexible work and the other student received three arguments supporting steady work.

All data, chats, and texts were analyzed on a propositional level. A *proposition* is defined here as a sentence or part of a sentence, which contains one key concept, or the description of the key concept. This gives us the possibility to score the chat and text on the research variables key concept and topic. A *key concept* is a unit of content linked to a topic of discussion. In total we distinguished 96 key concepts; dyads use on the average 33.4 concepts. We define *topic* as the position the concept is used to support. These topics are *flexible work* and *steady work*. The topic does not have to be mentioned explicitly in a proposition. In some cases, the topic is mentioned in an earlier proposition, and it is clear that the specific topic is the topic to which the concept is referring. To illustrate these variables, we give an example of a coded chat fragment in Table 10.3. With this coding system, we obtained interrater agreement percentages of 92% for topic and 65% for the key

TABLE 10.3
Example of Scored Protocol Fragment

Actor	Concept	Topic	Proposition
Client*	Specialization	Steady work	What do you think about the argument: With steady work people will become professionals in their work?
Server	Specialization		Yes, but it is restricted to the company where they are working. A person will get restricted on that working area.
Server	Commitment	Steady work	I think that he or she is more committed with the company or institute.
Server	Loyal employee	Steady work	And that is more important than for a flexible worker.
Client	Commitment	Steady work	Commitment because of steady work, I think.
Server	Contacts	Flexible work	Eeeeh. I think that is an argument supporting steady work. Because else (that is as flexible worker) you will have more contacts.
Client	Contacts	Flexible work	So, supporting flexible work: many contacts.
Server	Exchange	Flexible work	And supporting flexible work: easy exchange.

Note. *Students are named to the computer (client or server) they are working on.

concepts (Cohen's kappa's .77 and .63, respectively). Taking into account the complexity of interpreting semantic categories, these percentages and kappa's are acceptable.

Results

As a first step, we determined the number of key concepts used in each phase. Table 10.4 shows the mean number of different concepts discussed in the chats and used in the texts in each phase. In addition, we defined a measure for *information density* as the number of different concepts used in a phase divided by the number of propositions of that phase. Figure 10.4 visually displays the information density in chat and text in the three phases.

With respect to the number of concepts generated and discussed in the chat during each phase, we observe a steady decline over time. Furthermore, over time, discussion seems to become more focused on a smaller number of concepts. When we look at the texts, we see the greatest increase in number of concepts between the first and the second phase. With respect to the information density in the chat periods, we observe less discussion or more efficient discussion about a concept during later phases of text production. In the texts, the reverse case can be observed; concepts are dis-

TABLE 10.4
Mean Numbers of Concepts, Propositions, and Ratio
of Information Density in Chats and Texts
in the Three Periods of Collaborative Writing

Period	Mean Number of Concepts (sd)		Mean Number of Propositions (sd)		Information Density
Chat 1	16.36	(10.85)	32.00	(26.55)	.52
Text 1	5.28	(4.32)	6.00	(5.22)	.95
Chat 2	9.18	(4.77)	12.82	(8.57)	.74
Text 2	15.69	(4.33)	23.54	(7.89)	.65
Chat 3	6.57	(4.13)	9.29	(7.55)	.71
Text 3	22.57	(4.75)	38.64	(12.74)	.58

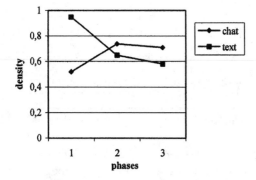

FIG. 10.4. Information density (concepts per proposition) in chats and texts of three phases.

cussed with single proposition at the beginning, but are more elaborated in later phases. All this seems in line with a model during which generating, formulating, and revising operate in consecutive phases. The generation phase (Phase 1) introduces new concepts, but does not include much attention to their realization in the text. Phase 2 shows text formulation, implying less new concepts being introduced, but more text. In Phase 3, the text is organized and reformulated in some respects, with some new concepts introduced, but not too many.

Correspondence of Concepts in Chats and Texts. The first research question concerns the correspondence of concepts active in chats and texts during the different phases. Correspondences between chat and text in the same phase (e.g. chat 1–text 1) reflect the parts of the landscape in which subjects agree, in other words, it reflects the contribution of effective co-construction to the text during a phase. Chat correspondences between different phases (e.g., chat 1–chat 2) reflect parts of the landscape that are reactivated. Correspondences between texts (e.g., text 1–text 2) allow assessing the relative impor-

TABLE 10.5
Proportions Corresponding Key Concepts
in Chats and Texts in the Three Periods

Period	No. of Concepts	Chat 1	Chat 2	Chat 3	Text 1	Text 2	Text 3
Chat 1	16.36		18.12%	14.25%	19.38%	33.51%	51.33%
Chat 2	9.18	32.29%		16.68%	9.80%	52.85%	68.46%
Chat 3	6.57	45.21%	29.69%		15.13%	25.10%	90.23%
Text 1	5.28	55.54%	15.74%	13.67%		79.93%	90.14%
Text 2	15.69	35.33%	31.25%	8.34%	29.41%		91.09%
Text 3	22.57	39.22%	29.35%	21.74%	24.04%	66.04%	

tance of a text production phase for the end result, which is another indication of co-construction. Note, however, that in the case of texts, differences between subsequent phases are to be taken cumulatively, because text 1 is for the most part included in text 2, and text 2 in text 3.

The rows of Table 10.5 display the proportion of corresponding concepts in a phase. For example, there are 16.36 concepts used in chat 1, 18.12% of these concepts correspond with chat 2, 14.25% correspond with chat 3, 19.38% correspond with text 1, and so on. Another conclusion of reading the table could be that, for example, 19.38% of the concepts discussed in chat 1 reappear in text 1, which comprises 55.54% of the total amount of concepts in text 1. We discuss the results for each phase.

Phase 1. Many concepts (16.36) are discussed during chat 1, but only 19.38% of these are taken over to text 1. It seems that during this phase, the subjects merely generate information, but they do not enter all this information in the first draft.

Phase 2. In chat 2, less concepts (9.18) are discussed than in chat 1, and ⅓ of these concepts are taken over from chat 1, so there is substantially less activation of new concepts. Conversely, more than ½ of the information discussed is transferred to text 2, indicating stronger agreement, a lower selection threshold, more efficient co-construction, and/or more effective decision making. It seems that compared to the previous phase, the subjects select information and include it in the text. This is the most important phase of co-construction and perhaps negotiation with regard to the actual writing of the text.

Phase 3. In chat 3 even less concepts are being discussed (6.57, or 21.7%), and ¾ of these concepts are taken over from chats 1 and 2. Almost all concepts discussed end up in the text (90.23%). Text 3 is for ⅓ based on text 2, but still contains seven more concepts. It seems that during this phase, we find almost complete agreement, no selection criterion, perfect co-construction, and efficient decision making. This seems to be characteristics of an efficient completion process.

Influence of the Position Defended. With regard to the second research question, whether the correspondence between the concepts in the chats and texts relate to the position to be taken, we refer to Fig. 10.5. In Figure 10.5 the distribution of concepts related to the two topics, steady and flexible work, are shown for the two positions.

In the chats and texts of dyads defending the flexible work position, the majority of the concepts that are mentioned relate to the flexible topic. In the texts in the three phases, almost all of the concepts (about 98%) are bound to this topic. In the chats, 86% of the concepts are about flexible work, whereas only 14% are related to steady work. It seems safe to conclude that in texts defending the flexible position (remember that the positions were assigned), chats and texts are merely focused on one side of the position. However, the students defending the alternative position (steady work) refer to both topics in a more balanced way. In the chats, about $\frac{1}{2}$ of the concepts (55%) are focused on steady work. However, while discussing how to defend steady work, participants frequently mention concepts related to flexible work (45%). In the texts, concepts related to the alternative position are emphasized even more (57%).

Probably differences in knowledge and attitude of the students with respect to the different positions affect both the discussion and the selection of information. When the students have to write an argumentative text supporting flexible work (a more familiar topic for our students, we suppose), concepts will enter the collective landscape and can be used directly in the construction of the text. However, the activation of concepts about flexible work will also occur in the case of students having to defend the alternative position. The dispositions of the students about this topic

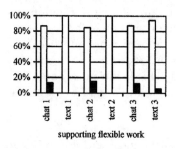 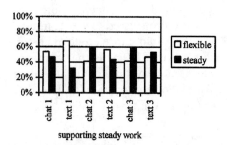

FIG. 10.5. Distribution of concepts between the topics in chats and texts for three phases.

will be less elaborate. Because of the assignment, they will have to put more effort to generate arguments with regard to steady work. So, forced to elaborate on a less known topic, their discussion and texts will be more differentiated and balanced.

Discussion

The comparison between phases in terms of concepts allows some straightforward conclusions. During Phase 1 of collaborative writing, the focus of co-construction is on the generation of new information. Generation takes place in every phase, but its main activity is in Phase 1. This has the form of discussion at the level of the chat, and does not lead to much text during this phase. Nevertheless, content and shape of the landscape are largely determined in Phase 1. In Phase 2, co-construction revolves around already generated content, already present in the landscape. There is not much continuity for the chat, as chats do not overlap very much between Phase 1 and Phase 2. Neither is much new information added to the landscape. Instead, most of the text is generated during this phase, which requires agreed-upon information. This process seems in part to rely on reinstatement of concepts from earlier discussion because much information in the text is based on earlier chats. This finding can be interpreted as support for the utility of the notion of a landscape as a collective space for negotiation. In contrast with general expectations, Phase 3 does not seem to involve extensive revision or discussion but rather very efficient decision making. Additional analyses are needed to confirm such conclusions, especially with respect to interaction and communication.

As for the influence of the content of the positions to be defended, we have found important differences between the two positions. The assignment to defend steady work results in the activation of more concepts for the alternative position than the assignment to defend flexible work. We suppose that university students have more knowledge and first-hand experience with flexible work. So, the activation of the concepts in the collective landscape may be related to this disposition of the individual students. Public discussion refers to flexible work. To defend a less publicly known position will enforce elaboration and may profit from the activation of concepts of the alternative position. An alternative explanation may be that steady work is the old, status quo position and flexible work the new, changing position in society. To defend the new, changing position, it is necessary to elaborate on the pros and to refute the cons related to this position, as everybody is familiar with the status quo. Whereas in defending the status quo, it is not sufficient to elaborate on the pros of this position and to refute the disadvantages, but one should also attack the alleged advantages of the seducing, new "revolutionary" alternative.

GENERAL DISCUSSION

In this chapter, we started with the claim that for understanding electronic collaboration, it is important to get more insight into the relationship between interaction and task performance. Our interest in collaborative learning is about its role in increasing understanding by students of the concepts and beliefs in a domain. To investigate the process of co-construction of understanding, a step-by-step analysis of interaction and performance is necessary. An important problem in this type of research is the establishment of the units of analysis necessary to answer this type of question. Collaborative learning situations and the roles of computers therein may vary tremendously and may require different systems of analysis. Our conclusion is that the content involved in the assignment is a very important factor to deal with when analyzing collaboration. A related conclusion is that the pragmatic level of analysis (discourse actions) is not sufficient to explain the role of collaboration for co-construction of understanding. Coordination processes in discourse essentially deal with content matters, so a semantic analysis (concepts discussed) is also required. Finally, we claim that such studies should involve open tasks that give space for negotiation of meaning and for co-construction of knowledge. In the context of two research projects, we present two examples of systems for the analysis of cognition and interaction during collaboration. In a first study we found three coordinating activities of special importance, as they are related to both interaction and performance: focusing, checking, and argumentation. The main proposal put forward in our chapter is that coordination processes serve to establish a collective space that serves as a common ground to be used during task execution. To illustrate our main points, we present a second study analyzing the use of concepts in a collaborative writing situation. For the case of collaborative writing, the conceptual dimension of interaction can be described as operating in a collective landscape of concepts, differing in activation level. As a first step, the content of this landscape is analyzed as a function of the content of the chat discussion, taken as an expression of individual dispositions of the participants, and of the content of already produced text during writing.

The landscape conception seems an appropriate metaphor for discussing what participants do; that is, to activate and focus on concepts in a process of co-construction. Moreover, it seems appropriate to grasp characteristics of what is collective in collaboration. While individual dispositions serve to produce content for the landscape, and the landscape may affect new content to be generated from individual dispositions, negotiations are about ideas and concepts that are collectively available. Concepts generated and produced during the chat remain active for a while, even when not discussed straightaway, to be reactivated later for discussion and selection for use in the text. An interesting question would concern the order in which such concepts are reactivated: Does linearization take place at the level of negotiation, or is it part of the formulation process? Many more such questions can be asked. Indeed, a general model of collaboration at the conceptual level with respect to the coordinated construction of content could be powerful enough to provide some answers.

REFERENCES

Alamargot, D., & Chanquoy, L. (2001). *Through the models of text production.* Amsterdam: Amsterdam University Press.

Andriessen, J., Erkens. G., Overeem, E., & Jaspers, J. (1996, September). *Using complex information in argumentation for collaborative text production.* Paper presented at the UCIS '96 Conference, Poitiers, France.

Andriessen, J., Erkens. G., Van der Laak, C., & Peters, N. (2001). Argumentation as negotiation in electronic collaborative writing. In J. Andriessen, M. Baker, & D. Suthers (Eds.), *Arguing to learn.* Manuscript in preparation.

Baker, M. (1996). Argumentation and cognitive change in collaborative problem-solving dialogues. *COAST* [Research Rep. No. CR-13/96]. France.

Baker, M. (1999). Argumentation and constructive interaction. In J. E. B. Andriessen & P. Coirier (Eds.), *Foundations of argumentative text processing* (pp. 179–203). The Netherlands: Amsterdam University Press.

Baker, M., & Bielaczyc, K. (1995). Missed opportunities for learning in collaborative problem-solving interactions. In J. Greer (Ed.), *Proceedings of AI-ED 95—7th World Conference on Artificial Intelligence in Education* (pp. 210–218). Charlottesville, VA: Association for the Advancement of Computing in Education.

Barnes, D., & Todd, F. (1977). *Communication and learning in small groups.* London: Routledge & Kegan Paul.

Bereiter, C., & Scardamalia, M. (1987). *The psychology of written composition.* Hillsdale, NJ: Lawrence Erlbaum Associates.

Breetvelt, I., Van den Bergh, H., & Rijlaarsdam, G. (1996). Rereading and generating and their relation to text quality. An application of multilevel analysis on writing process data. In G. Rijlaarsdam, H. Van den Bergh, & M. Couzijn (Eds.), *Theories, models and methodology in writing research* (pp. 10–20). Amsterdam: Amsterdam University Press.

Brown, A. L., & Palincsar, A. S. (1989) Guided cooperative learning and individual knowledge acquisition. In L. B. Resnick (Ed.), *Knowing, learning and instruction: Essays in honor of Robert Glaser* (pp. 393–453). Hillsdale, NJ: Lawrence Erlbaum Associates.

Brown, J., Collins, A., & Duguid, P. (1989). Situated cognition and the culture of learning, *Educational Researcher, 18,* 32–41.

Burton, D. (1981). Analysing spoken discourse. In M. Coulthard & M. Montgomery (Eds.), *Studies in discourse analysis* (pp. 61–82). London: Routledge & Kegan Paul.

Chan, T. W., & Baskin, A. B. (1990). Learning companion systems. In C. Frasson & G. Gaulthier (Eds.), *Intelligent tutoring systems: At the crossroad of artificial intelligence and education* (pp. 6–34). Norwood, NJ: Ablex.

Clark, H. H., & Brennan, S. E. (1991). Grounding in communication. In L. B. Resnick, J. M. Levine, & S. D. Teasley (Eds.), *Perspectives on socially shared cognition* (pp. 127–150). Washington, DC: American Psychological Association.

Cognition and Technology Group at Vanderbilt (1990). Anchored instruction and its relationship to situated cognition. *Educational Researcher, 19*(6), 2–10.

Cohen, E. G. (1994). Restructuring the classroom: Conditions for productive small groups. *Review of Educational Research, 64*(1), 1–35.

Coirier, P., Andriessen, J. E. B., & Chanquoy, L. (1999). From planning to translating: The specificity of argumentative writing. In J. E. B. Andriessen & P. Coirier (Eds.), *Foundations of argumentative text processing* (pp. 1–29). Amsterdam: Amsterdam University Press.

Cooper, C. R., & Cooper, R. G., Jr. (1984). Skill in peer learning discourse: What develops? In S. A. Kuczaj, II (Ed.), *Discourse development: Progress in cognitive development research* (pp. 77–97). New York: Springer.

Dillenbourg, P. (1999). Introduction: What do you mean by "collaborative learning"? In P. Dillenbourg (Ed.), *Collaborative learning: Cognitive and computational aspects* (pp. 1–19). New York: Pergamon.

Dillenbourg, P., & Self, J. A. (1992). A computational approach to socially distributed cognition. *European Journal of Psychology of Education, 3*(4), 353–372.

Doise, W., & Mugny, G. (1984). *The social development of the intellect.* New York: Pergamon.

Duffy, T. M., & Jonassen, D. H. (1991, May). Constructivism: New implications for instructional technology? *Educational Technology,* 7–12.

Erkens, G. (1997). Cooperatief probleemoplossen met computers in het onderwijs: Het modellerenvan cooperatieve dialogen voor de ontwikkeling van intelligente onderwijssystemen [Cooperative problem solving with computers in education: Modelling of cooperative dialogues for the the design of intelligent educational systems]. Unpublished doctoral dissertation, Utrecht University, the Netherlands.

Erkens, G., Tabachneck-Schijf, H. J. M., Jaspers, J., & Van Berlo, J. (2000, September). *How does computer-supported collaboration influence argumentative writing?* Paper presented at the Workshop on Argumentative Text Production, Earli SIG Writing Conference 2000, Verona, Italy.

Galbraith, D. (1999). Writing as a knowledge-constituting process. In M. Torrance & D. Galbraith (Eds.), *Knowing what to write: Conceptual processes in text production* (pp. 139–159). Amsterdam: Amsterdam University Press.

Gere, A., & Stevens, R. S. (1989). The language of writing groups: How oral response shapes revision. In S. W. Freedman (Ed.), *The acquisition of written language: Response and revision* (pp. 85–105). Norwood, NJ: Ablex.

Giroud, A. (1999). Studying argumentative text processing through collaborative writing. In J. E. B. Andriessen & P. Coirier (Eds.), *Foundations of argumentative text processing.* Amsterdam: Amsterdam University Press.

Grice, H. P. (1975). Logic and conversation. In P. Cole & J. Morgan (Eds.), *Syntax and semantics* (pp. 41–58). New York: Academic Press.

Grosz, B. J. (1978). Discourse knowledge. In D. E. Walker (Ed.), *Understanding spoken language* (pp. 269–286). New York: Elsevier North Holland.

Hayes, J. R., & Flower, L. S. (1980). Identifying the organization of writing processes. In L. W. Gregg & E. R. Steinberg (Eds.), *Cognitive process in writing* (pp. 3–30). Hillsdale, NJ: Lawrence Erlbaum Associates.

Hayes, J. R., & Nash, J. G. (1996). On the nature of planning in writing. In C. M. Levy & S. Ransdell (Eds.), *The science of writing* (pp. 29–55). Mahwah, NJ: Lawrence Erlbaum Associates.

Henri, F. (1995). Distance learning and computer mediated communication: Interactive, quasi-interactive or monologue? In C. O'Malley (Ed.), *Computer supported collaborative learning* (pp. 145–165). [NATO ASI Series, Vol. No. 128]. Berlin: Springer.

Johnson, D. W., & Johnson, R. T. (1975). *Learning together and alone.* Englewood Cliffs, NJ: Prentice-Hall.

Kanselaar, G., & Erkens, G. (1994). Interactivity in cooperative problem solving with computers. In S. Vosniadu, E. De Corte, & H. Mandl (Eds.), *Technology based learning environments: Psychological and educational foundations* (pp. 55–66). [NATO ASI Series F]. Berlin: Springer.

Katz, S., & Lesgold, A. (1993). The role of the tutor in computer-based collaborative learning situations. In S. P. Lajoie & S. J. Derry (Eds.), *Computers as cognitive tools* (pp. 289–317). Hillsdale, NJ: Lawrence Erlbaum Associates.

Kellogg, R. T. (1993). Observations on the psychology of thinking and writing. *Composition Studies, 21*, 3–41.

Kolodner, J. (1993). *Case-based reasoning.* San Mateo, CA: Morgan Kaufmann.

Lehnert, W. G. (1978). *The process of question answering.* Hillsdale, NJ: Lawrence Erlbaum Associates.

Petraglia, J. (1998). *Reality by design: The rhetoric and technology of authenticity in education.* Mahwah, NJ: Lawrence Erlbaum Associates.

Quignard, M., & Baker, M. (1999). Favoring modelable computer-mediated argumentative dialogue in collaborative problem-solving situations. In S. P. Lajoie & M. Vivet (Eds.), *Artificial intelligence in education* (pp. 129–136). Amsterdam: IOS Press.

Rijlaarsdam, G., & Van den Bergh, H. (1996). The dynamics of composing—An agenda for research into an interactive compensatory model of writing: Many questions, some answers. In C. M. Levy & S. Ransdell (Eds.), *The science of writing* (pp. 107–125). Mahwah, NJ: Lawrence Erlbaum Associates.

Roussey, J. Y., & Gombert, A. (1992). Ecriture en dyade d'un texte argumentatif par des enfants de huit ans. [Writing in dyads of an argumentative text by 8-year-old children]. *Archives de psychologie* [Archives of Psychology], 297–315.

Salomon, G. (1993). On the nature of pedagogic computer tools: The case of the writing partner. In S. P. Lajoie & S. J. Derry (Eds.), *Computers as cognitive tools* (pp. 289–317). Hillsdale, NJ: Lawrence Erlbaum Associates.

Scardamalia, M., Bereiter, C., & Lamon, M. (1994). The CSILE-project: Trying to bring the classroom into World 3. In K. McGilly (Ed.), *Classroom lessons: Integrating cognitive theory and classroom practice* (pp. 202–229). Cambridge, MA: MIT Press.

Schiffrin, D. (1987). *Discourse markers. [Studies in Interactional Sociolinguistics 5].* Cambridge: Cambridge University Press.

Sharan, S., & Sharan, Y. (1976). *Small-group teaching.* Englewood Cliffs, NJ: Educational Technology Publications.

Slavin, R. E. (1983). *Cooperative learning.* New York: Longman.

Suthers, D., & Weiner, A. (1995). GroupWare for developing critical discussion skills. Pittsburgh, PA: University of Pittsburgh. Available at http://www.pitt.edu/~suthers/belvedere.

Teasley, S., & Rochelle, J. (1993). Constructing a joint problem space: The computer as tool for sharing knowledge. In S. P. Lajoie & S. J. Derry (Eds.), *Computers as cognitive tools* (pp. 229–257). Hillsdale, NJ: Lawrence Erlbaum Associates.

Van den Bergh, H., & Rijlaarsdam, G. (1996). The dynamics of composing: Modeling writing process data. In C. M. Levy & S. Ransdell (Eds.), *The science of writing* (pp. 207–232). Mahwah, NJ: Lawrence Erlbaum Associates.

Van den Bergh, H., & Rijlaarsdam, G. (1999). The dynamics of idea generation during writing: An on-line study. In M. Torrance & D. Galbraith (Eds.), *Knowing what to write: Conceptual processes in text production* (pp. 99–120). Amsterdam: Amsterdam University Press.

Van den Broek, P. W., Risden, K., Fletcher, C. R., & Thurlow, R. (1996). A 'landscape' view of reading: Fluctuating patterns of activation and the construction of a stable memory representation. In B. K. Britton & A. C. Graesser (Eds.), *Models of understanding text* (pp. 165–187). Mahwah, NJ: Lawrence Erlbaum Associates.

Van den Broek, P. W., Young, M., Tzeng, Y., & Linderholm, T. (1999). The landscape model of reading: Inferences and the online construction of a memory representation. In H. van Oostendorp & S. Goldman (Eds.), *The construction of mental representations during reading* (pp. 71–98). Mahwah, NJ: Lawrence Erlbaum Associates.

Webb, N. M. (1982). Student interaction and learning in small groups. *Review of Educational Research, 52*(3), 421–445.

Chapter 11

Science Inquiry in a Digital World: Possibilities for Making Thinking Visible

Susan R. Goldman
University of Illinois at Chicago

Richard A. Duschl
King's College London

Kirsten Ellenbogen
King's College London

Susan M. Williams
University of Texas, Austin

Carrie Tzou
Northwestern University

An important issue in education generally, and science education specifically, is understanding how to modify classroom learning environments to encourage cultures of inquiry rather than cultures of fact memorization. One fruitful approach researchers are taking is to look closely at the language of the classroom. The language of the classroom is important precisely because it provides the basic information for how knowledge is being constructed and on what grounds knowledge claims are being judged. In brief, the promotion of language-based activities helps make thinking visible. In turn, making thinking visible enables formative assessment opportunities for teachers that help students learn. To be sure, learning in any content area requires the mastery of a body of factual knowledge. However, for this knowledge to be useful, flexible, and usable, it must be represented and organized in ways that facilitate its use in context and under appropriate conditions (Bransford, Franks, Vye, & Sherwood, 1989; Simon, 1980; Whitehead, 1929). In science classrooms, the context and conditions of importance are the ways evidence is related to models and explanations and how arguments are constructed to link these three together. Not only facts must be represented; the processes by which disciplines generate new "facts" and knowledge need to be learned. These processes are as much social as they are cognitive. Individuals contribute ideas, thinking, and reasoning to a community-based, collaborative, knowledge construction process. Knowledge emerges as these ideas, thoughts, and reasoning "bump up against" one another in a dialectical process.

Of course, individuals engage in individual inquiry. However, their inquiry reflects the norms, values, and assumptions about the nature of knowledge that are held by the larger community of which they are a part (e.g., historians, scientists, mathematicians). For example, a scientist adheres to the rules of evidence and argumentation to which the community of scientists adheres. Individual scientists have a responsibility to take into account the knowledge generated by those who came before them. Thus, even individual inquiry is essentially a dialectical process in which one grapples with the ideas, thoughts, and reasoning of others as part of the social and epistemic process of convincing and understanding others.

Dialogue was one of the earliest venues for knowledge construction, as demonstrated by the Socratic Dialogues (van Eemeren, Grootendorst, & Henkemans, 1996). Dialogues typically take place between two (or more) individuals and their content is typically transient. Specific segments of talk fade from memory rather quickly, unless measures are taken to preserve them (e.g., by recording them on flip charts, paper, or magnetic tape). These recordings are useful as communal, external memories of the process and may become the object of reflection in further efforts to build knowledge. Electronic technologies open up new possibilities for knowledge construction venues and for making thinking visible. Some electronic technologies are specifically designed for dialogue. Examples include E-mail, online forums, threaded discussions, and communal databases.[1] As a group, these technologies afford the opportunity to transcend time and space constraints that set limits on who can participate in dialogues. There is a written record of the dialogue that is generated as part and parcel of the process of exchanging ideas and that is available for inspection and reflection at any time and by anyone who wants to join the discussion. As such, thinking is made visible and can be used to formatively assess emergent knowledge and knowledge-building processes.

A number of electronic conversation environments have been specifically developed for the purposes of supporting collaborative knowledge building and learning (Edelson, Pea, & Gomez, 1996; Guzdial, Turns, Rappin, & Carlson, 1995; Scardamalia & Bereiter, 1994; Scardamalia, et al., 1992). In addition to providing a written record of the thinking and reasoning processes of the community, they encourage members of the commu-

---

[1]Chat rooms, or MOOs, are another example. These are typically used synchronously and transcend place but not time, although some chat rooms can also be used asynchronously.

nity to build on each other's ideas, thinking and reasoning. To do so, they provide learners with opportunities to organize and reorganize information, using techniques for linking, cross-referencing, or grouping information in multiple ways. Examples of electronic conversation environments that have been developed specifically for use with science content are the Collaboratory Notebook (Edelson et al., 1996), CaMILE (Guzdial et al., 1995), SpeakEasy (Hoadley, Hsi, & Berman, 1995), Sensemaker (Bell, 1997), the BGUILE data reporting section (Tabak, Smith, Sandoval, & Reiser, 1996), and Knowledge Forum/CSILE[2] (Scardamalia, Bereiter, & Lamon, 1994). Several of these occur in the context of more encompassing science learning environments, for example, SpeakEasy and Sensemaker in Knowledge Integration Environment and WISE (Linn & Hsi, 2000); or BGUILE for Darwinian theories of evolution (Tabak et al., 1996). These environments provide information and support the manipulation of that information for purposes of creating opportunities for scientific discourse and scientific inquiry. The Collaboratory Notebook (Edelson et al., 1996), CaMILE (Guzdial et al., 1995), and Knowledge Forum (Scardamalia et al., 1994) can also be used in this way but offer the advantage of being somewhat more flexible in how they are incorporated into classroom-based scientific inquiry.

The focus of our research is to obtain a richer understanding of science language in use by students during inquiry instructional sequences. Specifically we are interested in understanding the patterns of knowledge construction and of evidence use among individuals as well as that found in the collaborative processes of knowledge building and learning among groups. The research reported here is a beginning step toward understanding how face-to-face small group and whole-class conversations mediate and are mediated by electronic conversation environments. We focus on young adolescents in the age range of 12 to 14 years. Specifically, we focus on the use of Knowledge Forum (KF) as an example of electronic environments for scaffolding student argumentation in science. We first describe in more detail our orientation toward scientific inquiry and discourse. We then describe preliminary findings from a science inquiry unit that occurred in two middle-school classrooms that were also using Knowledge Forum. We specifically compare the evidence and reasons used in the discourse during whole class, small group, and KF electronic environments. Based on the comparison, we discuss some implications for scaffolds that might foster and support science inquiry. We conclude with a discussion of important theoretical and empirical issues related to roles for electronic technologies in supporting scientific inquiry.

---

[2]Knowledge Forum is the second generation of CSILE (Computer Supported Collaborative Learning Environments). CSILE has been used for knowledge building in a variety of domains, including science (see Scardamalia et al., 1992, 1994, for discussion).

SCIENCE INQUIRY

Science, like many other disciplines, defines a culture of inquiry with respect to the nature of explanation, rules of evidence, and the form by which scientific arguments are made. Becoming acculturated to a scientific community means coming to understand and operate according to the norms and languages of that community. Such norms can be epistemic in nature when evidence is considered in the construction of explanations. Such norms can be social in nature when such explanations are presented and represented to other members of the scientific community via conferences and or refereed academic journals. Although there exist many genres and forms of science communication, one in particular serves as a foundation—argumentation. Unfortunately, given the focus of many science education classrooms in the United States that emphasize teaching what we know, we are currently failing to provide the language development support essential for the promotion of scientific inquiry processes. This is the case in spite of the fact that there are many science curricula that provide demonstrations and hands-on activities that resemble "real science." However, many of these curricula fail to provide support for the development of scientific inquiry and argumentation skills. These skills require students to not only "do" hands-on activities but to be mindful in their doing. That is, learners need to understand how activities relate to scientific argumentation, explanation, and evidentiary reasoning. Learners need to learn how to coordinate and evaluate a set of complex processes associated with transitioning from evidence to explanation. Successful students in science classrooms are able to coordinate concept learning and the construction of knowledge claims with metacognitive processes and the evaluation of knowledge claims.

Coordination, construction, and evaluation are processes that must be modeled for students and students need opportunities to "practice" them. Small group and whole-class configurations provide opportunities for the instruction and for the practice. The very process of making thinking visible creates opportunities for the exchange and explanation of ideas. Teachers can select and use these as exemplars that can extend students' scientific reasoning. Scaffolded whole-class conversations grounded in students' work and ideas and guided by exemplars of emergent scientific reasoning are, like scientific research groups, the crucible where guiding conceptions, meanings, criteria, and understandings are forged. Thus, the framing and scaffolding of discourse across small group, whole-class, and computer environments can facilitate students' discussions on the more subtle aspects of reasoning from evidence to explanation.

Complicating the process is the fact that students come to science investigations with well-established, although informal, theories about the world. These theories are frequently at variance with dominant scientific theories.

Many science educators and cognitive science researchers believe that it is important to deal with this informal knowledge. Several have developed various approaches to eliciting students' thinking prior to beginning instruction and using these beliefs as starting points for student inquiry (e.g., Minstrell, 1989; Osborne & Freyberg, 1985; R. White & Gunstone, 1992).[3] Students engage in inquiry in efforts to provide evidence and explanations in support of their ideas. This process can lead to the successive refinement and development of their thinking toward more normatively accepted theories and explanations for scientific phenomena. However, critical to the successful development of students' argumentation and inquiry skills are learning environments that provide modeling and coaching of these linguistic forms.

Learning Environments That Support Science as Inquiry

There is evidence to suggest that successful science education depends on students' involvement in forms of communication and reasoning that models the discourse that occurs in scientific communities. Gee (1994) and Lemke (1990) unpacked the variety of subtle discourse practices embedded in "talking science" in classrooms, as students and teachers use concepts, evidence, models, and explanations to advance positions of knowing. Roseberry, Warren & Conant (1992) and Schauble, Glaser, Duschl, Schulze, and John (1995) are two examples of research that shows how important the context of learning is to promoting science talk and the appropriation of scientific ways of knowing for purposes of understanding hypothesis testing (Roseberry et al., 1992) and of the role of experiments in science (Schauble et al., 1995). Hence, scientific inquiry requires immersion into the language, culture, and tools of scientific activity, a language and culture that is grounded in certain logical and epistemological assumptions that make science different from other ways of knowing. Science has particular ways of considering evidence; generating, testing, and evaluating theories, and communicating ideas. A goal of science education is to help students participate in these inquiry practices of science. Achieving this goal involves providing models and scaffolds that help students move from their informal forms of argumentation to scientific forms of argumentation. Modeling and scaffolding can come from the teacher (e.g., Roseberry et al., 1992; Schauble et al., 1995) and from scaffolds built into electronic environments (e.g., Edelson et al., 1996; Linn & Hsi, 2000; Scardamalia et al., 1994).

A critical element to inquiry is the reliance on evidence or empirical information to guide the construction and evaluation of knowledge claims.

---

[3]Some highly successful interventions explicitly do not start with students' alternative conceptions (e.g., White & Frederiksen, 1998).

In addition, Driver, Leach, Miller, and Scott (1996) called attention to the importance for scientific inquiry of understanding the "role of theoretical and conceptual ideas in framing any empirical inquiry and in interpreting its outcomes" (p. 12). For learning environments to support learning the contents and processes of science elements through inquiry, B. White and Frederiksen (1998) advocated for the presence of at least one of several conditions. These conditions include (a) the linkage of knowledge claims to evidence, especially through examination and extraction of patterns in data; (b) student discussion of guiding theoretical conceptions, other established knowledge claims, and purposes/goals/context of the inquiry; (c) methods/tools of investigation; and (d) clear criteria for including or excluding data.

Both Driver et al. (1996) and White and Fredericksen (1998) contended that it is important for students to see scientific inquiry as an epistemological and a social process in which knowledge claims can be shaped, modified, restructured, and at times, abandoned. Thus, learners need to have opportunities to discuss, evaluate, and debate the processes, contexts, and products of inquiry. Such discussions and debates expose the members of the community to each other's ideas, opinions, sources of evidence, and reasoning. They also make thinking visible to participants in the discourse. This visibility can, in turn, provide a formative assessment opportunity. Argumentation theory provides a fruitful way to approach the analysis and interpretation of these discussions and debates, especially for purposes of understanding how teachers and students engage in the construction and evaluation of scientific knowledge claims.

Argumentation as Central to Science as Inquiry

Argumentation is a genre of discourse central to doing science (Driver, Newton, & Osborne, 2000; Kelly, Chen, & Crawford, 1998; Kelly & Crawford, 1997; Kuhn, 1992; Lemke, 1990; Siegel, 1995; Suppe, 1998). Three forms of argumentation are typically recognized in the sciences—analytical or formal logic; dialectical or informal logic; and rhetorical or persuasive logic. Whereas the final reports of science that appear in journals and textbook typically portray science as purely analytical and logical, studies of science in the making (e.g., ethnographies of research groups) reveal that much of science involves dialectical and rhetorical argumentation schemes. Dunbar (1995), for example, showed how important the use of analogies is for the advancement of scientific discourse in research groups. Latour and Woolgar (1979/1986), in their case study of scientists, stressed the importance of inscriptions, special domain-specific forms of representing scientific information through graphs, formulas, and diagrams, in scientific discourse. In turn, Longino (1994) made a strong case for the impact the social network of scientists has on estabishing the grounds for objective knowledge claims.

With respect to philosophical studies of scientific discourse, Toulmin (1958) showed that the critical dynamics of arguments (i.e., locating warrants, evidence, and reasons) seem to be field or domain dependent. The implication for teaching science as inquiry is to recognize the importance of enabling learners to engage in argumentation and to do so in a well-defined field or domain. Doing so necessarily entails coming to understand the central concepts and underlying principles (e.g., the "facts") important to the particular domain. In other words, good arguments depend on knowing the facts of a field; however, argumentation does not necessarily follow from merely knowing the facts of a field. It is equally important to understand how to deploy the facts to convincingly propose sound arguments about the link between evidence and explanation.

The learning environment design issue becomes how to make the discourse practices of science in classrooms reflect or model discourse practices and processes employed in science. Although scientists employ a wide variety of discourse practices, in a typical classroom two types of discourse dominate, that which occurs during whole class settings and that which occurs during small group activities. Research has shown that whole-class discourse is more often than not dominated by a teacher-led structure that focuses on the facts and follows the pattern of teacher Initiation, student Response, and teacher Evaluation (called I-R-E by Mehan, 1979; or triadic dialog by Lemke, 1990). Such a strategy may contribute to students learning facts. However, it does not function well when the goal of instruction is to promote reasoning skills, "doing" science, or learning about science. Thus, part of the challenge in science education is helping teachers develop instructional discourse forms that do promote the science inquiry process.

Small-group discourse (n = three or four students) in science classrooms is not well understood, in spite of the long-standing tradition to have science students work in cooperative groups (Driver et al., 2000; Hogan, 1999; Mercer, 1996; Wegerif, Mercer, & Dawes, 1999). Traditionally, science teaching has not focused on argumentation and controversy but rather has focused on the collection of facts about the world. Thus, the hands-on science lessons taught in classrooms typically serve to reinforce concepts introduced via lecture or textbook. When this kind of "teaching to reinforce claims" occurs, there is little occasion for the discussion, evaluation, and debate necessary for inquiry or making thinking visible.

The learning environment design challenge for promoting inquiry in classrooms is how to nurture and facilitate argumentation. This process involves taking the private knowledge claims of individual students and small groups of students and making them public. Of course, we would not expect the sophistication of knowledge claims made by middle and high school students to be of the same caliber as those of scientists. Nevertheless, analyses of the discourse of middle school students indicate that there is a form of argumentation occurring (Duschl, Ellenbogen, & Erduran, 1999). This form of classroom argumentation should be recognized as an entry point to facilitate the development of more complex argumentation skills. The research and design challenge is providing teachers and students with tools that help them build on these nascent forms of argumentation, including science lessons that support argumentation. Such tools need to address the construction, coordination, and evaluation of scientific knowledge claims. From our point of view, scientific knowledge claims include claims about theory (what knowledge is important), method (what strategies for obtaining and analyzing data are appropriate), and goals (what outcomes are sought and how to determine if the outcome has been attained). In the next section of this chapter, we discuss one attempt to create a learning environment to support argumentation discourse. It relies on science lessons developed in the context of Project SEPIA (Science Education through Portfolio Instruction and Assessment; Duschl & Gitomer, 1997) and used the Knowledge Forum electronic environment to scaffold students' dialogue.

SUPPORTING ARGUMENTATION DISCOURSE IN SCIENCE INQUIRY: PRELIMINARY FINDINGS

Duschl and colleagues (Driver et al., 2000; Duschl et al., 1999; Duschl & Erduran, 1996; Jimenéz-Aleixandre, Rodríguez, & Duschl, 2000; Smith, 1995) explored argumentation in middle school classrooms that use an innovative science unit format developed in the context of Project SEPIA. As a research program, SEPIA attempts to improve science education in middle school classrooms through students' involvement in specially designed instructional sequences that promote scientific reasoning and communication. The principles of SEPIA are realized in several prototype curriculum units that have been developed in collaboration with project teachers. Students are presented with authentic problems and then led through a sequence of investigations, demonstrations, discussions, and reports. The sequence develops both a conceptual understanding of a domain as well as specific reasoning strategies common to science as a way of knowing.

Public sharing of students' ideas is a critical element of SEPIA because it is a primary means of assessing knowledge claims and stimulating argumentation among students (Duschl et al., 1999; Duschl & Gitomer, 1997). SEPIA uses the pedagogical tool called the *assessment conversation* as a means of making public student thinking. However, public sharing of ideas is only the beginning of the complex task of coordinating students' knowledge claims and facilitating the development of scientific argumentation (Bruer, 1993; Duschl & Gitomer, 1997). Current practices in most classrooms provide little instructional scaffolding that would support this development. A major focus of the work in Project SEPIA has been on helping teachers develop the strategies and skills for modeling science argumentation in the context of the assessment conversations and other portions of the SEPIA units.

As we noted earlier, providing scaffolds for argumentation, especially in science, is one of the goals for which electronic tools have been created. In the research we discuss here, we used the *Knowledge Forum* (KF) environment (Scardamalia et al., 1994) for this purpose. KF is networked computer software that provides a conferencing system and communal database for students, opportunities for individuals to contribute ideas to class discussions, and more agency to students. Students have access to the thinking of other members of the community asynchronously in a nontransient medium, two properties that support metacognitive reasoning. Finally, KF has a mechanism that suggests different kinds of thinking to students. This is done through stems or labels that are affixed to different notes that students enter. These labels reflect different types of thinking and act as prompts to students to classify their ideas with respect to whether they are stating a claim (e.g., "My theory is . . ."), asking for help with something (i.e, "I need to understand . . ."), or are reporting an observation or datum (e.g., "What I observed . . ."). In the current version of KF, this mechanism has been made flexible and users can customize these stems. Accordingly, this flexible mechanism could be used to provide instructional scaffolds for scientific argumentation.[4]

In integrating the electronic technology with the SEPIA unit, our long term goal was to understand how the argumentation that occurred in both small group and whole class could be used to guide the construction of scaffolds in the KF environment. However, the data we report here specifically focus on knowledge claims and the kinds of reasoning about them evident in students' discourse in the three contexts (small group, whole class, and KF). The relationships among these discourses suggest implications for scaffolding argumentation in electronic environments such as KF.

Instructional Context

We studied the discourse of argumentation in the context of implementing the SEPIA Vessels Unit. In the Vessels Unit, the problem is to design a vessel hull from a 10" × 10" square sheet of aluminum foil that maximizes load-

---

[4]The KF environment actually calls thinking types *scaffolds*. In this chapter, we are using the term scaffolds more generally.

carrying capacity. The problem requires the application of the physics of flotation and buoyancy to an engineering design problem and the development of a causal explanation. The student must relate design features (e.g., the height of vessel sides and surface area of the vessel bottom) to vessel performance and ultimately, to buoyant forces, buoyant pressure, and water pressure.

The Vessels Unit begins with the presentation of the problem through a letter soliciting (a) designs of vessel hulls for hauling construction materials, and (b) a causal explanation for how vessels float. The class works through a series of iterative cycles in which some form of exploration is conducted, either through demonstration or investigation, often working in small groups. Students represent their understanding in some form (e.g., written, oral, graphical, or design product) and these representations become part of their class folder from which end-of-unit portfolios are constructed. Throughout the unit, the SEPIA instructional model calls for an *assessment conversation*. These conversations are structured discussions in which student products and reasoning are made public, recognized, and used to develop questions, challenges, elaborations, and discourses that can promote conceptual growth for students and provide assessment information to the teachers. Assessment conversations have three general phases: receive student ideas: recognize the diversity of ideas through discussion that is governed by a set of scientific criteria (i.e. rules of of argumentation); and use the diversity of ideas and scientific criteria as a basis for leveraging and achieving consensus on knowledge claims consistent with unit goals. It is during the consensus-building phase that students must grapple with contradictory and competing claims, provide and question the quality of evidence associated with various claims, and make compelling and coherent cases for their claims in a scientifically sound way.

Table 11.1 shows the specific instructional sequence that occurred in the two middle school classrooms we discuss in this chapter. The students in these classrooms ranged in age from 12 to 14 years, with approximately equal numbers of males and females in each class. In Part 1, students read a letter from city planners specifying their need to build a fleet of vessels. Students were to design vessels with features that maximized each vessel's capacity to carry a load, and identify and communicate the principles for design. The first activity was a "benchmark" activity: each student was asked to draw and then write about what makes a boat float and what makes a boat sink. During a whole class discussion, the first assessment conversation, students shared their ideas, from which 11 distinct ideas were recognized. These 11 ideas were then the focus of small group discussions. In small groups of four, students were directed to consider each of the ideas, ask questions about each idea, and determine if it was either a plausible or nonplausible reason for why a boat floats or sinks. Following the small

TABLE 11.1
Instructional Sequence

Lesson Sequence in a Floatation Unit	Short Description
Part 1	
Problem presentation	Read letter soliciting vessel designs.
Benchmark activity	Draw a floating vessel and explain what makes a boat float.
Assessment Conversation 1: Whole Class	Discussion of 11 ideas for why boat floats.
Small group discussion	Discussion of plausibility of each of 11 ideas.
Knowledge Forum 1—first entry, individually	Individual students entered most plausible and least plausible ideas in the database.
Part 2	
Design vessels	Students used 10″ square of aluminum foil to design vessels.
Exploration of design features	"Pressing Cups" activity.
Part 3	
Design and construct experiments to test four design features.	Students test load/cargo capacity for different designs.
Part 4	
Assessment conversation 2: Whole class	Designs of two students are discussed/ critiqued.
Knowledge Forum 2—second entry, individually	Individual students entered most plausible and least plausible ideas in the database.
Report Preparation	Students write prepare their packets in accord with criteria in the letter.

group discussion, students individually entered their most plausible and least plausible ideas in the KF database, along with an explanation of why they selected that particular idea.

In Part 2, students engaged in several explorations and used a 10″ square piece of aluminum foil to create various designs that they tested for load capacity. The subsequent assessment conversation asked students to determine which design features seemed to "influence" performance. Size of bottom, height of sides, shape, and thickness of foil (layers) are proposed as influencing performance. The results were recorded and stored in their class folders. One exploration in particular, Pressing Cups, allows students to explore assumptions about (a) how the downward-pulling gravity forces and upward pushing bouyant forces act on objects in water at different depths; and, (b) a mechanism for how the bouyant force can increase with depth.

In Part 3, students applied the knowledge and evidence from Part 2 to conduct experiments. After reviewing the evidence from Part 2, students generated ways they could experimentally test the four design features (size of bottom, height of sides, shape, and thickness of foil) through controlled experimentation. Results of these experiments were recorded in investigation reports that were designed to help students realize that there is a trade-off in maximizing the volume of the vessel (i.e., either higher sides and smaller bottom surface area or lower sides and larger bottom surface area). (The ideal vessel is one that makes a compromise between the two variables such that the volume is maximized.)

Part 4 of the unit is the culmination of the inquiry process. It begins by allowing the students to construct their final vessels using the knowledge and understanding they have acquired over the course of the unit. After constructing the second set of vessels and testing them, the students prepared their reports. The whole-class discussion we examine took place prior to the students writing their reports. Following this discussion, students entered a second KF note, responding to the same *most* and *least* plausible probes as the first time.

During implementation of the Vessels Unit, we videotaped whole-class discussions and audiotaped and videotaped small group discussions. As well, we took field notes throughout the implementation of the unit. (At least two of us were present for each class period.)

Forms of Argument in Individual, Small Group, and Whole-Class Contexts

Reported in this chapter are our analyses of the forms of argumentation present in the KF entries, one small-group discussion, and one whole-group discussion. In comparing the small group and first KF entries, we were interested in the relationship between the forms of argument present in the small group as compared to those in the KF entries of individuals. The analyses show that there is not much sophistication in the argumentation schemes at this point in the unit. We then shift to a whole-class session that occurred in Part 4, the last part of the unit. Our focus in the analysis of that discussion is on the kinds of reasoning modeled by the teacher and whether the discussion provided scaffolds for evidence-based explanation. Finally, we look at students' reasoning in their second KF entries to determine whether their explanations reflect use of more sophisticated argument schemes than their first entries. We find some evidence of change, consistent with the modest support provided by the whole-class discussion.

Analytic Framework for Forms of Argument

The whole-class and small-group argumentation discourse was analyzed employing a dialectical, or informal argumentation scheme that was derived from Walton's (1996) presumptive-reasoning framework. *Dialectical arguments* are those that occur during dialogue or debate and involve reasoning with premises that are not entirely grounded in evidence. Walton defines *pre-*

TABLE 11.2
Informal Argumentation Schemes

Argument Scheme	Definition	Sample Discourse
Request for Information	There is insufficient information to make a judgment. Spoken or written claims are used to infer the existence of the missing information. Otherwise, the need for the missing information is highlighted.	"Well before you can have holes, you have to design the boat and test it, so . . ." (Group 1)
Example	Reference to an example to support a generalization. Often supports a personal view.	"Are you going to sit there with your row things?" "Well, they did in Roman days." (Group 1)
Inference	Characterized by inferential presumptions. May include a conjecture. May include a premise that is causally linked to an observable effect.	"OK, if the boat is just a big square, it's going to sink." (Group 1)

sumptive reasoning as that reasoning which occurs during a dialog when a course of action must be taken and all the needed evidence is not available. Such a scenario of reasoning from a partial set of experiences and evidence reflects quite well what typically occurs in middle school science classrooms. Table 11.2 identifies and provides examples of the informal argumentation schemes that we used for purposes of the analyses presented here.

The three categories differentiate among three forms of reasoning. The first, request for information, recognizes that additional information is needed. The second, example, justifies a generalization with a single instance or analogy, often based on personal experience. The third, inference, reflects presumptive reasoning in that premises, conjectures, and observable effects are linked.

Analysis of the Small-Group Discourse

The small-group discourse analyzed here occurred following an initial assessment conversation in which students made known their claims about reasons boats sink or float. The claims made by the students were ultimately reduced through the discussion to 11 claims (Part 1; see Table 11.1.) The 11 claims were quite diverse and contained many relevant ideas that would be taken up during the course of the investigations in the rest of the unit. They were materials, shape, holes, density and gravity, air pressure and water pressure, placement of engine, design, weight of boat, too much cargo, engine, propeller, sails, and hollow bottom. Small groups then discussed these 11 ideas to determine which were least and which most plausible.

The small group discussion analyzed here is illustrative of the kind of reasoning in which students engaged. The four students in this group disagreed on the plausibility of 5 of the 11 claims and agreed on 6. Four of the ideas on which students disagreed generated argumentation discourse, as shown in Table 11.3. There was no argumentation discourse for the obvious (e.g., holes, too much cargo) nor was there argumentation discourse on the unfamiliar science concepts (e.g., density and gravity; air pressure and water pressure). We used the informal argumentation schemes shown in Table 11.2 to characterize the argumentation segments for the four ideas. The presumptive reasoning categories and distribution of comments are shown in Table 11.3.

The example used in this group was typical of that in the other small groups and drew on personal experiences, sometimes vicarious. In this particular small group, one member brought up the Titanic as an example of the plausibility of *design* as a cause of sinking. The group members then engaged in inferential reasoning about this example:

S2: "The Titanic sunk because one part of it . . ."
S3: "That's a movie."
S2: "Still it was in real life."
S3: "It was made right."
S4: "Because it hit an iceberg. If it didn't hit an iceberg no it wouldn't sink."
S2: "Well if it was a good boat, it wouldn't just crack."
S3: "I know, but the design, it still, it wasn't ready."

The inferential reasoning in which the students engaged in this segment provides clear evidence of the social dynamics of argumentation. The students were reasoning in terms of cause–effect and hypothetical situations, although they did not do so in terms of scientific principles. Rather, the discussion centered on the idea that design matters—if the Titanic had been designed correctly, the iceberg would not have mattered.

TABLE 11.3
Presumptive Reasoning in Small Group Session

Argument Scheme	Materials	Placement of Engine	Design	Engine, Propeller, Sail
Requests for Information	2	0	4	3
Example	0	0	1	0
Inferences	1	2	5	2
Total	3	2	10	5

In general, the inferences were logical and based on prior knowledge and personal experience rather than being explicit, empirical evidence statements. For example, "If a boat was made out of sand it would sink" is an inference used to justify *materials* as important to whether a boat sinks or floats. Although it could be based on empirical evidence, it is not stated in that way.

The small-group discourse at the beginning of the unit reflected informal reasoning strategies based on knowledge derived from personal experiences and are consistent with the forms of presumptive reasoning observed in students in this age range and who have had little exposure to the formal principles that operate in this domain of science. Although we can characterize the discourse of the small group, it is difficult to tell from the small-group discussion what knowledge claims each individual holds and how these are justified. The KF entries provide insight into this issue.

Analysis of the First KF Entries

The individual KF entries regarding which ideas students thought least plausible and which most plausible reasons a boat would float or sink were classified into three categories, as shown in Table 11.4. We distinguished among unsupported claims and claims for which an explanation was provided. Explanations were of two types: (1) evidence referred to students mentioning the results of experiments conducted in class or stated as em-

TABLE 11.4
Categories for Classifying the Reasoning in the KF Entries

Reasoning Type	Example for Idea "Design of the Boat"
Claim only	The design really doesn't matter.
Claim + reason	I think that the design is important because if you don't build it right, it will not float.
	Well, the design counts for different kinds of boats for different things. Tall walls and large boats are for heavy loads. Canoes most of the time hold people to float around but like a barge holds a big load its all in the design.
Claim + evidence[a]	I think it is still the design that is important because the bigger the surfaces are, the more the boat will hold. When we tested the aluminum foil boats, the ones with larger bottoms held more pennies" (based on in-class experiment).

[a]Not all claims plus evidence drew on in-class experiences. For the variable *hollow bottom*, one student drew on prior experience but stated it as an empirical claim: "I think its plausible to have an air tank in the bottom part of the boat because it will keep the boat afloat. For example, if you place a rock on water its going to sink, but if you attach pontoons (air tanks), it will float. Same thing with the boat but the air is on the bottom."

pirical claims; and (2) reasons referred to justifications based on examples, personal experience, or logical inference.

A total of 41 students from both classes contributed 103 entries to the KF database during the first KF session. In this sample, the entries were dominated by claims plus reasons (58%). Claims only were provided 41% of the time. This distribution was similar across the two classes. Of the specific ideas, the dominant response for the most plausible reason a boat would sink or float was *holes* (51%) and the least plausible was *placement of the engine* (38%). None of the justifications were stated as empirically based claims, although there was one that reflected an elaborated causal explanation: "The reason why I think holes are most plausible is because holes cause boats to sink in less than a few hours. Since the hull is hollow when there is a hole in it and the water goes in, it makes the hull heavier which then makes the boat sink." The vast majority of the justifications were statements of the impact of water getting in a boat, for example, "I think that holes are the most plausible because water can go through the holes and fill up the boat." These statements provide reasons based on personal experience, observations, and examples, as illustrated by the samples provided in Table 11.4. Similarly, for the dominant, least plausible idea, *placement of the engine*, students reasoned from their experiences as in this entry: ". . . if you [have] ever seen a fishing boat, the engine is in the back or the front." Those ideas that reflected more of the scientific concepts (density, pressure) were not given as either plausible or nonplausible reasons. Thus, the reasoning evident in the KF entries for the sample as a whole indicated presumptive reasoning based on observations and examples from personal life experiences or the assertion of claims with no justifications provided.

Examining the subset of KF entries from the four students who participated in the small-group discussion just analyzed, we see some parallels with what the face-to-face discussion suggested: All four students chose Holes as the most plausible reason a boat would sink; two students provided reasons ("because water would come in") and the other two just made the claim. Thus, the lack of argumentation discourse about holes, an idea they all agreed was plausible, is reflected in the KF entries. The small group's least plausible responses were more diverse and revealed student beliefs not evident in the face-to-face discussion. One student selected density as the least plausible: ". . . because when a boat is in the water, you want (won't) have to worry about air pressure cause you will float." Although providing a reason that brings in a scientific concept, the logic is flawed. Two students gave *placement of the engine* and provided as the reason the information that another member of the group raised in the small-group discussion, "[the boat] will work properly wherever it [the engine] is placed." Finally, one student reported that shape was least plausible "as long as the boat floats," a response that does not seem to address the question.

Comparison of Small Group and KF Argumentation

Comparing the argumentation in the small group with that in the KF entries reveals some similarities and some differences. The KF environment requires each student to make their thinking visible in contrast to the small-group conversation where there is ambiguity as to the beliefs held by individual students. Both contexts reflected an absence of science content and a reliance on personal observations and examples from everyday life in their reasoning about knowledge claims. Given that both the small-group discussion and the KF activity occurred very early on in the unit and ahead of any concept development lessons, the absence of science content is not surprising (cf. Hogan, 1999). However, the existence of presumptive reasoning argumentation patterns in both the group discussion and the individual entries reinforces the claim made by Duschl et al. (1999) that middle school children do indeed possess the ability to participate in argumentation lessons. These reasoning patterns provide a foundation on which to build. Although research by Wegerif et al. (1999) showed that social interactions in small groups can have a significant positive effect on individuals' reasoning, the challenge is how to direct or leverage the discourse to promote scientifically based argumentation (Pea, 1993).

Indeed, one of the intended functions of assessment conversations in the SEPIA framework (Duschl & Gitomer, 1997) is to model and scaffold the use of scientifically determined content in the construction of arguments. Such modeling and scaffolding could also occur in electronic environments. Assessment conversations are frequently preceded by teacher-led demonstrations that introduce and reinforce important science content principles. The demonstrations often reiterate the principles that underlie experiments students have conducted. Selected results of experiments are the focus of assessment conversations during which claims and the data behind them are supposed to be discussed. In the next section, we provide a whole-class discourse that includes both demonstration and assessment conversation segments. Our interest is in the forms of reasoning and argumentation that are modeled and scaffolded in the discourse and whether the individual KF entries that are made subsequent to the whole-class meeting reflect "uptake" of these argument schemes and or the scientific content.

ANALYSIS OF THE WHOLE-CLASS DISCOURSE

The whole-class lesson we analyze occurred at the beginning of Part 4 of the Vessels units, wherein students are to prepare the packet of material requested in the letter they had read in Part 1. We first describe the structure and content of the lesson at a macrolevel and then provide a more in-depth look at selected segments of it. The lesson had five segments. In the first, the teacher set the overall objective of the day's class: "Today we are going to spend some time kind of refocusing, kind of taking a look at where we are, kind of taking a look at where we've been, and looking at—in the next week or two—(what) we need to do to successfully complete this project." The remainder of the lesson focused on the scientific principle underlying the Pressing Cups activity, namely Newton's First Law (An object at rest remains at rest unless an uneven force or unbalancing force is applied). This focus is achieved by moving between a demonstration using the apparatus the students had used for the pressing cups activity (an aquarium tank filled with water and containing a cup; Segments 2 and 4) and an assessment conversation around the drawings two students had produced based on the pressing cups activity (Segments 3 and 5). In the drawings, students were to represent the forces acting on the cup when they had pushed it to three different depths in the tank of water.[5] Throughout the lesson, the discussion was heavily guided by the teacher as he continuously attempted to have the students "see" the instantiation of Newton's First Law in the demonstration segments: an object at rest (cup in a state of flotation) was being acted on by equal and opposite forces (gravity and buoyancy). He wanted them to see how this needed to be represented in the diagrams that were the focus of the assessment conversations.[6]

In taking a more microanalytic perspective on the lesson, we were interested in the argument schemes that became part of the public discourse and thus available as potential models students might adopt. The first model was provided by the teacher when he reinstated the elements of the reports students were to prepare, as specified in the letter the students had received at the start of the unit, and described how reports might read:

I started with an idea that the boat should look like this. I tested it, and after testing the boat, and after talking to my friends, and after looking at their boats, and after seeing the boats up on the wall, and after talking about things in class, I decided that I should make my sides taller, or my bottom bigger, or change the shape, or whatever you change from boat 1 to boat 2. And then I tested boat 2, and boat 2 held so many pennies, and I thought to myself, I bet if I changed this, I can hold even more. Or, I talked to George, and George said you know if you just did this. Or I talked to John and John said well my

---

[5]The Pressing Cups activity directs students to place a cup, bottom down, into the tank of water and to press the cup to three depths—shallow, middle, and deep positions. A graphic representation of the cup in these three positions is provided and students are asked to draw arrows to represent the forces they feel acting on the cup, label the drawing, and write a brief statement to explain the drawing.

[6] The introduction of scientific principles in this way is within the realm of the instructional strategies SEPIA recommends. However, the approach taken by the teacher in this particular case is more directive than the typical SEPIA discussion.

boat held 400 pennies and I did this. And so I learned from everybody else how I should design my boat differently. And I made my third boat. That's all your report is.

What is notable about this "model" is the emphasis on events and consequences rather than on why various decisions were made. However, the model did provide students with a reminder about the sequence of experimental tests they had made, the data they had collected, and that these were relevant and needed to be included in the reports.

The first introduction of explanation into the class discourse occurred in response to a question from a student that occurred a few minutes after the teacher's description of the report. The student asked about the relevance of the Pressing Cups task: "What did the cup thing have to do with the . . . ?" The teacher's response emphasized the importance of getting to the underlying explanatory principles:

> T: That's a good question. That's a good question. And it goes back to the idea, why would you design an airplane if you don't know why an airplane flies. OK—why would you design a boat if you're not sure what makes a boat float. And, uh, that's something we're going to talk about.

The teacher then segued into the demonstration (Segment 2) directing students' to the cup floating in the tank of water and asking them "How do you describe the relationship, or the phenomenon, what's going on in the fish tank?" After the first student responded, "The cup is floating and sitting on top of the water," the teacher asked if the cup was moving, to which several students said "No." He used the consensus as a springboard for reintroducing flotation-relevant scientific concepts and principles, specifically Newton's first law of motion. In so doing, the teacher provided a model of argumentation that draws on established principles as explanatory tools.

> T: Everybody will agree the cup is stationary. Stationary. Stationary. Stationary. Let's see. I tend to remember something that we studied not too long ago. About a man named Newton. And he had this idea about things that were stationary. And he called it the first law of motion. Somebody—Connie—refresh my memory here, what did he say about things that were stationary?
>
> Connie: If something is not in motion it will not stay. If something is not in motion, it will stay not in motion. If it is in motion, it will stay in motion. Unless an uneven force is applied.
>
> T: Unless a what?
>
> Connie: Unless an uneven force . . .
>
> T: An uneven or unbalancing force. Very nice, very nice.

What she's saying is this coffee cup is sitting still. It's at a state of rest. It's going to continue that way until something unbalances, unevens, until something acts upon it to make it change. We can say that right now this cup is balanced. All the forces that are acting on this cup are balanced. Would you agree with that?

An extended, teacher-led discussion ensued that followed a typical teacher-initiated question, student response, but an atypical appeal to the rest of the class for consensus on the response. The practice of seeking consensus is characteristic of SEPIA units; however it occurs more typically when students have put forth different responses. Nevertheless, the notion of seeking consensus was introduced into the public discussion.

Finally, the teacher summarized the explanatory principle he wanted the students to apply in the upcoming assessment conversation segment.

> *T:* " . . . every object that is at rest is balanced. The force pressing up is equal to the force pressing down. The force pressing left is equal to the force pressing right. The force pressing back is equal to the force pressing forward. Would you all agree with that?"

There is general assent to this statement but subsequent student comments during the first assessment conversation suggest that the students did not "own" the principle of balance of forces and understand its importance to explaining flotation.

The teacher showed the first student work sample (shown in Figure 11.1, upper diagram) and asked the students in the class to figure out with what in the diagram they agreed, with what they did not, and what the student might do to improve the drawing. He then had one of the students (Nina) say what she thought the author of the drawing had been trying to say and guided her to a conclusion that he co-constructed with her. The interchange models a process of drawing a conclusion from observations.

> *Nina:* With the first one (diagram) he pressed down a lot, and it only went down a little. . . . With the second one, he pressed down half and half, and it came up, and well, when he pressed down, and then it came up a little more. And then with the last one, he pressed down a little, and it, and the arrow points that it went . . . I guess it went down a lot."
>
> *T:* OK. OK. Tell me, Tell me more. What do you see in this picture?
>
> *Nina:* OK, when he's pressing down, there's more force pushing down than there is pushing up in the first picture.
>
> *T:* OK.
>
> *Nina:* Then in the second picture when it's down halfway, there's equal amount of force pushing it to keep it in the middle. Then on the last one, there's less force pushing down on it, and more pushing up on it.

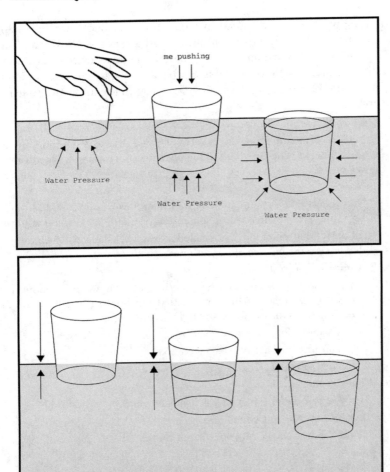

FIG. 11.1.   Drawings of the student work that was the focus of the assessment conversation during the whole-class discourse. The upper panel was
the topic of the first assessment conversation (Segment 3) and the lower of
the second (Segment 5).

T: So, the length of the arrow has something to do with how strong the
        force is.

Nina: Yea.

Two other students offered interpretations of the drawing that brought in
water pressure and air pressure but in ways that appeared to cue the teacher
that he needed to have the students think more about balance of forces and
how to represent these balance of forces. He returned to demonstration

mode (Segment 4) and engaged in a dialogue that began with principles that they had previously agreed on and asked a series of "Why" and "Why not" questions. This exchange culminated in more explicit statements about implications of Newton's First Law because the teacher expanded the responses the students were providing, bringing in the appropriate science concepts.

T: Let's look at something for a second 'cause I have a question about something . . . The cup that's in the uh, aquarium right now is it moving, yes or no?

Ss: No.

T: No, when I take the cup and I move it half down, and . . . hold it very, very still, is it moving? (After some disagreement, Ss decide it is not.)

T: An object that is not moving is called at rest. Or balanced, which means that *what* must be true about an object that's at rest?

S: It must stay at rest.

T: It must stay at rest, but not only that, but, what do we know about the forces? It's balanced. Which means that I'm holding it halfway down. What's true about the force up and the force down?

S: There's more force up and down.

T: OK. You just told me it is balanced.

S: . . . They're equal.

S: They're not equal.

T: They're not equal. Then why is it not moving?

S: Because they're not equal.

T: If they're not equal, why does it not move?

S: Force.

T: Force. So my force is down, which is equal to what force?

S: Water pressure

T: Force of the water up. When I hold it farther down, is that easier or harder?

S: Harder.

This sort of interchange continued and the teacher guided the students to the point where they were saying that if you push the cup down with increased force, the water will push back up with increased force. A central conceptual element of these interchanges is that they are grounded in the data from the students' own Pressing Cups activities, with the teacher at times asking them whether they had to push harder to submerge the cup more deeply and why. As a result of this grounding, the role of evidence in argumentation schemes is being made more explicit. Through the dialogic process illustrated in the previous segment, the teacher helped the group make public the idea that the reason it requires more force to push the cup farther down is because the further down in the tank, the greater the water pressure. After an extended discussion of how to equalize forces, the teacher returned the focus of the conversation to providing advice to the student who had generated the drawing.

In the final segment of the lesson, the teacher used another strategy for deepening the students' reasoning. He intentionally selected a second student's work sample (Fig. 11.1, lower portion) that introduced a new element into the discussion of balanced forces. As the teacher put it, "All of a sudden we have a whole new thing to think about." In the selected drawing, the student had actually drawn his own hand and showed the strength of different forces with different numbers of arrows. Students more actively participated in generating suggestions for improving this second student's drawing but focused on equalizing the numbers of arrows, for example, "Put the same number of up arrows as down arrows." Then the teacher directed their attention to the new element introduced by this student's drawing, the arrows showing pressure on the sides of the glass. As the students thought about these "sideways" pressures, the teacher asked them for evidence that there are sideways forces. He said:

> Somebody give me something that tells you that there are forces that press sideways. Think about your boat. Somebody give me something. Tell me something about your boat and what you saw that lets you know that yes, indeed, not only are there forces that press up and down, but there are also forces that press in from the side.

This prompted at least one of the students to describe the results of the pennies activity; as she put more and more pennies in the boat, it sank because the sides caved inward. The teacher supported and reflected this insight to the group:

> What she's saying is the thing that I saw a lot of you do. The sides of your boat started to cave in. And you didn't sink the boat from a hole in the bottom; you sunk the boat because your sides caved in. What was the pressure that was taking place? Pressure of the water pressing in from the sides.

The discussion continued with students offering ideas about how to show this in the diagram and the teacher prompting them to consider all the forces acting on the cup and how those forces were in balance. The teacher concluded the lesson by indicating to the students that he wanted to see balanced forces in their diagrams.

In this whole-class discourse, the teacher used a combination of demonstration and assessment conversation formats to engage in a highly scaffolded discussion of the balance of forces and their representation. Al-

TABLE 11.5
Analysis of the Argumentation of the Whole-Class Discussion

	Segment of Whole Class Discussion			
Argument Scheme	Demo, Segment 2 (274–449)*	Assessment Conversation, Segment 3 (505–687)	Demo, Segment 4 (688–806)	Assessment Conversation, Segment 5 (809–1238)
Request for Information	7	11	12	22
Example	1	0	0	0
Inference	7	6	4	21
Total	15	17	16	43

*Lines of transcript.

though the discourse was predominantly teacher led, he built off of the students' comments and introduced several aspects of scientific argumentation schemes into the public discourse. The most important of these were the role of principles or laws in constructing explanations, the value of considering counterexamples (e.g., the *why* and *why not* exchanges), and the importance of providing evidence for claims by using observations to ground inferences or claims.

A more formal analysis of the demonstration and assessment conversation segments of the whole-class discourse produced the data shown in Table 11.5. First, notice that over the course of the lesson, the discourse becomes more dominated by the need for information, reflected in the requests for information. As well, by the second assessment conversation segment, inferences are relatively frequent. These are significant because they related premises (claims) to observables (data) and reflect the availability in the public discourse of an important scientific argumentation principle. Although the whole-class discourse was teacher dominated and conformed to Lemke's (1990) triadic dialog or Mehan's (1979) I-R-E sequence, it did bring into the public discourse argumentation schemes that students were not using. In this sense, the teacher scaffolded more sophisticated forms of argumentation. The second KF entries indicate the kind of student "uptake" of these forms of argumentation.

Analysis of the Second KF Entries

During the second KF session, a total of 33 students from both classes provided 66 entries. The same three categories shown in Table 11.4 were applied to these entries. Differences between the first and second KF entries indicate that students thinking changed in two significant ways from the beginning to the end of the unit. First, there was a shift away from making claims only. The second KF entries indicated 26% claims only compared to the 41% for KF 1; 48% claims plus reasons compared to 58% on KF 1; and 26% claims plus evidence compared to 1% on KF 1. Thus the difference between the distributions for KF 1 and KF 2 reflects an increased tendency to justify a claim and to use evidence based on empirical observations to do so. These shifts are consistent with the argumentation schemes found in our analysis of the exemplar whole class discourse.

The second interesting trend was toward a greater use of ideas connected to the science concepts central to buoyancy and flotation. For example, holes declined from 50% on the first session to 32% of the most plausible claims on the second session. Claims about most plausible reasons increased for design (from 10% to 20% of the claims) and air/water pressure (from 0 to 12% of the claims). Although modest, these changes reflect important shifts in conceptual understanding of content introduced through the activities and argumentation schemes in which data from the activities was revisited. Of course, mastery of the concepts was far from complete. In the 66 entries, there was explicit mention of balance of forces and pressure by only three students. One of the students, who was part of the whole-class discussion just analyzed, wrote the following:

> I think this (air pressure/water pressure) is the most plausible because if the boat is still then that means all of the pressure is even. If the pressure is uneven than the boat will either float or sink like in the first law of motion. Newton said that any object in motion will stay in motion and any object at rest will stay at rest. The activity that made me think this was the cup activity. When we discussed the activity we talked about if the pressure is not equal all around the ship, it will sink.

This was a change from her initial, "most plausible" idea, which was engine, propeller, and sail.

The KF data from the individuals in the small group discussed earlier also reflected some movement toward more scientific argumentation in the children's thinking. Rather than the universal response of holes as the most plausible on the first entry, there was greater variability on the second entries. The variability was reflected within students as well as across the four. That is, two of the four students gave multiple responses for most plausible, holding onto their everyday idea about holes but also entering an additional reason that reflected a greater awareness of scientific concepts related to flotation. One student cited *density* and the other, *design*. Even the one student who continued to claim that holes were the most plausible provided a more sophisticated justification than he had on the first entry: "Because if holes are in the boat, as soon as the boat hits water it's going to start sinking. But even though the boat does not have holes, it could sill sink. If a boat has holes, it will start to sink slow."

Finally, the fourth student in this group was able to justify her claims of least and most plausible using argumentation that clearly reflects greater understanding of scientific criteria for evidence.

> I think that the weight of the boat was least plausible because when I made the boat, it was always the same weight. The only thing that I changed about my boat was the shape, and the way it was designed. The weight was always the same and it just held more weight because of the way it was designed.
>
> I think the shape is now the most plausible because every time that I made a boat, the way it was designed was different, and it held different amounts of weight.

Thus, the KF entries prove extremely valuable for taking the pulse of students' scientific thinking and argumentation approaches. In the KF context, it can be easier to "see" this pulse than in the context of a whole-class discourse where, as we have seen, teachers may tend to dominate the discourse in their efforts to communicate the scientific principles and concepts that underlie phenomena in the physical world.

IMPLICATIONS FOR ROLES OF ELECTRONIC ENVIRONMENTS IN SCIENTIFIC INQUIRY

A primary goal of our attempt to integrate the KF environment with the SEPIA unit was to explore ways in which such electronic environments might contribute to supporting the development of scientific argumentation skills in middle-school students. Before we discuss the implications we draw from our work to date, we must point out that the use of KF was less than optimal and certainly not the way its creators intended for it to be used. We would have liked it to be used differently. However, the reality test for us may prove informative to others attempting to pursue similar types of classroom-based investigations. In attempting to do the SEPIA–KF integration, we were confronted with a number of pragmatic constraints. These resulted in a shorter than optimal time frame for the whole SEPIA unit and placed severe constraints on the students' access to the KF environment and database. The students had only 2 weeks for the SEPIA unit and only two opportunities to work in the KF environment (beyond the sessions they spent learning how to use the KF tool). During both KF sessions, the students only had time to make their own thinking visible through their entries. They did not have the opportunity to examine the entries of their classmates nor of students in other classes.

Yet, precisely this consideration of other peoples' views is at the heart of the assessment conversations built into the SEPIA units. Small group discussions have the potential for peers to confront and challenge each others' ideas. However the group needs some means for validating their thinking and seeking sources of expertise external to the group. During small-group discussions and whole-class assessment conversations, teachers must be actively processing the reasoning of the students and intervening with questions, comments, and prompts for additional student input that are oriented toward evidence-based consensus building. This is a new role for most teachers and one that they need support to effectively assume. What we saw in the illustrative whole-class discourse that we discussed was the overarching tendency of the teacher to dominate the discussion, regardless of whether it was a demonstration segment or an assessment conversation segment. Although the direction the lesson took and the movement back and forth between assessment conversation and demonstration mode reflected the teacher's "reading" of student thinking, it was not clear that the teacher heard *all* students or all the ideas the students had. Even under optimal conditions, during whole-class discussions, many student voices are silent. Teachers, and the one we worked with is no exception, are aware of the problems inherent in tracking student understanding during such discussions. Indeed, at several points in the lesson we analyzed, the teacher turned to the students for help by asking them for some type of signal as to who was "with him" and who was not. Clearly, this teacher was aware of some of the difficulties of assessing student thinking "in the moment."

What might have occurred had the initial assessment conversation from the whole-class lesson taken place in the KF environment? In terms of assessment that informs instructional decision making, one of the main advantages of the KF environment is that individual student thinking can be made visible. Individuals can be asked to respond independently of one another. This means that the explicit knowledge claims and the forms of justifications used are available to the teacher, as well as to other students, in time frames that permit reflection. At the same time, we and others using the KF environment or other environments with similar functionality have consistently seen greater student willingness to offer ideas (Secules, Cottom, Bray, & Miller, 1997). For whatever reasons, the electronic venue seems to call forth more informative comments than students make in the context of face-to-face, whole-class and small-group discussions, and in some cases even when they write out their responses and hand them in. Perhaps the electronic environment seems less testlike to them. Perhaps it is being part of a community engaged in the same activity. Perhaps it is the ability to see their own responses in relation to those of their peers. These are empirical issues that bear further investigation as we continue to explore the value of electronic environments of the KF variety.

From the teachers' point of view, having a written record of what individual students think might prove quite valuable in terms of gauging and documenting individual student progress in forms other than standardized tests. In the future, it is possible that information entered in KF-like electronic environments could be copied to electronic portfolios and constitute a learning profile for the individual. Not only would this be useful for accountability purposes but it would begin to create a database from which we might begin to better understand developmental progressions from presumptive reasoning to formal, scientific argumentation.

The KF environment might also provide a more effective venue for scaffolding consensus building than the face-to-face, small-group or whole-class discussion. One of the main advantages of the KF environment is that the visibility of student thinking is nontransient. It is available for inspection and reinspection by the teacher and students alike, provided there is adequate time allotted for working with the information. Given time to do so, students can actively treat the ideas of their peers as objects of the students' own thinking and do so over extended periods of time. Students could potentially group and regroup the ideas, trying out different explanatory frameworks and hypotheses. The physical juxtaposition of ideas that occurred in disparate notes and at different points in time could lead to new insights and hypotheses about the scientific phenomena in question. In turn, sharing these thoughts with peers and getting their reactions creates a scientifically oriented learning community. Whole-class discussions of the type illustrated in this chapter often seem to lack the "thinking space" that many students need in order to respond to the comments of their peers and the suggestions and guidance offered by the teacher. From the teacher's perspective, instructional guidance and scaffolds could be more individualized and responsive to the individual student. As well, the student responses to efforts to move thinking forward would provide the teacher with more sensitive feedback regarding the success of particular efforts.

The uses and benefits of KF-like environments are not to our knowledge easily realizable in current systems, KF included. In most systems it is presently difficult to rearrange notes, link them in multiple ways, and annotate these different arrangements because most are some form of threaded discussion. That is, notes are hierarchically linked and not easily rearranged. Although the present KF environment does permit the rearrangement of notes by any user, the rearrangement changes the database for all users. In other words, changes to the database cannot be done "privately," at least not without creating a copy of the database and working in the copy. This process presently requires a sophistication with the software environment that is unrealistic for teachers and students. Clearly, however, for electronic environments like KF to support scientific inquiry, their designs and functionalities will need to support flexible "thinking spaces" of the type described.

At the same time, there are definite limits on electronic conversations. There are multiple cues that are missing, notably affective and gestural. The social dynamics offset in time may make it more difficult to co-construct ideas, a phenomena that seems to occur in small-group discussions such as the one we analyzed. One issue that our study raises and that needs more intensive study concerns synergies and unique roles for the various discourse contexts. Consistent with the focus of the volume, in this discussion we have concentrated on the contributions that newly available electronic environments make to the development of scientific inquiry and efforts to study the same. However, optimizing the integration of these new technologies with knowledge-building practices that have been operating for centuries requires more intimate understanding of the relationships among information exchange and knowledge building when it is distributed across a variety of discourse contexts and contents.

ACKNOWLEDGMENTS

The work discussed in this chapter was supported, in part, by a U.S. Department of Education grant, *Student Achievement Across the Whole Day and Whole Year*, and by a grant from the Center for Innovative Learning Technologies (CILT) to Susan R. Goldman and Richard A. Duschl while they were at Vanderbilt University. CILT is a distributed center supported in part by the National Science Foundation. We thank our collaborating teacher and students for their participation in this work.

REFERENCES

Bell, P. (1997). Using argument representations to make thinking visible for individuals and groups. In R. Hall & N. Miyake (Eds.), *Proceedings of the Computer Supported Collaborative Learning Conference '97*, (pp. 10–19). Toronto, Canada: University of Toronto.

Bransford, J. D., Franks, J. J., Vye, N. J., & Sherwood, R. D. (1989). New approaches to instruction: Because wisdom can't be told. In S. Vosniadou & A. Ortony (Eds.), *Similarity and analogical reasoning* (pp. 470–497). New York: Cambridge University Press.

Brown, A., & Campione, J. (1994) Guided discovery in a community of learners. In K. McGilly (Ed.), *Classroom lessons: Integrating cognitive theory and classroom practice* (pp. 229–272). Cambridge, MA: MIT Press.

Bruer, J. (1993). *Schools for thought: A science of learning in the classroom.* Cambridge, MA: MIT Press.

Cognition and Technology Group at Vanderbilt (1990). Anchored instruction and its relationship to situated cognition. *Educational Researcher, 19*(6), 2–10.

Cognition and Technology Group at Vanderbilt (1994). From visual word problems to learning communities: Changing conceptions of cognitive research. In K. McGilly (Ed.), *Classroom lessons: Integrating cognitive theory and classroom practice* (pp. 157–200). Cambridge, MA: MIT Press.

Driver, R., Leach, J., Millar, R., & Scott, P. (1996) *Young people's images of science*. Philadelphia, PA: Open University Press.

282 GOLDMAN ET AL.

Driver, R., Newton, P., & Osborne, J. (2000). Establishing the norms of scientific argumentation in classrooms. *Science Education, 84* (3), 287–312.

Dunbar, K. (1995). How scientists really reason: Scientific reasoning in real-world laboratories. In R. J. Sternberg & J. E. Davidson (Eds.), *The nature of insight* (pp. 365–395). Cambridge, MA: MIT Press.

Duschl, R. A., & Erduran, S. (1996). Modelling the growth of scientific knowledge. In G. Welford, J. Osborne, & P. Scott (Eds.), *Research in science education in Europe: Current issues and themes* (pp. 153–165). London: The Falmer Press.

Duschl, R. A., Ellenbogen, K., & Erduran, S. (1999, April). *Understanding dialogic argumentation.* Paper presented at the annual meeting of American Educational Research Association, Montreal.

Duschl, R. A., & Gitomer, D. H. (1997). Strategies and challenges to changing the focus of assessment and instruction in science classrooms. *Educational Assessment, 4*(1), 37–73.

Edelson, D. C., Pea, R. D., & Gomez, L. (1996). The collaboratory notebook: Support for collaborative inquiry. *Communications of the ACM, 39,* 32–33.

Gee, J. (1994, April) *"Science talk": How do you start to do what you don't know how to do?* Paper presented at the annual meeting of the American Educational Research Association, New Orleans.

Guzdial, M., Turns, J., Rappin, N., & Carlson, D. (1995). Collaborative support for learning in complex domains. In J. L. Schanse & E. L. Cunnius (Eds.), *Proceedings of CSCL '95: Computer supported collaborative learning* (pp. 157–160). Hillsdale, NJ: Lawrence Erlbaum Associates.

Hoadley, C. M., Hsi, S., & Berman, B. P. (1995). The multimedia forum kiosk and speakeasy. *Proceedings of ACM Multimedia '95* (pp. 363–364). New York: ACM Press.

Hodson, D. (1992). Assessment of practical work: Some considerations in philosophy of science. *Science & Education, 1,* 2.

Hogan, K. (1999). Thinking aloud together: A test of an intervention to foster students' collaborative scientific reasoning. *Journal of Research in Science Teaching, 36*(10), 1085–1109.

Jimenez-Aleixandre, M. P., Rodríguez, A. B., & Duschl, R. A. (2000). Doing the lesson or doing science: Argument in high school genetics. *Science Education, 84*(6), 757–792.

Kelly, G. J., & Crawford, T. (1997). An ethnographic investigation of the discourse processes of school science. *Science Education, 81*(5), 533–560.

Kelly, G. J., Chen, C., & Crawford, T. (1998). Methodological considerations for studying science-in-the-making in educational settings. *Research in Science Education, 28*(1), 23–50.

Kuhn, D. (1993). Science as argument. *Science Education, 77*(3), 319–337.

Latour, B., & Woolgar, S. (1986). *Laboratory Life: The construction of scientific facts.* Princeton: Princeton University Press. (Original work published 1979)

Lemke, J. (1990). *Talking science: Language, learning, and values.* Norwood, NJ: Ablex.

Linn, M. C., & Hsi, S. (2000). *Computers, teachers, peers: Science learning partners.* Mahwah, NJ: Lawrence Erlbaum Associates.

Longino, H. (1994). The fate of knowledge in social theories in science. In F. F. Schmitt (Ed.), *Socializing epistemology: The social dimensions of knowledge* (pp. 135–158). Lanham, MD: Rowan & Littlefield.

Mehan, H. (1979). *Learning lessons: Social organization in classrooms.* Cambridge, MA: Harvard University Press.

Mercer, N. (1996) The quality of talk in children's collaborative activity in the classroom. *Learning and Instruction, 6*(4), 359–378.

Minstrell, J. (1989). Teaching science for understanding. In L. Resnick & L. Klopfer, (Eds.), *Toward the thinking curriculum: Current cognitive research. 1989 Yearbook of the Association for Supervision and Curriculum Development* (pp. 129–149). Reston, VA: Association for Supervision and Curriculum Development.

Osborne, R., & Freyberg, P. (1985). *Learning in science: The implications of children's science.* London: Heinemann.

Pea, R. (1993). Learning scientific concepts through material and social activities: Conversational analysis meets conceptual change. *Educational Psychologist, 28*(3), 265–277.

Roseberry, A. S., Warren, B., & Conant, F. R. (1992). Appropriating scientific discourse: Findings from language minority classrooms. *The Journal of the Learning Sciences, 2*(1), 61–94.

Scardamalia, M., & Bereiter, C. (1994). Computer support for knowledge-building communities. *The Journal of Learning Sciences, 3*(3), 265–283.

Scardamalia, M., Bereiter, C., Brett, C., Burtis, P. J., Calhoun, J., & Smith Lea, N. (1992). Educational application of a networked communal database. *Interactive Learning Environments, 2*(1), 45–71.

Scardamalia, M., Bereiter, C., & Lamon, M. (1994). The CSILE Project: Trying to bring the classroom into world 3. In K. McGilly (Ed.), *Classroom lessons: Integrating cognitive theory and classroom practice* (pp. 201–228). Cambridge, MA: MIT Press.

Schauble, L., Glaser, R., Duschl, R., Schulze, S., & John, J. (1995). Students' understanding of the objectives and procedures of experimentation in the science classroom. *The Journal of the Learning Sciences, 4*(2), 131–166.

Secules, T., Cottom, C. D., Bray, N. H., Miller, L. D., & The Schools for Thought Collaborative (1997). Creating Schools for thought. *Educational Leadership, 54*(6), 56–60.

Siegel, H. (1995). *Pedagogical challenges of instructional assessment in middle school earth science: Two case studies.* Unpublished doctoral dissertation, University of Pittsburgh.

Simon, H. A., (1980). Problem solving and education. In D. T. Tuma & R. Reif (Eds.), *Problem solving and education: Issues in teaching and research* (pp. 81–96). Hillsdale, NJ: Lawrence Erlbaum Associates.

Suppe, F. (1998). The structure of a scientific paper. *Philosophy of Science, 65*(3), 381–405.

Tabak, I., Smith, B. K., Sandoval, W. A., & Reiser, B. J. (1996). Combining general and domain-specific strategic support for biological inquiry. In C. Frasson, G. Gauthier, & A. Lesgold (Eds.), *Proceedings of the Third International Conference on Intelligent Tutoring Systems* (ITS '96) (pp. 288–296). Montreal, New York: Springer-Verlag.

Toulmin, S. (1958). *The uses of argument.* Cambridge, MA: Cambridge University Press.

van Eemeren, F. H., Grootendorst, R., & Henkemans, F. S. (Eds.). (1996). *Fundamentals of argumentation theory: A Handbook of historical backgrounds and contemporary developments.* Mahwah, NJ: Lawrence Erlbaum Associates.

Walton, D. N. (1996). *Argumentation schemes for presumptive reasoning.* Mahwah, NJ: Lawrence Erlbaum Associates.

Wegerif, R., Mercer, N., & Dawes, L. (1999). From social interaction to individual reasoning: An empirical investigation of a possible socio-cultural model of cognitive development. *Learning and Instruction, 9*(6), 493–516.

White, B., & Frederickson, J. (1998). Inquiry, modeling, and metacognition: Making science accessible to all students. *Cognition & Instruction, 16*(1), 3–118.

White, R., & Gunstone, R. (1992). *Probing understanding.* London: Falmer Press.

Whitehead, A. N. (1929). *The aims of education.* New York: MacMillan.

Author Index

L

M

294

Subject Index

A

Access, 133
Acquisition,
  of schema, 5
Addiction, 28
Affordance, 170
Aggressive behavior, 32
Aggressive play, 32
Archiving,
  Television/TV, 49–51
Argumentation, 232, 235, 248, 258–281
Assessment, 260, 262, 269–278
Asynchronity, 206
Attentional inertia, 29
Attention deficit disorder, 39
Automation, 5
Avatar, 118
Awareness, 113

B–C

Bookmarks, 104
Business managers, 141
Cataloguing, 49, 56, 59, 64
Checking, 232, 235, 248

Co-construction of meaning, 227, 247, 248
Cognitive Flexibility theory, 166
Cognitive load theory, 5
  extraneous, 5, 6
  intrinsic, 5
Cognitive psychology, 10, 12
Collaboration, 98, 113, 116, 118, 208, 255
Collaborative,
  learning, 225, 226, 248
  Text Production (CTP), 236
  Virtual Environment, 118, 119
  writing, 238, 241, 248
Collective Landscape model, 225, 239
Common ground, 106, 118, 179, 227, 241
Communication, 175–191
  asynchronous, 77, 80
  categorization, 177
  empathic, xii
  units of, 177
  Video-mediated, 219
Community,
  founders, 139
  leaders, 139
  members, 140
  practice of, 163
Community-centered design, 147
Competence development, 106, 107